The
Equal Opportunities
Revolution

James Heartfield

Published by Repeater Books
An imprint of Watkins Media Ltd

19-21 Cecil Court
London
WC2N 4EZ
UK
www.repeaterbooks.com
A Repeater Books paperback original 2017
1

Distributed in the United States by Random House, Inc., New York.

Cover design: Johnny Bull
Typography and typesetting: JCS Publishing Services Ltd, jcs-publishing.co.uk
Typeface: Minion Pro

ISBN: 978-1-910924-92-1
Ebook ISBN: 978-1-910924-83-9

Contents

Preface

Somewhere between 1965 and 2005 British attitudes on race and sex discrimination went through a sea-change. Broadly, the common belief that white people were better than black people, and that men were better than women, was challenged. There are many sides to that challenge, but this book just looks at one, equal opportunities in the workplace. Before the 1970s there were no workplaces that had equal opportunities policies. Today, the great majority of people at work are covered by such a policy – as they are covered by many acts of parliament drafted to guarantee equality at work.

There are a great many books written about diversity at work. Many of these are handbooks for employers and human resource managers, or they are addressed to employees and their representatives. As valuable as those are, they do not show the change that took place in the later part of the twentieth century. Talking to students about these questions many are generally aware that social attitudes in the past were very different. But it is harder for them to see how it was that things changed. The publications about discrimination at work do not address the question why equal opportunities policies arose, what the social conditions were that led to their success.

This book is written as a history, drawn from published sources. It also relies a lot on my own records and recollections of the time, and those of my peers. It is strange to see arguments that were only just developing when I was younger settle down to become the basis of policies and practices that govern society today. The questions of inequality were urgent as I was growing up, when the country was fixated on immigration, its supposed threat to jobs, and also on the growing numbers of women at work, and the imagined damage that would do to family life. As students we protested against discrimination – I was thrown out of college after one occupation demanding nurseries for students with children. In the 1980s I worked at Haringey Council, which was at the centre of a great row with the government about equal opportunities for ethnic minorities, and then again about gay rights. The industrial struggles that were common in the 1970s carried on, right up to year-long miners' strike against pit closures. But more and more, the argument in society was about oppression and discrimination, as well as about workers' pay and conditions. I was only a bit-player in the culture wars of the 1980s, but they did unfold around me. The book draws on my experiences, and those of the many people alongside whom I worked and campaigned over questions of discrimination and workers' rights over three decades. In particular I have leant on the advice and wisdom of Daniel Ben-Ami, Rosie Cuckston, Phil Hammond, Eve Kay, Chris Kyriakides, Kenan Malik, Munira Mirza, Mick Owens and Kevin Yuill. I am indebted too to Lizzie Terry and Tariq Goddard whose interest in this story helped the writing of it.

The book also draws on documents that I am embarrassed to think of now as historical sources, having seen them the first time around as so many surplus newsletters and policy briefs, often heading for the wastepaper bin. The work of the Commission for Racial Equality and the Equal Opportunities Commission, as well as the many local authority and employers' working groups on equality, were not well-respected at the time. They were often seen by conservatives as 'social engineering' and by radicals as tokenism — both criticisms that had some point. When I contacted the press office of the Human Rights Commission they were unaware of any history of their predecessor commissions (though there are in fact some retrospective accounts, as in the 25th Annual Report of the CRE). In reconstructing their history, and that of the other local government and workplace bodies dealing with equal opportunities, my argument is that these organisations did have a greater impact than they are credited for, though the changes they heralded were also pushed forward by other changes in the way that work is organised.

Back then, many of us were pessimistic about the likelihood that the market system, capitalism, could be reformed, most especially in its dependence on discrimination against women and against black people. The case against oppression was one that seemed to demand a revolution against the whole social order. A revolution did take place, but not the one that we were hoping for. The revolution in workplace relations has been profound. It was a revolution that did not overthrow the market system, but instead perfected it. Many of the things that we thought were unlikely to happen under capitalism, like a general belief in equality between men and women, and even a general belief in equality between white and black, did happen. The discrimination that we thought was going to get worse, got better. But the improvement of the position of women relative to men, and of black people relative to white people, took place in the context of a worsening of the position of all working people, relative to their employers. The position of the working classes overall, which we hoped would get better, has gotten much worse. Trying to understand the contradictions of the equal opportunities revolution is what we set out to do here.

Introduction

'Equal opportunities' policies were first modelled in Britain in the early 1980s. In 1980, the Commission for Racial Equality listed 73 employers who had adopted their draft equal opportunities policy. By 2004, three quarters of all workplaces had a formal written equal opportunities policy, up from 64% in 1998.[1]

Equal opportunities policies were designed to address discrimination against women and ethnic minorities at work. These are policies adopted by firms. They include promises not to discriminate, equal pay for equal work, oversight of recruitment policies and of promotions, and monitoring of the ethnic and gender mix of the workforce.

Before there were any such policies, there were laws against discrimination, notably the 1970 Equal Pay Act, the 1975 Sex Discrimination Act and the 1976 Race Relations Act (there were predecessors, and there have been reforms afterwards, but these are the most important). Both laws created quangos to enforce non-discrimination, which were known at the time as the Commission for Racial Equality and the Equal Opportunities Commission. Both had powers to investigate and to find against individual employers.

Though the EOC and the CRE were important enforcement bodies, the adoption of equal opportunities policies by firms signalled the dissemination and generalisation of a culture of equal opportunities. This is a sea change in British employment law and practice. Discrimination had been woven into the workplace to a remarkable degree in the later nineteenth and twentieth centuries.

Today women are nearly half the workforce, and the gender pay gap is shrinking all the time. Employers have taken on many more black people, too, and the racially segregated workplaces that were common up into the 1970s are today exceptional.

Catherine Hakim called this change an 'equal opportunities revolution', and she is right. Whatever problems remain, it is hard to gainsay that the explicit promises and beliefs of mainstream British society are for equality of opportunity. It is a revolution because oppression in the home, at the borders, and in the ghettos had been a mainstay of British society, and one that shaped the world of work. A gender and racial division of labour made a hierarchy in which women and migrants were marginal workers. That hierarchy is being dismantled. More importantly, it has no significant, explicit defenders among the political or business elite.

Whether the change was caused by the new policies, or whether those policies were only symptomatic of the extensive recruitment of women and of black people, the evidence is that a profound change has taken place. We are, of course, still impatient at the persistence of discrimination, and rightly so. All the same, the distance travelled over the last 30 years is remarkable.

The paradox of the equal opportunities revolution is that very few people expected it to succeed. Most of those who worked for equal opportunities from the late 1970s on were either liberal or radical. These were people, for the most part, who saw the 1980s and 1990s as a depressing time, when progress had been thrown into reverse. For workplace organisation this was a time when trade unions lost their legal privileges and were pointedly attacked by employers, with the support of the government. Anti-trade union laws put workers' representatives on the back foot. In the country, the tenor of government was hostile to working women and to ethnic minorities.

Curbs on welfare payments and social services as well as on nursery provision all hurt women who were trying to work. The governments of Margaret Thatcher and John Major talked about a return to 'Victorian values' and 'back to basics', seeming to suggest a far greater sympathy with traditional family life. At the same time harsh measures against immigrants, aggressive policing of inner cities, and a preoccupation with British values all seemed to point to a retrograde attitude toward black people.

And yet, the era of those Conservative governments, between 1979 and 1996, was just when the equal opportunities revolution was underway. This is the time when there was the greatest take-up of equal opportunities policies at work. The attitude of the government to those changes was mixed. Some in the Conservative Party were outspoken in their hostility to the equal opportunities policies adopted by local authorities, which they decried as 'social engineering'. There were moments when it seemed that both the CRE and the EOC would be targeted by a hostile government, and even abolished. The Greater London Council, which had been a pioneer of equal opportunities policies, was abolished, and much of the criticism of the GLC that preceded the abolition highlighted its 'loony-left' policies on race and gender.

For all that, the government never did abolish the CRE or the EOC, and the Department of Employment quietly supported their efforts to promote equal opportunities policies. More importantly, leading businesses, at first cautiously, and then enthusiastically, embraced the equal opportunities revolution. By 1998, 55% of all private business had equal opportunities policies (rising to 68% in 2004). All the other reforms of industry and employment law were pulling the country to the right. But the incremental reforms under the heading of equal opportunities carried on.

Most of the political left's policies seemed to be out of keeping with the times. There was not great support for economic planning, or trade union power — not even among trade unionists. But there was increasing sympathy for equal opportunities. These policies seemed to chime well with the other innovations that were taking place at work. Codes of practice, legalisation, tribunals, monitoring, all seemed commensurate with the new discipline of Human Resource Management. HRM saw personnel departments take on much of the work of managing relations between employers and employees that had formerly been done through negotiations with trade unions. Social scientist Alan Wolfe said that in the 1990s the right won the economic war and the left won the cultural war. One clear sign of that is the integration of the goal of equal opportunities within a restructured economy.

Trying to understand why the equal opportunities revolution happened, when the conditions seemed so hostile to such change, is one of the goals of this book.

All change at work

Between 1950 and 2015 the regime of workplace organisation has been through a sea change. Back then women made up just 35% of the workforce. Since then women's share in employment has climbed markedly to around 46% today.

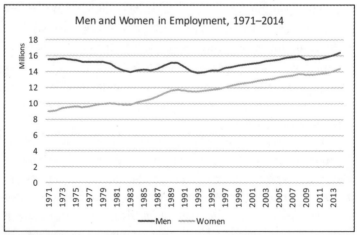

Source: ONS

Between 1991 and 2011 the percentage of 'White British' residents in England and Wales fell from 94% to 86%. In England and Wales, a workforce of 25.7 million now includes 3 million non-white workers.[2]

Go further back and see that in Britain at the start of the twentieth century just one tenth of married women worked, compared with 60% in 1990. Though Britain in 1900 governed an empire of 350 million, including India, much of Africa, and the Caribbean, the black presence in the United Kingdom was relatively small, until migration from the West Indies (from 1948), East Africa (of Asians from 1967), India, and Pakistan began. Net migration to the United Kingdom between 1961 and 2011 was 2,149,000, more latterly coming from Africa and Eastern Europe.[3]

On the basis of these changes, the Home Office claimed in 2002 that Britain was 'a more pluralistic society' and a 'multicultural society', and further that 'today very few people believe that women in Britain should stay at home and not go out to work'.[4]

The change in the make-up of British society, and most importantly in its workforce, has many causes. They are: agitation on the part of women and black workers, full employment and economic restructuring; and these changes are clearly marked by laws on race and sex discrimination, enforced by dedicated government bodies, and adopted as workplace codes by most employers. These legal codes forbid discrimination and unequal pay for equal work — and much more. Just what the forces were that gave rise to these changes is the subject of this book.

The change in the composition of the British workforce was sharply contested. As we will explain in Chapter One, the particular settlement between employers and labourers in the early twentieth century was exclusive, resting on an overwhelmingly white and male workforce that had established its rights and position over many years. Later, as women and then black workers were introduced into the workforce, labour relations were markedly hierarchical, as these newer recruits were employed in defined areas, and on worse terms.

The old labour regime was not deliberately constructed by any single agent to be the way that it was. Nobody sat down and planned a largely white, male labour force. Rather it came about out of the distinctive social position of the core industrial workforce, and the way that they fought to establish their authority within the workplace. But if it was not deliberately designed to be exclusive, discriminatory, and hierarchical, once in place it was. What is more, many agents, employers, governments, and even trade union representatives often used the shape of the settlement to defend their own positions, often to the detriment of those women and black people who were disadvantaged.

The unravelling of the established gender and racial ordering of the workforce, and its reconstruction, is a long and complicated story, and it is by no means complete. All the same that sea change in the working lives and broader society of Britain has been remarkable. In this book we look at the equal opportunities revolution as a real, historical event, to try to understand the actions and decisions that people took that made it happen.

The original meaning of 'equality of opportunity', and how it changed

Before the legislation of the 1970s the concept of 'equal opportunity' had a distinctive meaning. Equal opportunity, a shortening of 'equality of opportunity', came into use in the late nineteenth century as liberals sought to show how they were not like socialists. Henry Broadhurst explained the meaning of 'True Liberalism': 'Liberalism does not seek to make all men equal; nothing can do that. But its object is to remove all obstacles erected by men which prevent all having equal opportunities.'[5]

At that time, of course, the Liberals were facing down an emerging challenge from the labour movement, which was demanding equality. The liberal press parodied that as 'levelling'. Liberal Party-supporting trade union leader Henry Broadhurst was saying that he was not levelling all people down to the same point, but giving them 'equality of opportunity'. (Note that the inequality being looked at is social inequality, between 'men'.)

The Reverend J. J. R. Armitage, the Munitions Area Chaplain, lectured on the meaning of 'Equality' at the Empire Theatre, Coventry during the First World War. Armitage was sure that 'the doctrine of equality had no sanction from science or from experience'. On the other hand, the 'clergy and the Church of God, without fear or favour, had through the centuries preached to the all-powerful ruling classes that the lowest soul was in the eyes of Heaven of equal value with the highest'. He said 'they should endeavour to make it possible for every boy, without restraint of class privilege or birth, to go wherever his talent leads him'. If only we could 'grant equality of opportunity and the way was opened in competition'.[6]

In 1943, in the middle of the Second World War, Viscount Hinchingbrooke was talking to the Bradford Rotary Club about the Conservative Party of the future. Lord Hinchingbrooke 'urged the desirability of a society in which an individual, in whatever circumstances he might be placed, would have full scope to use his abilities in service of his fellow man'. 'Equality of opportunity', he said, 'therefore became one of our war aims — by which all might attain to positions of highest endeavour in service to their fellows'.[7] In raising the ideal of 'equality of opportunity' Viscount Hinchingbrooke was trying to head off the more socialistic aims of the Beveridge Report, of which he thought Britons ought to be wary.

In all these instances, equal opportunities are set out as the fulfilment of the free market; equality of opportunity is the counter-claim to the socialist demand for equality. To get rid of unfair discrimination is to make the labour market more perfect.

This was the meaning, too, of Milton Friedman's 1979 distinction between equality of opportunity and equality of outcome. Noting that the American Declaration of Independence seemed to put in train two rival principles, Liberty and Equality, Friedman explains: 'In the early decades of the Republic, equality meant equality before God; liberty meant the liberty to shape one's own life.' More, Friedman says: 'Equality came more and more to be interpreted as "equality of opportunity" in the sense that no one should be prevented by arbitrary obstacles from using his capacities to pursue his own objectives.' He goes on to say: 'Neither equality before God nor equality of opportunity presented any conflict with liberty to shape one's own life' — that is they were commensurate with a free labour market.[8] He expands, later on:

> Equality of opportunity, like personal equality, is not inconsistent with liberty; on the contrary, it is an essential component of liberty. If some people are denied access to particular positions in life for which they are qualified simply because of their ethnic background, color, or religion, that is an interference with their right to 'Life, Liberty, and the pursuit of Happiness.' It denies equality of opportunity and, by the same token, sacrifices the freedom of some for the advantage of others.[9]

Friedman contrasts equality of opportunity with another idea of equality that he differentiates by giving it different qualifier, 'equality of outcome':

> A very different meaning of equality has emerged in the United States in recent decades — equality of outcome. Everyone should have the same level of living or of income, should finish the race at the same time. Equality of outcome is in clear conflict with liberty.[10]

Equality of opportunity was a call often linked with education, as in 1914 when Mr Henry Davies, the Glamorgan Director of Mining, appealed to the Miner's Federation to get behind a school set up by mine-owners. 'There was to be equality of opportunity for all', said Davies, 'the miner's son, the checkweigher's son would have the same advantages of the manager's son'.[11] In 1917 a National Union of Teachers' leader Mr H. Walker called for the raising of the school leaving age, at a meeting of the Labour Club, backed by councillor J. Thicket, who said 'there should be equality of opportunity for the children of rich and poor alike'.[12]

The idea of 'equality of opportunity' had been worked out as a liberal answer to labour. Later on, the moderate left took it up themselves as a form of words that seemed to be a concession to egalitarianism. In the House of Lords, Labour peer Lord Haldane attacked an anti-union law proposed as a reaction to the General Strike of 1926. The General Strike was wrong, said Haldane — 'never again if it could be prevented would such a blow be struck at the heart of the country' — but things would never be satisfactory 'until workmen and employers come to be more of one mind than at present'. Arguing for such a meeting of minds, Haldane said 'workmen desired to have the opportunity of making the best of their lives and securing for themselves the best conditions of their labour... Working people asked not for luxuries, but for equality of opportunity, and they desired that still more on behalf of their wives and children.'[13]

The phrase 'equality of opportunity' was first used as a challenge against sex discrimination toward women teachers. For them, equality of opportunity had keen meaning because of the rule that they were to be laid off if and when they married (on the assumption that they would be supported by their husbands, and that their leaving would free up jobs for men). Miss S. M. Burls told the 1929 annual conference of the National Union of Women Teachers that they 'demanded freedom to apply for every post in the educational sphere', and 'impartiality which considered immaterial questions of sex or celibacy, and the justice which awarded equal remuneration and equal opportunities of promotion'. A woman's marriage, she said, should be treated 'as her private concern just as all the world treats a man's'.[14] At a meeting of the Plymouth Women's Hospital Fund, chair Dr Mabel Ramsay said 'medical women occupied an excellent position in Plymouth, but they would not be satisfied until they got the same opportunities as those given to men', and they 'could not stop until every avenue was open to all women'.[15]

Equal opportunities in an era of full employment

The Labour Party manifesto in 1950 said 'Our appeal is to all those useful men and women who actively contribute to the work of the nation'. They called on manual, skilled, technical, and professional workers, 'and housewives and women workers of all kinds'. The Labour Party set out its goal of realising the 'means to the greater end of the full and free development of every individual person'. In the context of full employment, the manifesto committed themselves: 'Labour will encourage the introduction of equal pay for equal work by women when the nation's economic circumstances allow it.'[16] The Conservatives were a little more cautious, restricting their offer of equal pay — 'principle of equal pay for men and women for services of equal value' — to public employees, and also limiting it to what could be afforded.[17] Five years later, Labour's promises were vaguer, offering that 'our goal is a society in which free and independent men and women work together as equals', but without any proposals to make that happen.[18] Women did not feature very much in the Labour Party's electoral appeals, though in 1964 the "New Britain" they foresaw would rely on 'encouraging more entrants to teaching and winning back the thousands of women lost by marriage' (it was an offer that was adopted by the Conservatives at the following election). Nancy Seear was an economist and former personnel manager, who had been on the Production Efficiency Board at the Ministry of Aircraft Production in the war. She advised that 'if we want to find an

unused reserve of potential qualified manpower it is among women
that it can most easily be discovered'.[19]

Two years later, and again with 'full employment' as the
background, Labour put down a marker:

[W]e must move towards greater fairness in the rewards for work.
That is why we stand for equal pay for equal work and, to this end,
have started negotiations.

We cannot be content with a situation in which important
groups — particularly women, but male workers, too, in some
occupations — continue to be underpaid.

In 1966 the Conservatives did say 'we intend that there should be
full equality of opportunity', though it was not linked to any specific
measures, but rather an argument for a more competitive economy
in which we should not 'all be equally held back to the pace of the
slowest'. At the same time, they appealed to women as homemakers
more than they did as potential wage earners, promising that 'we
want to see family life strengthened by our Conservative social
policies'.[20]

The TUC Congress in September 1965 followed this with a
resolution reaffirming

its support for the principles of equality of treatment and
opportunity for women workers in industry, and call[ing] upon
the General Council to request the government to implement the
promise of 'the right to equal pay for equal work' as set out in the
Labour Party election manifesto.[21]

Labour won office in 1964 and showed themselves willing to
adopt some cautious measures against discrimination in the 1965
Race Relations Act. Then in 1970 they made the following manifesto
statement on equal opportunities, which in its main outlines

anticipated the legislative framework that was to follow, and would shape our current employment regime:

> [W]e believe that all people are entitled to be treated as equals: that women should have the same opportunities and rewards as men. We insist, too, that society should not discriminate against minorities on grounds of religion or race or colour: that all should have equal protection under the law and equal opportunity for advancement in and service to the community.

Labour's commitments were ahead of the Conservatives' though these too were sharply opposed to discrimination. The Conservative Party under Edward Heath also committed itself: 'We have supported and sought to improve the equal pay legislation.' Heath's Conservatives said they wanted to 'ensure genuine equality of opportunity'. They despaired that 'many barriers still exist which prevent women from participating to the full in the entire life of the country', and that 'women are treated by the law, in some respects, as having inferior rights to men', promising 'we will amend the law to remove this discrimination'.[22]

In 1974, Harold Wilson put his name to Labour's election appeal. The main thrust of the manifesto was for greater control by the British people over the powerful private forces dominating economic life, and for an extensive incorporation of industrial relations.

Alongside those demands, Wilson set out another area of policy, saying 'it is the duty of Socialists to protect the individual from discrimination on whatever grounds'. Under the heading 'Women and Girls', he said that they 'must have an equal status in education, training, employment, social security, national insurance, taxation, property ownership, matrimonial and family law'. Further, he promised that 'we shall create the powerful legal machinery necessary to enforce our anti-discrimination laws'.[23] The following October, Labour could say 'new rights for women and our determination to implement equal pay have been announced'.

Britain's first Race Relations Act was passed in 1965, but its remit was modest. It was the Race Relations Act of 1976 that made race discrimination illegal and created the Commission for Racial Equality with powers to investigate employers to persuade them to redress the balance. Six years earlier, in 1970, the Equal Pay Act had been passed — following a strike by women machinists at Ford's Dagenham plant demanding parity with equivalent workers on the assembly line. A further act of 1975 created the Equal Opportunities Commission that had powers to investigate and reprimand employers and other institutions for discrimination. These Commissions were both non-departmental public bodies.

With the legislative commitment, the stage was set for the revolution in equal opportunities that was to follow. As we shall see, one of the most far-reaching consequences of the legislation, and the Commissions it created, was the adoption of equal opportunities policies by employers. These policies were the third leg of the stool alongside the law and the Commissions. In themselves they were just pieces of paper — though they also tended to reorganise and even lend greater importance to personnel management, particularly in larger companies, as managers committed to take on the responsibility of enforcing the policies. They might be actively embraced by far-sighted employers, or taken on without much thought, or even reluctantly, for fear of sanctions under the law. But once in place they were a framework through which employers and employees, unions and Commissions, could negotiate the new working conditions. Their widespread adoption in the 1980s and 1990s gave institutional form to the equal opportunities revolution.

The elusive victory

Agents of the equal opportunities revolution — activists, officials, analysts, politicians — more often talk down the successes than talking them up. How could one be satisfied with anything less than equality? As Rebecca Solnit writes, we need the 'ability to recognize a situation in which you are travelling and have not arrived, in which you have both cause to celebrate and fight'.[24]

The equal opportunities revolution has been superimposed upon the old corporatist order of business, and has never wholly eclipsed it. So too, the inequalities between men and women, and between white and black, are greatly moderated but have not disappeared. How could it be otherwise? Equal opportunities does not imply equality of outcome. Equality of opportunity in the sense of greater competition has increased social inequality in income, as measured in the 'Gini coefficient' (0=equality, 1=inequality).

Source: Mike Brewer et al, Accounting for changes in inequality since 1968, Institute of Fiscal Studies, 2009, p 1

The income gap between wealthy and less so has opened up, and to some extent that is associated with the inequalities of race and sex. Even if all racial discrimination were to cease, since socio-economic status tends to reflect the socio-economic status of parents, black people by their incomes, on average lower, will still raise children who are less likely to succeed than their white counterparts. That would be so because colour would still be a marker of class, even if there were no active discrimination. For women, the income penalty of leaving full-time employment to raise children persists stubbornly despite many measures (such as the legal right to paternal leave). But for the most part, women have improved their position relative to men, and black people have improved their position relative to white, over time. The distant horizon of equality of outcome has not been reached, and campaigners' determination to press onwards is both understandable and laudable. But the perspective of the campaigner is not one that illuminates just how far we have come over just a few decades.

On average women earned 36.5% less than men per hour in 1970, compared to 15% less than men in 2010.[25]

There are two ways to measure the gender pay gap. If you compare the earnings of men and women in full-time employment, the gap today is quite small, and has fallen over some years. The other way, which compares all hourly earnings, gives a larger pay gap because more women work in part-time employment, and part-time employment is less well paid by the hour. The striking thing, however, is that while hourly pay for all workers gives a larger gender pay gap,

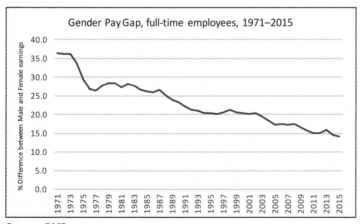

Source: ONS

Ethnic pay gap, men, 2004-7						
			Percentage pay gap			
	Indian	Pakistani	Bangladeshi	Black Caribbean	Black African	Chinese
All employees	-4	23	21	5	18	0

Note   The comparator is a white man

Source: Simonetta Longhi and Lucinda Platt, Pay Gaps Across Equalities Areas, Equality and Human Rights Commission 2008, p 18

the same trend towards convergence is there in both measures. The gender pay gap is closing.

The ethnic pay gap, by contrast has worsened somewhat in the last ten years. However, the position of some established ethnic minorities, at least as reflected in the ethnic pay gap, is more encouraging.

According to the estimates, the ethnic gap in hourly average pay between white men and Indians, black Caribbean, and Chinese men is statistically insignificant. These minorities are well established, and their disadvantage in employment in earlier times is well recorded, but more recently they appear to have overcome those barriers. Black Africans and Bangladeshis are more recent arrivals, and they are at a clear disadvantage in the jobs market, as are Pakistanis (suggesting that Muslims in particular are at a disadvantage in the workforce today). The social science researchers who looked at the ethnic pay gap saw one of the principle barriers to advance being the concentration of these minorities in particular, and precarious, occupations — black disadvantage being closely linked to class.[26]

This book is mostly about relations at work. The equal opportunities policy is a workplace policy. Like the sex- and race-based hierarchies that went before, equal opportunities policies are about managing *all* employees, white and black, men and women. In what follows we look first at the old regime that was overturned by the equal opportunities revolution, in Chapter One. This chapter is quite detailed, explaining how sex and race discrimination came to be built in to the old 'corporatist', or 'tripartite' order of industrial relations. Then we go on to look first at the question of race, the creation of the Commission for Racial Equality and the promulgation of equal opportunities policies at work in Chapter Two. In Chapter Three we go on to look at the question of women, the Equal Opportunities Commission and its impact upon employment practice. In Chapter Four we consider the revolution in workplace relations overall, and ask what the motives were for employers who adopted these policies. The fifth chapter looks at some of the critical reaction to equal opportunities policies, both conservative criticisms and radical ones. In Chapter Six we consider the way that equal opportunities policies came as part and parcel of the new Human Resource Management theory of workplace relations. Chapter Seven looks at the way that the organised labour movement was at odds with the changes at work, and how the economic cycle impacted on employment, for men and women, and for black and white. Many looking at these questions have showed that influences outside work, in particular the 'second shift' of domestic work for women and Britain's institutional racism, have entrenched discrimination — and we look at these in Chapter Eight, though drawing attention too to the ways that even those barriers are being moved. Chapter Nine looks at the different examples that British policy makers had to draw on, of native self-government in the British Empire, of the Fair Employment Commission in Northern Ireland, affirmative action in the United States, and the work of the European Union on women's equality. In Chapter Ten we look at how the equal opportunities model was generalised in workplace rights for lesbians and gays and for the disabled, and also how, paradoxically, the generalisation of the model made the EOC and the CRE redundant. Chapter Eleven looks at some of the contradictions in the system that has been created by the equal opportunities revolution.

There is a kind of awkwardness that comes from looking at all the social questions that fall under the equal opportunities category together. The two most important equal opportunities questions: those of discrimination against women, and of discrimination against black people, are matters in their own right. The case for considering them under the same heading is that they really are under the same heading, as the two substantial questions addressed in equal opportunities policies. They are very different, though. Sex cuts through society across the question of class, at a right angle to it, as it were. There are women in the upper classes, and women in the working classes. Race, while it is not the same as class, tends to track social inequality much more directly. Women's oppression in the family has been a feature of the life of elites, and of working-class people — the inequality is reproduced in each family unit. There have been wealthy black people, and even black people in the ruling elites (though very few might be counted as such in Britain). On the other hand, the social status of black people has been shaped by their relationship to a division of labour that is outside of the home (which is not of course to say that the question of the domestic economy and women's relationship to it is not an issue for black people). Proportionately, black and Asian people are fewer, pointedly fewer, than the white population (around 87% of the population of the United Kingdom), so that they have at times been referred to as 'the minorities'; there are fewer black and Asian people than there are women, who, though they have in occasional mistakes been referred to as a minority, are in fact the majority. For that reason, the question of equality for women has probably been more important, not morally, but in its weight within British society, and so too have changes in the balance of power between the sexes.

This book dodges between the two cases of sex discrimination and of race discrimination, sometimes seeming to read as if they were the same, but that is only because what is being addressed is the policy of equality of opportunity. Equal opportunities policies are not, of course, restricted to women and black people. The equal opportunities revolution has expanded outwards to take in new questions, such as sexual orientation, disability, and more. Those questions are given less weight in the treatment here, because it is largely historical, looking at the way that the ideas, campaigns, policies, and practices changed over the years. In driving those changes, the questions of sex and of race discrimination simply carried more weight. No moral judgment is intended in the priority given, only to tell the story.

The words we use about race are often awkward, and rightly so, since there really are no good grounds for sifting people out according to their colour. The words date quickly because they carry an unstated stigma. The National Association for the Advancement of Colored People was founded in America in 1909 and has fought for black Americans ever since — but few today would be happy with the choice of its title. C. L. R. James wrote many essays in support of 'negroes', where today we would say black people. In the 1970s some radical Asians called themselves 'black', and the radical Greek economist Yanis Varoufakis even served as president of the Essex University Black Students Society. The collective 'black' for all those who are not white, though, is not always right. British Asians are often differentiated from black Britons, and called Asians, or sometimes brown. Black would have done as a collective noun for all those who are not white in the 1970s, but less so today. In the text I have used 'black' as the generic word where the meaning is clear, sometimes 'black and Asian', 'black and brown', or the negative 'not white' — knowing that none of these are satisfactory. The American 'people of colour' strikes many as too close to 'coloured', and sounds demeaning, and 'black and minority ethnic', while accurate, strikes me too much as policy-makers' jargon. I have not changed terms in quotations, to keep the historical record. No words will ever satisfy, because the naming fixes what is fluid. Geneticists tell us that there is no biological foundation to the concept of race, fixing as it does on minor heritable features of skin colour and hair, and point out that the genetic variation within 'races' is greater than between them. Still the fetish concept of race is a social fact in that people treat it as if it were real, and so in their actions it becomes real. I hope that people will not get caught up too much in the language used here, which will no doubt be out-of-date already.

— ONE —

The Old Order

Between 1850 and 1950 British industry dominated the world. The factories that fed Britain's success were for the most part worked by white men. Most of what was traded was made by white men. Between 1850 and 1880 11,000 miles of railway track were laid mostly by white men. In 1850 men smelted 2.25 million tons of pig iron, rising to 7.75 million tons by 1880. In 1850 men forged 49,000 tons of steel rising to 1.44 million tons in 1880. And men dug 49 million tons of coal in 1850, rising to 147 million in 1880. The number of engineers doubled between 1851 and 1881, and carried on growing so that there were 1.1 million engineers in 1935, almost all of them white men.[1] Throughout that time Britain was making between 10% and 15% of all manufactured goods in the world, with greater output per worker than any country, bar the United States.

Britain's take-off was based primarily on industrial labour in factories, and, through two key changes, that labour was overwhelmingly the work of men. The first change was the move from domestic production to factory production. Seventeenth-century spinning and weaving was done indoors, like furniture-making and most other handicrafts. The factory system separated domestic work from wage labour under a different roof. Many of these early factories, though, had women working alongside men, and children too. The second change, which was driven by a moral revulsion at the exploitation of women and children in dangerous work, was a series of laws, clauses in the Factory Acts that restricted women's work (Mines and Collieries Act, 1842; Factory Acts of 1844, 1878, 1891, and 1895).

In the census of 1911 there were 13,662,200 men aged over ten years, and 14,857,113 women. Of those 84% of men and 32% of women were in work. More pointedly just 10% of married women (around half the total of all women) were in work.[2]

The men's labour in British factories depended on other work done elsewhere. There was the work done by women, mostly in the home — cooking, washing, cleaning, caring for children — that all added up to the raising and sustenance of the working men. Also, industrialising Britain gobbled up raw materials that were grown and harvested and mined by black and Asian people. Sugar, rubber, tin, and oil from the colonies fed the industrial revolution, as the profits of the slave trade and empire yielded the seed money that grew it. But in the second half of the nineteenth century the factory system was the primary source of its profits (profits that averaged around 25%).[3] The most important relationship, and the one that dominated social and political life in Britain, was that between the wage-earning class and the propertied classes. Those workers at that time were overwhelmingly male and white — factors that would influence the culture and organisation of the working classes that emerged between 1850 and 1950.

The forward march of labour

The growth of organised labour was bound up with a sharply gendered division of labour, first and foremost between paid factory work and unpaid domestic work; it was also based upon a demarcation of British industrial workers from toilers in the Empire, and from largely unorganised Irish labourers.

Today we might be tempted to call the centrality of white men to the factory system 'privilege' — though that is not really the word to use for the lives they led. Explaining that these industrial workers were the source of their employers' profits, Karl Marx said that 'to be a productive labourer is, therefore, not a piece of luck, but a misfortune'.[4] The hours worked in those days were long, generally more than 50 a week. The primitive extent of mechanisation also made working life dangerous, arduous, and dirty. The status of the nineteenth-century factory hand was low, and he was often dominated by his master, under threat of instant dismissal, subject to fines for misdemeanours.

In the earlier nineteenth century skilled craftsmen tried to control the work process by limiting the number of people in the trade, limiting membership of their associations, and so bidding up their wages. Women were not the main target — all rivals in the labour market were — but the strategy did institutionalise discrimination in employment. In South East England at that time, as many as 34% of all apprentices were women. But in 1796 the Spitalfields silk weavers excluded women from skilled work; in 1779 the journeymen bookbinders excluded women from their guild; the Cotton Spinners Union excluded women in 1829; and in 1834 London tailors struck work to force women out of the trade.[5] These defensive measures also sharply differentiated the skilled from the unskilled, the craftsmen from the labourers. It was a division that could take on a racial aspect: 'Every industrial and commercial centre in England now possesses a working class divided into two hostile camps, English proletarians and Irish proletarians', Marx wrote: 'The ordinary English worker hates the Irish worker as a competitor who lowers his standard of life.'[6]

Working-class organisation

The radical United Kingdom Alliance of Organised Trades formed in Sheffield in 1866 and the more moderate Trades Union Congress held its conference in Manchester in 1868. The establishment vilified the radicals as dynamiters, and rewarded the respectable head of the working-class household — but not his wife — with the vote in 1867. That year Lord Derby set up a Royal Commission on Trade Unions, and in a law of 1871 stopped them being classed as a conspiracy, and lifted the unions' liability for employers' losses in a dispute. The measure was meant to encourage responsible trade unionism, and it did.

The end of the Combination Acts was a thing that pulled in one way and another. On the one hand it made it possible for many more people to join unions. On the other hand, legalisation bedded down the more conservative side of working-class identity. They had offices and officers, standing agreements with employers, legal status, and a hearing in Royal Commissions. All of these cemented the more conservative outlook of organised labour. They laid a basis for a patriotic love of England, its parliament, and even its monarchy. Karl

Labour Force Survey, ONS — the dip in the middle is due to the recession between the two world wars

Marx wrote in 1883 that the English workers were participating in the country's success, and

> are naturally the tail of the 'great Liberal Party,' which for its part pays them small attentions, recognises trade unions and strikes as legitimate factors, has relinquished the fight for an unlimited working day and has given the mass of better placed workers the vote.[7]

Christopher Kyriakides and Rodolfo Torres make the point that the vote and the chance of reform 'was the British state's policy tool through which racial proximity and distance were institutionalised'.[8] The workers' patriotic identification with England and its institutions left them open to chauvinistic divisions, in particular against the Irish. 'He cherishes religious, social, and national prejudices against the Irish worker', Marx wrote of the English worker:

> In relation to the Irish worker he regards himself as a member of the *ruling* nation and consequently he becomes a tool of the English aristocrats and capitalists against Ireland, thus strengthening their domination *over himself.*[9]

Legitimacy did not only entrench conservative attitudes towards the Irish, it also kindled a more patrician idea of the family.

State intervention and the shaping of the working-class family

As we have seen, successive employment laws tended to differentiate men's and women's work, limiting the hours that women worked, and barring them from more dangerous trades. The debate over the regulation of factory life turned on gender. 'The public debate about enacting protective labour legislation in England', says researcher

Carolyn Malone, was all about the 'idea that women's work outside the home was dangerous to society and required state intervention'. She cites Peter Gaskell's book *The Manufacturing Population of England* (1833), where he warns that 'crowding together of numbers of the young in both sexes in factories, is a prolific source of moral delinquency'. Gaskell lauded 'the moral obligations of father and mother, brother and sister, son and daughter' and warned against the breaking up of these family ties; the consequent abolition of the domestic circle, and the perversion of all the social obligations which should exist between parent and child under the factory system. These warnings against women's work often turned on the harm to children — as they often do today. So Thomas Maudsley, of the nine-hour bill campaign, thought that 'prolonged absence from home of the wife and mother caused an enormous amount of infant mortality and it must cause the elder children to be more or less neglected'. To him women's work 'deadened the sense of parental responsibility'.[10] True as this was, women did not object to the protective laws, because the work conditions were exploitative and arduous. One factory inspector noted that 'no instances have come to my knowledge of adult women having expressed any regret at their rights being interfered with'.[11]

A more profound influence of the division of labour between the sexes than the formal bars on women working in mines and other dangerous trades, or the limitation on women's working hours, was the consequence of full-time, compulsory schooling for under-11s. Already in 1833 factories were forbidden from employing children under nine. The provision of free education under the Forster Act (1870) and the limit on children's working hours were without doubt a great step forward.

As great an advance as it was for society and the law to enforce the protection of children, the impact upon women was that it greatly increased the need for childcare, as one of the main tasks of housework. MP Charles Buxton, supporting Forster's education act, warned that 'No feeling of tenderness for the parents would deter him for one minute from adopting compulsion'. He added that 'Society was suffering grievously from their shameful apathy with regard to the education of their children'.[12] A Board School in Upper Holloway minuted that 'parents say they would be glad to send, but their girls' services were needed at home'. Later, truant officers took older children who did much of the caring for their younger brothers and sisters away from their homes and back to school.[13] There were campaigns, too, to police deviant sexual behaviour. The largely middle-class Social Purity Movement campaigned against prostitution and for 'fallen women'. Henry Labouchère's amendment to the 1885 Criminal Law Amendment Act outlawed 'gross indecency', and led to the imprisonment of thousands of homosexuals.

All of these interventions brought with them officials to police the newly created nuclear family — there were 250 NSPCC 'cruelty men', empowered under an act of 1889, truant officers, health visitors, and social workers, all making sure that an orderly home was being kept. This way women's domestic role was vigorously enforced.

The family wage as ideal and reality

In 1877 the Secretary to the Parliamentary Committee of the Trades Union Congress, the same Henry Broadhurst we met earlier, told the Congress that it was the duty of male trade unionists 'as men and husbands to use their utmost efforts to bring about a condition of things, where their wives should be in the proper sphere at home, instead of being dragged into competition for livelihood against the great and strong men of the world'. As a delegate of the Mason's Union, Broadhurst perhaps had one foot in the old protectionism of the craft unions. But his views were echoed later by Tom Mann, the Dockers' leader and champion of the 'New Unionism', who gave evidence to the Royal Commission of Labour in 1894 that he was 'very loth to see mothers of families working in factories at all', adding that he considered their employment to have 'nearly always had a very prejudicial effect on the wages of the male worker'.[14] Trade union leader and Liberal MP John Burns' speech in the Dock Workers' strike in 1889 was largely an appeal to the men to conduct themselves respectably, and not to beat their wives or drink.[15]

The ideal of the respectable male breadwinner had become established. Tory MP Charles Newdegate argued against votes for women, drawing on the case of those unions that had put in place rules against women. He told Parliament 'the rightful head of the family claims for himself priority in labour as the chief breadwinner', adding, 'If that be selfishness, it is selfishness for the family'. Another MP, the rather radical Liberal Edward Pickersgill of Bethnal Green, appealed to the idea of the breadwinner to defend his constituents' incomes, saying he 'wanted to impress upon the conscience of the House that there were thousands of his constituents, bread-winners, earning wages in many cases not more than 20s. per week'. Arguing against the founding of a women's college, the Liberal MP Stuart Rendel said that 'after all, the men are the breadwinners, and must have the prior consideration'.[16] In 1909 William Beveridge set out the meaning of the breadwinner role that had been set down in the later nineteenth century, saying that 'society is built on labour', and 'its ideal unit is the household of man, wife and children maintained by the earnings of the first alone'. The liberal administrator added that 'the wife, so long at least as she is bringing up children, should have no other task'.

In spite of these claims, it was not typical for any working-class family to survive on one wage alone. Sara Horrell and Jane Humphries estimated that male wage earnings as a share of all family income had risen from 55% in 1830 to 81% in 1865. Economist Arthur Bowley worked out that in 1911 — when the division of labour was most sharply based on gender — only 41% of working-class families were dependent on a man's wage alone, and that on average the man's wage made up just 70% of family income.[17] What the family wage model did was not to exclude women entirely from paid work, but rather pushed them down the scale into less well-paid, less organised and less secure work. Substantially work inside the home had become women's work; while outside the home paid work was segregated on gender lines, with women in the role of the 'reserve army of labour', that employers could draw upon more or less as the business cycle demanded. For those at the lower end of the income scale, the male breadwinner ideal fell apart, and poorer families took what work they could.

The marriage bar

The idea of the family wage was in Edwardian England hardened up into a custom that was in effect a marriage bar — 'the prohibition on married women's employment which ensured that jobs, especially white-collar jobs, were reserved for men'. The Fabian Society's Chiozza Money, in 1905, wrote that 'the nation must set its face against the employment of married women, and gradually expand the period of legal prohibition'. To his mind 'there is only one proper sphere of work for the married woman and that is her

TUC Library Collection

own home'. Catherine Hakim says that 'strong social norms' against women working were 'sometimes institutionalised in company rules and policies', as for example the BBC's marriage bar, introduced in 1935. The marriage bar for teachers was not abandoned until 1945, and those in the civil service and the post office were not removed until 1954.[18]

While men and women were divided into different roles, the true winners were the employers, who had the advantage of a male workforce that was committed whole-heartedly to the workshop, having been fed and kept by the unpaid work of women; and they had on top of that an additional reserve of labour that, being less organised and already dependent, was more malleable.

Labour and empire

Between 1815 and 1914 Britain was at the centre of a transformation in the organisation of the global order. Ten million square miles of territory and 400 million people were colonised by Britain. The imperial economy secured raw materials for Britain's industrial surge, and increasingly native labour was working to enrich Britain. Now it was Britain's surplus capital that was overflowing, and rushing into the new territories.

At first it was the well-to-do who profited by the expansion, which the radical John Hobson called 'a vast system of outdoor relief for the upper classes'. Britain's imperial grandeur was also a powerful draw upon the imagination of working people. In the first half of the twentieth century, social reforms bound the British worker more closely to the Empire project, while at the same time raising up a great barrier between the British worker, who enjoyed greater rights, and colonial labourers who had very few. The 'new Liberals' of the turn of the century brought in a policy of social reform with investment in municipal and public utilities that

was known as 'Gas and Water Socialism'. Lloyd George overcame
Tory opposition to a tax-raising budget that paid for pensions and
primitive schemes of worker's compensation and pensions. Trade
union officers were drawn into the administration of social reforms
through local boards, solidifying their identification with the state.

There had been a spate of conciliation boards — as on the railways
and in the cotton industry — set up to moderate trade disputes in
the 1860s. These were enshrined in law in the 1896 Conciliation
Act and a special Labour Department in the Board of Trade set up
in 1911 brought government directly into industrial relations. The
conciliation boards gave union representatives recognised official
status, and were conceded by employers as a part of the 'routinisation
of social conflict'.[19]

Herbert Asquith's Liberal administration passed an act in 1909
that set up Labour Exchanges, and then in 1911 the National
Insurance against unemployment and sickness. Unions were asked
to help work the National Insurance fund, so that the militant
labour activist Jack Murphy would write that 'the unions were
drawn closer to the state by the ingenious means of giving them
a share in the administration of the state insurance funds'.[20] Home
Secretary Winston Churchill voiced the hope that reform would
moderate labour: 'With a "stake in the country" in the form of
insurance against evil days these workers will pay no attention to
the vague promises of revolutionary socialism.'[21]

The sociologist Robert Michels, looking at English and German
labour organisation in 1915, said:

There already exists in the proletariat an extensive stratum
consisting of the directors of co-operative societies, the secretaries
of trade unions, the trusted leaders of various organisations, whose
psychology is entirely modelled upon that of the bourgeois class
with whom they associate.[22]

This new layer of labour bureaucracy became the foundation of the Labour Party, and an essential support to the corporate society that was built after the Second World War. It would also bind organised labour ever-closer to the fortunes of the British Empire.

Against immigration

One sign of organised labour's identification with Britain was its opposition to immigration and hostility to foreigners. In 1889 union leader Ben Tillett published a pamphlet, *The Dock Labourer's Bitter Cry*, which carried this attack on the migrants:

> The influx of continental pauperism aggravates and multiplies the number of ills which press so heavily on us… Foreigners come to London in large numbers, herd together in habitations unfit for beasts, the sweating system allowing the more grasping and shrewd a life of comparative ease in superintending the work.[23]

Tillett welcomed new immigrants at the dockside: 'Yes, you are our brothers and we will do our duty by you. But we wish you had not come.'[24] In 1894 and 1895 William Inskip and Charles Freak, officers of the National Union of Boot and Shoe Operatives, put forward resolutions against Jewish immigration — a 'blighting blister' upon the English worker — to the Trades Union Congress, and won.[25]

A Royal Commission on Alien Immigration of 1902 became the focus of a lot of hostility, as its hearings were reported in the press. Another Tory MP, William Evans Gordon, started the British Brothers League, which paraded in military fashion to protest against the influx of Jews.[26]

From all of this one might get the idea that the new unionism was a step backwards, hopelessly reactionary, sexist, and racist. But that would be wrong. This was a movement that fought and won rights for working people and defended their interests. The very idea of equality was defended and promoted by the labour movement. The new model unions took up the cause of the Bryant and May Match Women's strike, and in 1925 Tom Mann helped organised a seaman's strike that spanned the Empire, from London to Cape Town and Australia.

Bryant and May strike committee

The union movement was limited. It was limited to what was achievable within the relationship between capital and labour. Trade unionism was a bargain between two parties. Its achievements were what was possible within those terms. The gains for working people — English men for the most part — were circumscribed. The gains for working people were concentrated amongst those who were key to the relationship: industrial labourers. The enlargement of the wages, resources and rights of that one section marked out the difference between them and those women and immigrants who had not broken through. It was the greater *equality* afforded English working-class men that opened up the *inequality* between them and the oppressed.

The corporate system comes into its own

After the 'new Liberalism', it fell to the wartime coalition of 1914-19, and then the 1940-45 coalition and the post-war Labour government of 1945-51, to consolidate the corporate system. War mobilisation into the army and the munitions factories greatly increased the demand for labour, both in the First World War, and in the Second. Between the wars, though, a terrible slump led to mass unemployment and the 'hungry Thirties'.

Between 1914 and 1919, and again from 1939 to 1945, the emergency suspended all the normal rules of balanced budgets and free markets. Asquith's Munitions Minister Christopher Addison relished the idea of directing the work of industry, and often leveraged workplace strife into a case for government taking over.[27]

Ruby Loftus screwing a breech ring, Laura Knight, 1943

As well as the great increase in the numbers working, there was a marked change in the make-up of the workforce. Millions of women were mobilised to work in munitions factories and on the land, wholly changing the sociology of work.

The use of women in munitions and engineering factories caused serious conflict. The Clyde Workers Committee led by Davy Kirkwood and John McLean trod a fine line between defending the rights of skilled workers and pushing for the exclusion of women. This was a live issue, and Charlotte Drake told a Conference of Women's Organisations at the Board of Trade 'that the men's trade unions should be asked to take in women members and the women paid just as if they were men'. That way, she said, 'there would be no reason to talk of the undercutting of the men by "women blacklegs"'.[28]

The Labour Party

The movement towards a more corporate capitalism, though, would need a political vehicle that working people could trust, and that was not the Liberal Party. Politically, the new century saw the formation of the Labour Party. The party was formed on the initiative of the trade unions who created a Labour Representation Committee in 1905, followed in 1918 by a more strictly disciplined party. This was the party that would in the 1970s bring in equal opportunities legislation. Labour was in government in 1924, and 1940-45, and as a governing party between 1945 and '51, from 1964 to 1970, and 1972 to 1979. Over that period British industrial relations were transformed with the creation (and eventual collapse) of the 'tripartite system' that institutionalised the partnership of capital and labour, with government, the third party, playing a role between umpire and organiser of industry.

Even more so than the 'new Liberals', Labour argued for the state to regulate private industry to defend workers. 'The state assumed a new importance to the unions', said J. T. Murphy: 'State socialist ideas spread like wildfire. The demand for the nationalisation of this and that industry became popular.'[29]

It was not, however, until the Second World War that Labour's instincts for a corporate capitalism could be put in motion. Even though they were junior partners in the wartime coalition, the Labour Party, by virtue of its intimate connection with the unions, carried great weight with working people. The Cabinet Office closely — and secretly — monitored popular opinion for signs of disaffection from the war effort, fearing the worst, but the results were largely approving. War mobilisation gave working people a feeling that they had a much greater stake in the fortunes of British society than they did in the era of mass unemployment.

During the war Ernest Bevin was Minister of Labour and second only to Churchill in the Cabinet. Bevin directed production, and cancelled the free movement of labour with 'Essential Work Orders', with a central register of all workers. Hours worked rocketed and consumption was cut by rationing — all of which could happen not just because of the widespread sympathy with the war, but also because working people were given a say in the organisation of work through Joint Production Committees. Workers and their representatives sat on Joint Production Committees, often with an official from a government department to meet the targets set in the Essential Work Orders. By the end of 1943, over 4000 Joint Works Production Committees had been established in the engineering and shipbuilding industries. Though the idea was that the Joint Production Committees were about increasing output and preventing bottlenecks, workers' representatives often interpreted that to include their own goals. Canteens were a hot topic of discussion. But most of all skilled workers had their own views about how to do the work well, and were glad to be asked, having so rarely had their understanding of the processes recognised in the past. Under the common moral mission of winning the war, labour, management, and the government officials came close to embracing each other as partners. The wartime Joint Production Committee experience was the foundation of the corporatist, tripartite system of industrial relations in Britain, and a touchstone for most later iterations of that idea, right up to the mid-1980s.

Patriotism was re-worked to make the idea of Britain a popular, everyman version. Through the war, and in the peace that followed, the party of trade unionism was called upon to govern not just at home, but in the colonies, and to manage Britain's relations to the wider world. Both the former trade unionists and the Fabian civil servants embraced the Empire project. So it was that the Labour Party objected to the clauses in President Roosevelt's Atlantic Charter that promised decolonisation on the grounds that 'the inhabitants of the African territories are backward' and 'not yet able to stand by themselves'. Labour's 'Marxist' food minister John Strachey was blunt:

> By hook or by crook the development of the primary production of all sorts in the colonial territories and dependent areas in the Commonwealth and throughout the world is a life and death matter for the economy of this country.

Or as one young Labour Tribune supporter asked, 'what would happen to our balance of payments if we had to take our troops out of Malaya?'[30]

The post-war Labour government took one fifth of British industry into public ownership, including coal, steel, and rail — representing a quarter of the industrial workforce — as well as creating the National Health Service and extending compulsory state schooling from age 11 to 14. A significant share of the workforce was working directly for the state, and, though there was conflict between government managers and employees, workers, and in particular their unions, largely shared the identification with the ideal of nationalised industries.

Organised labour and officialdom

Workers' representatives took part in a wide array of official bodies, panels and inquiries

- Wages Councils (operating industry by industry, 1945-93)
- National Wages Board (1950-65)
- National Board for Prices and Incomes (1965-70; policed pay norms and productivity agreements; separated into a Prices Commission and a Wage Board in 1970)
- National Joint Industrial Council (first created in 1919, these bodies were known as Whitley Councils in white-collar occupations)
- Advisory, Conciliation, and Arbitration Service (known by various names since 1960, as ACAS since 1975)
- Commission on Industrial Relations (1969-74)
- National Industrial Relations Court (1971-74)
- Employment Tribunals (set up under the Industrial Training Act, 1964)
- National Economic Development Council (1961-92)

There were also industry-wide negotiation bodies, like the Railway Staff National Tribunal, and factory-based consultations, and negotiations between unions and management.

There were as well a number of Royal Commissions dealing with trade unions over the years, including

- Royal Commission on Trade Unions (Lord Derby, 1867)
- Royal Commission on Labour (1894)
- Royal Commission on Trade Disputes (1906)
- Royal Commission on Trades Unions and Employers Associations (Lord Donovan, 1968)

And unions gave evidence to a great many Royal Commissions that they were interested in, such as the Royal Commission on National Health Insurance (1926); the Royal Commission on Unemployment Insurance (1931); and the Royal Commission on Mines (1906).

There was also the provision for Courts of Inquiry, like that into the newspaper dispute in 1955, into the power dispute in 1971, and into the dispute at Grunwick in 1977.

Trade unionists were drawn into a dizzying array of official bodies, which dealt with pay, prices, productivity, and industrial disputes.

Many of these bodies were set up with the express goal of disciplining labour, though where that was too explicitly so, as with the National Industrial Relations Court, the body failed. They were also very effective at drawing workers into the administration of capitalist industry. The legitimation of organised labour drew on 3000 full-time union officials and as many as 175,000 voluntary shop stewards. Though industrial disputes were commonplace, the conflict between the classes was largely contained in what the authorities often referred to as 'constitutional' actions. Employers told the Donovan Commission that the shop steward was not generally 'trouble maker' and 'more of a lubricant than an irritant'.[31] A Ford's directive advised that 'a shop steward holds his position by virtue of being a company employee and his first responsibility is to carry out the duties for which the company pays him'.[32] Trade union officers could also serve on school governing bodies, as Justices of the Peace, as labour councillors, MPs, or even Ministers, and could take seats in the House of Lords and sit on government quangos.

Mark Freedland and Nicola Koutaris explain that between 1945 and 1970 the Department of Employment identified itself as 'the seat and location of a tri-partite approach to the governance of the labour economy', which rested on the 'regulation of employment relations by collective bargaining of various sorts and at various levels between employers and organised labour, brokered and supported by the State'.[33] In a Commons debate on the aerospace industry, Ealing MP Bill Molloy lauded the 'record of British trade unionists in achieving industrial peace', and Minister Gerald Kaufman agreed, saying that the British trade union movement 'sets an example in patriotism' — and they had a point.[34]

The new corporatist capitalism rested on a kind of social contract between private industry, organised labour, and government. The promise of job security and reasonable wages, coupled with extensive consultations and negotiations, cemented the deal. Managers took on the new arrangements and worked with them. The policy coalescence around full employment and corporatism was dubbed 'Butskellism' after its main proponents, the Tory 'Rab' Butler, and Labour's Hugh Gaitskell. [35]

The recognition of the status of the core, skilled, and organised industrial workforce also meant by implication the subordinate status of those who were less organised, and whose skills were not certified. They were not covered by the same contract. The corporatist system institutionalised discrimination in employment. It created a hierarchy in employment where unskilled labour, immigrant labour and women workers were underpaid, aggressively managed, and insecure. The status of women workers in the new corporatist model was carefully set out for them, and given institutional shape by the post-war welfare system put in place after the Beveridge Report of 1944.

The Beveridge Plan

Central to the post-war compromise was the creation of the 'welfare state', set out in William Beveridge's report, Social Insurance and Allied Services, in 1944. This was the bible for Labour Party supporters, the outline of a comprehensive welfare plan to create 'freedom from want'.[36] The plan was a great step forward for working people at the end of a terrible war, who had experienced the insecurity and hunger of the 1930s. 'The aim of the Plan for Social Security is to abolish want by ensuring that every citizen willing to serve according to his powers has at all times an income sufficient to meet his responsibilities.' But the responsibilities that Beveridge outlined were very different for men and women, seeing the latter first and foremost as housewives, whose responsibilities were in the home, while the former were breadwinners, who would be expected to provide for their wives.

According to the Beveridge Plan the population falls into four main social classes: 1) Employees; 2) Employers and the self-employed; 3) 'Housewives, that is married women of working age'; and 4) the Unemployed.

Unemployment benefit stated that 'there will be a joint rate for a man and wife who is not gainfully employed'; 'every citizen of working age will contribute in his appropriate class according to the security he needs, or as a married woman will have contributions made by the husband'.[37]

> Most married women have worked at some gainful occupation before marriage; most who have done so give up that occupation on marriage or soon after; all women by marriage acquire a new economic and social status, with risks and rights different from those of the unmarried. On marriage a woman gains a legal right to maintenance by her husband as a first line of defence against the risks which fall directly on the solitary woman; she undertakes at the same time to perform vital unpaid services.

Beveridge could be sure that his judgments were based on sound evidence:

> At the last census in 1931, more than seven out of eight of all housewives, that is to say married women of working age, made marriage their sole occupation; less than one in eight of all housewives was also gainfully occupied.

Beveridge acknowledged that 'there has been an increase in the gainful employment of married women since 1931' — but that was to understate the importance of women workers in both world wars, and to take the contraction of employment in the interwar period, and the forcing of women out of the job market, as the norm. Beveridge went on to say that 'even if a married woman, while living with her husband, undertakes gainful employment', she is not in the same position as other employees, in two important ways. The first is that her work is 'liable to interruption by childbirth', and, he adds, 'in the national interest it is important that the interruption by childbirth should be as complete as possible'. Second, the 'housewife's earnings in general' are 'a means, not of subsistence but a standard of living above subsistence' — he does not say 'pin money', but the meaning is close to that.[38]

In Beveridge's vision, the housewife's 'home is provided for her either by her husband's earnings or benefit if his earnings are interrupted'. He criticised the 'existing insurance schemes' because they have 'not recognised sufficiently the effect of marriage in giving a new economic status to all married women'. Evidence of the problem was that under the National Insurance scheme women 'carry into marriage claims in respect of earlier contributions with full rates of benefit' (though these were already disallowed under the Married Women's Anomalies' Regulations). Instead, Beveridge said, 'the principle here is that on marriage every woman begins a new life in relation to social insurance', and 'she does not carry on rights to unemployment or disability benefit in respect of contributions before marriage' — though she would receive a 'marriage grant'.[39]

Beveridge knew that there would be criticism. 'The decision to pay less than the normal rate of unemployment and disability benefit to housewives who are also gainfully employed is likely to be questioned', he admitted. But 'the case for it is strong'. 'It is undeniable that the needs of housewives in general are less than those of single women when unemployed' — because they would be dependent on their husbands. Given the maternity benefits and marriage grant, thought Beveridge, 'housewives cannot complain of inequity'. Rather, he says, 'Taken as a whole, the Plan for Social Security puts a premium on marriage, instead of penalising it', and 'the position of housewives is recognised in form and substance'.[40]

The Beveridge Plan was rightly celebrated for the commitment to social security it represented. But even as the welfare state offered help, it enshrined the role of the housewife in the organisation of the economy as a distinctive class, rewarding marriage and penalising those married women who worked, on the assumption that they would be dependent upon a male breadwinner.

Not just welfare law, but tax law too, institutionalised gender segregation. Before the Second World War only around 20% of the population paid tax, but alongside National Insurance, workers were subject to 'pay-as-you-earn' income tax, bringing the tax base up to 12 million. The tax system aggregated married couples' incomes and gave a married person's tax allowance that assumed women's work was secondary, and incentivised the nuclear family. From 1969 married couples got tax relief on mortgages (Mortgage Interest Relief at Source), and from 1945 they got child benefits. There were benefits for lone parents, including free school meals, though these came with a great deal of social shaming. From 1948 the National Health Service took on the policy of 'confining' women in hospital wards for the last weeks of pregnancies to shield them from work and to cut infant deaths. A division of labour based on gender was written into the welfare state, and was a guide to employers.

Segregated workforce

After the war, women's employment grew steadily, much more than Beveridge had anticipated. But the tenor of government policy mirrored the attitude of both employers and trade union leaders, that women had a subordinate place in the jobs market. One clear sign was that the growth in the numbers of women in work went hand in hand with sex-segregated workplaces. At Ford UK's plant in Dagenham there had since the war been many women working alongside men on the assembly line, but a big shake-out in 1951 forced them out. Afterwards, women at Ford worked stitching seat covers with sewing machines, or in the canteen. Women worked in biscuit factories, like

Women on Cadbury's production line

Peek Freans in Bermondsey, making sweets at Rowntree's in York, and in the clothing trade working sewing machines. Many worked, too, as nurses in the new National Health Service — 194,900 in 1952, alongside doctors who were almost all men.[41] Researcher Carolyn Vogler found that gender-segregated workforces are associated with more traditional roles in the home: 'men living in households with a more traditional division of labour were more likely to be working in segregated jobs'.[42]

In the post-war expansion of the economy, employers took advantage of the low wages women were expected to work for — expected by Beveridge and the Labour government, amongst others. With this outlook common in the labour movement the unions failed to recruit. Trade union membership rose from 7.8 million in 1944 to 10 million in 1966, but throughout the share stayed at four fifths men to one fifth women. Around half of all men in work over those years were members of a union, but only one quarter of all women were.[43] As was common, the National Union of Tailors and Garment Workers negotiated a differentiated pay rise of 5d an hour for men and 4d an hour for women in 1969 — even though 93,000 of its 111,000 members were women.[44] It was common up until the 1990s to find largely female workforces represented by male trade union convenors, and often male shop stewards, too.

'Coloured immigration'

In 1948 the British Cabinet was looking in alarm at the arrival of 492 Jamaicans on a ship called the Empire Windrush, bound for Tilbury. The Cabinet Economic Policy Committee regretted that the migrants were 'private persons travelling at their own expense' and that they could not be turned back, though they did look at whether they could

John Hazel, Harold Wilmit & John Richards arrive at Tilbury docks from the Caribbean on the ex-troop ship Empire Windrush (1948).

be sent on to East Africa. The committee asked for a report on 'the incident' from Colonial Secretary Arthur Creech Jones, and asked how any more like it could be stopped. Creech Jones accepted that the arrival was a 'problem' but that as a 'spontaneous movement' the government did not have the 'legal power' to stop it. Instead they would have to take special measures to manage the migrants.[45]

Britain's post-war economy grew at a healthy average of 3% per year between 1948 and 1973. Demand for labour tightened and for the first time significant numbers of immigrants came from the British West Indies, and from the Indian sub-continent. They were joined by Asians forced out of Uganda and Kenya in the 1960s. More than a quarter of a million black West Indians arrived in Britain between 1953 and 1962, along with 143,000 from India and Pakistan.

The legal and moral basis for the right of migration to Britain was set out in the 1948 Nationality Act. The British Empire had been re-organised as a Commonwealth after the war. Where the Empire nominally had common citizenship, each country was allowed to make their own laws afterwards, but Britain at first operated something like an 'open door' in recognition of the rights of former subjects. Practical restraints made migration between Commonwealth countries rare, except where there was labour recruitment.

Booming Britain took on West Indians and Asians as nurses and midwives, on the buses and the Underground, as labourers, as cleaners, and in catering. West Indian teachers were called on to fill places in the new Secondary Modern schools, after the school leaving age was raised. Indians and Pakistanis found work in textiles in West Yorkshire and Lancashire. Indian doctors found work in the new National Health Service, as did West Indian and some Asian nurses. Most jobs that migrants filled were unskilled, though many who came had good training and education.

From the outset the political establishment were nervous about the new migrants. When the Windrush arrived at Tilbury in 1948 a group of Labour MPs wrote to the Prime Minister that 'an influx of coloured

---

Caribbean nurses

In 1949 the Ministries of Health and Labour, together with the Colonial Office, the General Nursing Council, and the Royal College of Nursing, started recruiting in the West Indies. By 1955, 16 British colonies had set up selection and recruitment schemes for the NHS.

In its first 21 years, between one quarter and one third of all NHS staff were recruited from overseas.

By 1954 more than 3000 Caribbean women were training in British hospitals, rising to 6,450 in in 1968.

In 1969 the *Nursing Times* pointed out that only 5% of overseas recruited nurses were reaching the top grades of the profession.

— Ann Kramer, *Many Rivers to Cross*, London: The Stationery Office, 2006

---

people domiciled here is likely to impair the harmony, strength and cohesion of our public and social life and to bring discord and unhappiness to all concerned'. After the Attlee government's reaction, the Conservative leader, Winston Churchill, planning the 1955 Conservative Manifesto, told the Cabinet that the best slogan would be 'Keep England White'.[46] Birmingham Labour MP Roy Hattersley argued that 'unrestricted immigration can only produce additional problems'. In 1964 he thought that 'we must impose a test which tries to analyse which immigrants are most likely to be assimilated into our national life'.[47]

Government hostility was in time mirrored by race attacks in Notting Hill and the Midlands in 1958. These disturbances were taken as a justification for the first in a succession of laws to restrict immigration, the 1962 Commonwealth Immigration Act. Under the Act, a set number of vouchers were issued through which migrants could enter, therefore controlling the numbers coming into the country from each Commonwealth country. More laws were passed in 1968 and 1971, all aiming to 'tighten' controls on immigration.

The practical impact of the immigration law was that it established a hierarchy in which black people were of lower status than those who were white. The hierarchy was ideological in that it embodied racial superiority. It was also practical in that black people were subject to treatment by public authorities that white people were not. Black workers were investigated by an Illegal Immigration Intelligence Unit of the Police Force, the immigration police, which raided scores of workplaces from its foundation in 1973. At the same time police paid special attention to younger black men on the streets, searching and arresting them for public order offences. Even schools were unofficially segregated, by local catchment areas, and by excluding many West Indian boys under disciplinary rules; in 1986, Calderdale Education Authority was investigated by the Commission for Racial Equality for keeping Asian children out of mainstream schools, by testing their language proficiency and pushing them into special language units.[48] When Bernard Coard wrote a small booklet titled *How the West Indian Child is Made Educationally Sub-Normal in the British School System*, 'the whole community' was 'galvanised'. (Schools today show some evidence of segregation by choice.)[49]

Discrimination against black people shaped their lives and the work they did. Overall, the numbers working in manufacturing fell by 745,000 between 1961 and 1971; but the number of manufacturing workers born outside Britain rose by 272,000. By 1971 79% of West Indian men and 78% of Pakistani men of working age were manual workers, compared to 50% of working men as a whole. Three quarters of immigrants' wives worked compared to just 43% of all married women.[50]

A third of all the workers at the Courtaulds Red Scar mill in Preston, by 1964, were Asians: 'Two departments of the mill were wholly immigrant, organised in ethnic work-teams under white supervisors.'[51] The authorities' differential treatment of black and Asian people in Britain made it easier for employers to treat them differently, too. One Asian Ford worker described the assembly line at Langley:

[W]alking along the Body line at Langley truck plant, on either the day shift or the night shift, is like walking around the world. The bottom section is where the work is hardest and there is hardly any overtime: the workers are mostly Asian with only the occasional white and West Indian worker. The middle section involves less arduous and slightly more skilled work. There you will see a mixture of African, West Indian, Asian and white workers. The top section is the repair area, an area where the pace of the work is not determined by the speed of the line, and where there is the most overtime. The area is predominantly white.[52]

Ford were well known for taking on black workers, and in their southern plant at Dagenham, West Indians were moving up the skills grade. Ford's race relations would become a battleground for many years.

In 1982 Leila Hassan looked at 'ancillary work in the National Health Service — catering, portering, washing up, cleaning jobs and laundry jobs done by some 70,000 blacks (mainly women), a third of the total workforce'. The women she talked to told her:

The government and ministers know that ancillary workers are more low paid than any other workers in the NHS or in the country and we are living below the poverty line, and never has the government offered us anything.

They added, 'it is not the nurses doing the dirty jobs, it is the ancillaries, and without us the nurses couldn't function, it's we keep the nurses'.[53]

West Indian nurses were mostly taken on at the less qualified State Enrolled Nurse position while the better paid State Registered Nurse position was kept for whites. 'The NHS reminds me very much of a colony in the way it's run', one nurse told Beverly Bryan and her fellow researchers: 'the white sister will act as manager, organising the work for her black nursing staff, and then spend the morning sitting in the office'.[54]

Black workers were generally taken on in subordinate roles and discriminated against at work. Trade union offices would insist that they were 'colour blind'; but they were also patriotic for British industry in a way that their officials took to mean 'British jobs for British workers'. In 1965 a local union branch opposed jobs for black nurses at Storthes Hall Mental Hospital; the following year Asquith Xavier was barred from working at Euston station under an agreement between the Staff Association and the employers — colour bars were operating at Camden and Broad Street, too. In Keighley in 1961, engineers struck when two Pakistanis were put to work, and in the same year shop stewards at Alfred Herbert Machine Tools sought assurances from management that black workers would not be promoted.[55]

The end of corporatism

The problems of race and sex discrimination were important markers of the limits of the corporate society, of the outer boundaries beyond which the social contract no longer applied. But these problems were not its core dynamic. The basis of the system was the relationship to organised labour. It was that relationship that was tested to destruction in the 1970s and 1980s. The crisis, and the subsequent dismantling of the corporatist system, would shake up all relations.

In the 1960s Britain's competitiveness with its industrial rivals was slipping, and its profit rates were under pressure. British workers had been driven hard to produce more in the post-war years. But ever-greater capital investments gave, to the frustration of the employers, a declining rate of return. Labour-saving machinery increased the product efficiency of industry, but in lowering prices reduced profit margins too. The National Board for Prices and Incomes saw the barrier to increased profits as workers' reluctance to raise productivity, a view that echoed managers' resentment at the imagined encroachment on their right to manage under agreements with the unions.

Over the years from 1965 to 1979 governments and employers tried different ways to address what they saw as a 'productivity gap' through the corporate system they had built. Harold Wilson's government tried to enforce a wage freeze in 1966 alongside increased productivity. Then Labour tried to stop unofficial strikes with their 'In Place of Strife' white paper: proposals to manage industrial conflict through a quasi-legal framework. Labour's working-class supporters were put off, and Edward Heath's Conservative government was elected — only to try put in place a yet more coercive Industrial Relations Act. The attempt to impose pay restraint and limit industrial conflict through the corporate system only tended to provoke a greater reaction. Using it to restrain labour militancy and force up productivity strained the corporate system to breaking point.

The first sign of the crisis of corporatism was a rising crescendo of industrial conflict, and unnervingly for the system's defenders, of unofficial strikes, rising to 24 million in 1972. According to the government white paper, 'In Place of Strife', '95 per cent of all strikes in Britain were unofficial and were responsible for three quarters of working days lost through strikes'.[56]

Militant strike action was always a possibility in a system that relied on negotiating agreement between employers and labour. The subjective collaboration of the workforce was what the system was there to engage, so the prospect that it might be withheld was a perennial danger. Institutionalised conflict might break out of its boundaries. The incorporation of the union leadership in the management of British industry put them in the front line of the conflict. They were at once trying to hold the support of the union members, and put forward the case for the terms they had negotiated with management. Opposition to the leadership opened up. In many instances, the local shop stewards became an alternative leadership, leading strikes that were not sought, and often not supported by the convenors and union leaders. On other occasions *ad hoc* rank-and-file movements challenged the stewards as well as the convenors.

Employers were not surprisingly outraged at what they called 'unconstitutional' action. They felt that they had already conceded more authority to unions than they would have liked, and were angry to find that the union leaders could not deliver their members' support. Employers, though, had provoked the conflicts, driving workers to increase productivity, and trying to hold down wages while putting up their own prices. The workplace relationship was only superficially one of agreement. Agreements and negotiations

Strike for the 'Pentonville 5' dockworkers jailed for picketing

would hardly be necessary if the workers' interests truly coincided with their employers' interests.

Baron Geddes of Epsom had been General Secretary of the Post Office Workers' union from 1944 to 1957, and President of the Trades Union Congress in 1955. On 18 March 1969 he told the House of Lords that 'the men who ran the trade union movement... could be called patriots':

> They believed that they supported the Government of the day, not because they were, in the Left-wing words, 'capitalist lackeys' but because they believed that the good of the country in the long run, in the long term, was for the good of their members. It seems to me to-day that we cannot be so certain that that is true.[57]

Women were also taking strike action. In 1968 187 women working as machinists making seat covers at Ford went on strike to get their jobs regraded. Around that time many women were taking part in the workplace disputes that were raging, such as the London night cleaners' fight for union recognition, the disputes of 20,000 Leeds clothing workers, and women taking part in the teachers' strike. The Ford machinists' strike set down the ideal of 'equal pay for equal work'.

The 1974-79 Labour government pushed the corporate system to its limit. The social contract between organised labour, employers, and government was used yet more forcefully to hold down wages and boost productivity. In its programme of 1973 Labour argued for 'a great contract between government, industry and trade unions, with all three parties prepared to make sacrifices to achieve agreement on a strategy to deal with the problems'. The trade union leaders agreed a wage rise limit of £6 in 1975, followed by a second phase of limit of 4.5%. The 'third phase' was imposed against an all-out strike by firefighters in 1977. The view of the trade union movement was that government had forfeited their trust by its use of legal compulsion in labour organisation.[58]

The announcement of another 5% limit — 'Phase 4' — in 1978 provoked an open rebellion. The low-paid workers of the National Union of Public Employees struck out rubbish collection and even burials; railway workers and road haulage drivers struck. More people were out on strike than in 1972: 4.6 million, with a loss of 29.4 million working days.

Engineers' leader Reg Birch looked back over the record of Labour's 'In Place of Strife', Health, and Industrial Relations Acts, 'the various forms of wage restraint and compulsion': 'After 33 years of the oppression of the working class by social democracy there is now a bursting out.'[59] The feminist Beatrix Campbell took an altogether different view. To her it seemed that the revolt was against the egalitarian pay award under the Social Contract, an across-the-board £6 per week, that was sabotaged when 'the redoubts of macho Labourism had mutinied and insisted on the "restoration of differentials" — the gap between skilled, unskilled and women'.[60]

The crisis of the corporate economy was felt sharply by ethnic minorities. Unemployment rose overall, but black unemployment climbed even faster. Black people made up 2.3% of the unemployed in 1973, but by 1982 that number was 4.1%. For a social group that was heavily dependent on manufacturing and the public sector, the contraction of both those spheres was a blow. Unofficially trade union branches often adopted the line 'last in, first out', meaning that where there were lay-offs, black workers would be first. Black children were demotivated at school by the limited job prospects of their older peers, and by the low expectations of their teachers. Asian workers were militant in defence of their jobs and conditions. In the Midlands Motor Cylinder Company in 1968, at Mansfield Hosiery Mills in Loughborough in 1973, in the Imperial Typewriters strike in Leicester 1974, and in the strike by photographic processing workers at Grunwick's in 1977, they took action against employers. These strikes were all provoked by bullying management, and the promotion of white workers over Asians. Often the local union negotiators dismissed the workers, as TGWU negotiator George Bromley did when he complained that the Imperial Typewriters employees 'have not followed the proper disputes procedure', and 'have no legitimate grievance'.[61]

With greater pressure on household budgets in the later 1970s women were taking on more work, often part-time. Economic pressures, though, were leading to more reactionary ideas. The *Sunday Times* editorialised that 'unemployment and inflation have made it imperative to convince women that their place is in the home because the country cannot afford to employ them or pay for the support facilities they need'.[62]

The strike wave of the low-paid was called a 'peasant's revolt', and also a 'winter of discontent', and the widespread disaffection saw Labour lose the 1979 election to a Conservative government committed to dismantling the post-war consensus.

Dismantling the consensus: 1979-92

Soon after winning the election in 1979, Margaret Thatcher signalled that the days when government would broker talks between industry and unions were over, saying there would be 'no more beer and sandwiches at Number Ten'. The Labour government, she said, had offered 'the joint oversight of economic policy by a tripartite body representing the Trades Union Congress, the Confederation of British Industry and the Government'. But 'we were saved from this abomination', which she called 'the most radical form of socialism ever contemplated by a British government'; corporatism and the tripartite talks between government were a trap. As Neil Millward et al summarised:

The government's aim — highly controversial at the time — was to weaken the power of the trade unions, deregulate the labour market and dismantle many of the tripartite institutions of corporatism in which the trade unions played a major part.[63]

Chancellor Nigel Lawson, limiting the powers of the wage councils, said that in a 'free society it is plainly a matter for business and industry itself to determine rates of pay'.[64] As Linda Dickens and Alan Neal explain, 'institutional arrangements seen as underpinning... structured collective bargaining and/or imposing rigidities on the operation of the free market were eroded or ended'.[65] Employment laws were passed in 1980, 1982, 1984, 1986, 1988, 1989, 1990, 1992, and 1993 — all limiting the power of trade unions to strike, making them liable for company losses, outlawing the 'closed shop' agreements with employers, and enforcing ballots before strike action could be taken.

With the encouragement of the Department of Trade and Industry, British industry set about a marked reorganisation. Not only were 60% of government holdings privatised, but many larger and more established industries were slimmed down — some, like shipbuilding and coalmining, to the point of extinction. Industries were restructured, often contracting out all but their core activities, leaving employees to compete for their old jobs in new service-sector businesses. Many companies de-layered and down-sized their workforces, taking advantage of anti-union laws. Bypassing union negotiators, employers made their own contracts with individual employees. Workforces were encouraged to agree 'flexibility', working hours that suited their life obligations or, more often, the needs of the employers. Many new contracts were for part-time and temporary positions. There would be 'no more job for life', workers were told. One change that would prove important for the spread of equal opportunities policies was the growing appeal of the paradigm of 'Human Resource Management', 'the banner under which increasing numbers of employee relations specialists marched', according to Neil Millward. Human Resource Management would mean a much more individuated relationship between employee and employer, but also one that was all procedure, and so depersonalised.[66]

Though they claimed to be taking the state out of industry, and out of wider society, the Conservative government used state power extensively. Police power and the law courts were used to prevent workers from striking and protesting, having outlawed 'secondary' picketing and mass picketing. Between 1980 and 1988 520 separate acts of parliament were made law, along with 18,893 statutory instruments — around 7000 pages of legislation every year; civil liberties were reined in over everything from horror films on video, to schools' treatment of homosexuality, dangerous dogs, football fans, and raves.[67]

Most of all, though, the meaning of trade union reform and the effective end of the tripartite system was that the national consensus that had been established in the post-war period was ended. The end of consensus had profound effects on social attitudes, leading to a marked individuation and even a disaffection from public life. One of the more pointed features of the Conservative governments in the years from 1979 to 1997 was an appeal to a robust patriotism. But in a sense, that appeal to national sentiment was a sign that its substantial basis had been eroded. The post-war consensus bound people to the national project, through a wide span of bodies: trade unions, mass political parties, municipal councils, in addition to the charities, church groups, and women's institutes that appealed to the more middle-class Britons. Most of those groups and clubs withered as the government tore up the old social contract. As 'the Nation' had less and less substance, the establishment appealed to it even more.

Targeting immigrants

One dramatic focus of the stridently national rhetoric that the government adopted in the 1980s was a renewed focus on restricting immigration. Margaret Thatcher had said at the election that many people felt 'that this country might be rather swamped by people of a different culture'. A new Nationality Act of 1981 limited the rights of those citizens of the Commonwealth, and William Whitelaw said the law was 'to dispose of the lingering notion that Britain is somehow a haven for all those whose countries we used to rule'.[68] The immigration police were encouraged to re-double their efforts and in 1980 there were 910 removals and 2,472 deportations, around twice the amount in previous years, and a rate that was kept up through the 1980s. Newspapers sent photographers to the landing gates for flights coming in from India and Pakistan to illustrate headlines like 'they're still flooding in' (*Evening Standard*). 'In former times such invasions would have been repelled by armed force', reported the *Daily Mail*. When Tamil refugees arrived from Sri Lanka in 1985, Home Secretary Leon Brittan said they were a threat to British workers' jobs and living standards. The *Financial Times* trumpeted that 'the last thing the country needs is a flood of new immigrants'.[69] Official sanction for anti-immigrant feeling encouraged a long spasm of race attacks against brown and black people living in Britain.

In March 1986, 36 police officers raided the British Telecom offices in the City of London, interrogating cleaning staff on their legal status, with the collaboration of the BT managers. It was just one of hundreds of 'fishing raids'.[70] Black and Asian people were asked to show their passports at work, and at hospitals and unemployment benefit offices. People deemed 'illegal' under the nationality laws were subject to detention and deportation.

It was not just immigrants from the Indian sub-continent who were caught out by the renewed emphasis on Britishness. West Indians stood out as far as the authorities were concerned. Metropolitan Police Chief Kenneth Newman said in 1982 that 'in the Jamaicans you have people who are constitutionally disorderly... it's simply in their make-up'.[71] The year before, London police had launched a campaign against 'street crime' called 'Swamp 81', under which they stopped and searched scores of young black men in

Brixton in South London. The operation provoked a riot that lasted two days. A sustained campaign to criminalise black people provoked disturbances in Toxteth, Liverpool, and Bristol in that same year. In 1985 police assaulted Cherry Groce in a raid nearby the Broadwater Farm that ended in prolonged rioting in which Police Constable Kenneth Blakelock was killed. Winston Silcott, imprisoned for the killing, was vilified as the face of hatred on the front cover of the newspapers, though later his conviction was quashed.

Britain's unhappy row about what was and what was not 'British' was a sign that the old social compact had broken down. Without many positive gains to engage their citizens, the elite chose to define the nation negatively, targeting foreigners with darker skin. The consequences for equality of opportunity seemed very slim. According to Sociologist Yaojun Li,

> in 1981, unemployment rose to 10% for White men, but jumped to 26% for Pakistani/Bangladeshi men. When the recession was at its highest in 1982, Black and Pakistani/Bangladeshi men's unemployment rate reached nearly 30% as compared with only 12% for White men.[72]

The impact of a patriotic Britain was destructive, but it was also limited in its appeal to a nation that felt less and less engaged.

Victorian values

Alongside the emphasis on nation, Prime Minister Margaret Thatcher thought that her government ought to be 'concentrating on strengthening the traditional family', and 'never felt uneasy about praising "Victorian values"'.[73] In 1979 the new Conservative Minister for Health and Social Security, Patrick Jenkin, said that 'Mothers should be encouraged to look after their children full-time instead of going out to work'. According to Jenkin, 'the increasing turbulence of modern life, with rising crime, industrial disruption, violence and terrorism is rooted in the separation of children from their parents'.[74]

Legislation cutting social security entitlements to under-25 year-olds was based on the idea that families would support young people for longer. Cuts in many services assumed and depended upon the work of families — overwhelmingly of wives and mothers — to make up what was taken away. So the limited spending on care for the elderly assumed that women would take up the slack.

In 1988 it seemed to be a real possibility that abortion rights would become more limited. Liberal MP David Alton's Private Member's Bill (which was ultimately unsuccessful) would have outlawed late-term abortions. At Dame Jill Knight's urging a clause

Margaret Thatcher

was added to the 1988 Local Government Act forbidding teachers from saying that homosexual relations could be 'a pretended family relation'. The restriction, first demanded by the Parents' Rights' Group in Haringey, passed.

That social compact that had been made in the post-war years between capital and labour, brokered by the state, was breaking down in the 1980s. The circumstances suggested that the times were hostile to equality in the workplace.

The Conservative governments of 1979-83 and 1983-87 kept up a strongly traditionalist and xenophobic rhetoric, backed up with laws hostile to migrants and women. The end of the industrial consensus seemed to signal an even harsher iteration of the gender and racial inequality than before. As things turned out, though, other changes were pulling in an altogether different direction.

— TWO —

The Commission for Racial Equality

'There are two problems in world politics today which transcend all others', *Sunday Times* editor Harry Hodson told the Foreign Office audience at Chatham House in 1950: 'the struggle between Communism and liberal democracy, and the problem of race relations'.[1] Hodson called for the founding of the Institute of Race Relations. Back then, race relations were mostly about the colonies, but with the beginnings of Commonwealth migration in the 1950s the question of race relations, and the fear of race conflict, came to be a domestic issue.

Britain's first race relations law did not cover discrimination at work. The Race Relations Act of 1965 was mostly about public order. When the Houses of Parliament argued over the need for laws on race relations they were mostly worried about the threat of disorder and of Britain's reputation abroad, in the Commonwealth, and in Washington.

Home Office Minister Frank Soskice told the House of Commons, 'basically, the Bill is concerned with public order':

> Overt acts of discrimination in public places, intensely wounding to the feelings of those against whom these acts are practised, perhaps in the presence of many onlookers, breed the ill will which, as the accumulative result of several such actions over a period, may disturb the peace.

The Bill was also put through with one eye on Britain's standing in the world:

> It would be a tragedy of the first order if our country, with its unrivalled tradition of tolerance and fair play as between one man or woman and another and perfect respect for the rights and personal worth and dignity of the individual, should see the beginnings of the development of a distinction between first and second class citizens and the disfigurement which can arise from inequality of treatment and incitement to feelings of hatred directed to the origins of particular citizens, something for which they are not responsible.[2]

The legislation on race relations in Britain was closely tied to the laws stopping immigrants from coming to Britain. In opposition, the Labour Party leader Harold Wilson had spoken out against the 'colour bar' raised by the 1962 Immigration Act, 'strongly opposed to its terms because it was based on racial and colour discrimination'. Wilson was aware of the suggestion that race discrimination was damaging to Britain's reputation, as had been shown by the protests and boycott of Bristol's bus service over its colour bar — condemned throughout the Commonwealth.[3] As Prime Minister, he said that: 'In 1964 the world cannot live with a division between first-class and second-class citizens differentiated by the colour of their skins.'[4]

Patrick Boyle, the Earl of Cork and Orrery, warning of the dangers of the 1968 Commonwealth Immigration Act, asked the House of Lords: 'Apart from the justice or the legality of the matter, what does it look like to the rest of the world?'[5]

Harold Wilson recoiled from open race discrimination, but he still kept the limits on non-white immigration in place, pleading 'we accept in this congested island the need for control'.[6] The race conflict was inflamed by the debate over immigration, which was why the 1965 Act was brought in. It was a widely shared fear, so that even the chairman of the Immigration Control Association, John Sanders, welcomed the Race Relations Act: 'The most positive statement he makes is that he would introduce legislation to bar incitement of racial strike. Every responsible citizen in the country would be behind him on that.'[7]

Some black activists, though, were sceptical. Paul Stephenson, who had organised the Bristol Bus Boycott, remembered worrying that 'the government wanted to take the sting out of the racial protest we had started'.[8] There were grounds for thinking that the Race Relations Act was not there to help black people but to defeat militant activism. Those who were first investigated under the clauses on incitement to race hatred were black radicals Michael de Freitas and Obi Egbuna (who were both imprisoned) and the visiting American black power leader Stokely Carmichael (who was told to leave the country).[9]

The 1965 Act criminalised discrimination in shops and on the streets, but not, initially, in employment, which was seen as too great an incursion on the individual liberty of employers.

In 1968 a tougher act to outlaw race discrimination in employment was brought in by Home Secretary James Callaghan, though its first goal was 'to protect society as a whole against actions which will lead to social disruption'.[10] Under these laws ethnic leaders were asked to join Community Relations Councils and act as go-betweens to the government and the community.

In 1976 Home Office Minister Roy Jenkins looked again at the policy. The chairman of the Select Committee Frederick Willey saw the need to address the problems that 'job levels are substantially lower for the immigrant communities, that earnings are lower and that we have an alarming proportion of young West Indians unemployed and homeless'.

The Select Committee concluded that:

Race discrimination and race prejudice are still widespread. The fact that much of the discrimination and prejudice is covert,

Prince Charles, David Lane of the CRE, and Norman Gardner, 1979

negligent, or unintentional does not make this less harmful, and it is aggravated by growing lack of confidence among the ethnic communities, especially the young — the second generation non-immigrant population. Consequently, there is a risk of the communities becoming permanently alienated. What is needed, above everything else, is a clear and demonstrable Government commitment to equal rights.

Conservative William Whitelaw thought that 'the main requirement for the Bill's success is that the Home Secretary gives the public real confidence in his approach to race relations policy as a whole'. What he meant was that the management of race relations meant first and foremost that 'he must demonstrate clearly that there is strict and effective control of the numbers entering the country'.[11]

The Select Committee, taking account of the cost to the public purse, argued for a more targeted approach, which justified the setting up of the Commission for Racial Equality. The head of the Commission was David Lane, who had been a Tory junior minister for immigration at the Home Office, after working for the Confederation of British Industry.

Grassroots anti-racism

While the officials were talking about containing the race problem, many people were doing something much more practical. They were speaking out against race discrimination, both on the part of the government, and by bigots.

When the 1965 Commonwealth Immigration Act was being argued for, students, black Britons and trade unionists protested against the laws. Among them was Claudia Jones. Originally from Trinidad, Jones had been in Harlem until she was barred from the United States for her radicalism, and took refuge in London. Jones saw that the far-right British Movement was stirring up hostility against West Indian migrants in Notting Hill. After a young carpenter Kelso Cochrane was murdered, Jones had the idea of starting a West Indian carnival to showcase the best of Caribbean society for Londoners. In 1963 the West Indian Development Council and their spokesman Paul Stephenson led a four-month boycott of a Bristol bus company over its bar on black crews.

In 1968 there were a few groups that took their inspiration from the Black Panthers in the United States, including those led by the playwright Obi Egbuna, another led by Michael de Freitas, who set up the 'Black House' on Holloway Road and styled himself 'Michael X', and a group based in North London led by Althea Jones-Lecointe and her husband Eddie. This last group campaigned with great effect when Frank Critchlow's Mangrove restaurant was raided many

British Black Panthers on
the march in Brixton / Neil
Kenlock

times on spurious charges of drug-dealing. The Black Panthers'
marches were broken up, and when they were charged under public
order offences, they fought a strident campaign around the trial at
the Old Bailey.[12]

Another group of migrants was organised by the Indian Workers
Association. Drawing on the ties with Communist and Socialist
parties, and trade unions in India, they related awkwardly with trade
union officials and Labour Party members in Britain. Recruiting
especially among the textile workers in Lancashire and West
Yorkshire, the Indian Workers Association leaders were active in
many industrial disputes. In Birmingham, IWA leader Avtar Jouhl
fought against the colour bar, and against the racist candidate in the
Smethwick by-election.

Another militant group were those around Darcus Howe, of the
Race Today collective. With him, Howe had an impressive team of

activists and writers, including his uncle, the veteran left-wing activist C. L. R. James, the poet Linton Kwesi Johnson, Mala Sen and Farrukh Dhondy, the radical educationalist Gus John, and Leila Hassan. Sen and Dhondy played a key role in a housing campaign in the Seventies, with squatting activist Terry Fitzpatrick, under the banner of the Bengali Housing Action Group. Opening up scores of vacant homes to Bangladeshi families who had been shut out by Tower Hamlets' surreptitious colour bar against Asian families, the prolonged protests won the Greater London Council to release additional housing to the homeless families.[13]

On 18 January 1981 a fire was started at a birthday party in New Cross Road, Deptford, killing 13 young people, all West Indian. Around that time there had been many firebomb attacks on black venues, like the Moonshot Club, and it seemed clear that this was another.[14] The New Cross Massacre Action Committee galvanised a remarkable movement of protest. Twenty thousand mostly black marchers left from Deptford on Monday, 2 March 1981. When the police tried to stop them crossing the river to go to parliament, the numbers were too great and the police line was pushed aside. When I was a boy at Kingsdale School, black school-leavers barricaded themselves into the headmaster's office, announcing themselves as 'Radio Revolutionary Kingsdale', and played Bob Marley and Tapper Zukie records over the school tannoy, to the delight of all the children (nearby Tulse Hill School had its own Black Panther chapter).[15]

Grassroots resistance to racism in Britain was strong and effective. It did, though, have one pointed weakness. For the most part black people in Britain marched alone. White opposition to racism was not often attempted by activists. There were some important exceptions. The left wing of the trade union movement organised protests in support of the Grunwicks strikers, and joined large protests outside the firm, in support of the mostly Asian women workers. At Ford, black stewards like Jupiter Harry tried to organise with white

National Union of Mineworkers join the picket line at Grunwicks

counterparts to challenge racism in the company (and in the 1980s, Ford workers refused to handle goods from South Africa). There were attempts, too, to organise defence against racist attacks, with the group East London Workers Against Racism. Protests against the National Front, organised by the 'Anti-Nazi League' and 'Rock Against Racism', were also popular with a broad range of younger people, though pointedly these tended to emphasise the alien, un-British character of the 'Nazis', rather than identifying a problem of British racism.

The trade union leaders endorsed the Anti-Nazi League, and sponsored other campaigns like the Campaign Against Racial Discrimination. These though were mostly top-down campaigns that relied on letter writing and middle-class sponsorship. Those campaigns would relate well to the Commission for Racial Equality, as well as the Community Relations Councils that preceded it. Grassroots activism, though, was at odds with the official approach.

Propagation of equal opportunities policies

The new Commission for Racial Equality was established under the 1976 Race Relations Act under chairman David Lane with the duties of:

a) Working towards the elimination of discrimination;

b) Promoting equality of opportunity between persons of different racial groups generally; and

c) Keeping under review the working of the Act, and, when required by the Secretary of State or when it otherwise thinks it necessary, to draw up and submit to the Secretary of State proposals for amending it.[16]

In 1977, the Commission for Racial Equality announced that:

We intend to adopt a vigorous, firm approach. We shall make full use of our powers to ensure the twin objectives of eliminating discrimination and promoting equal opportunity. In pursuance of our statutory duties we shall seek to identify every area where blacks are the victims of undisguised or thinly disguised discrimination, or of indirect discrimination or discriminatory practices... as well as tackling the deeper causes of disadvantage.[17]

At a conference in Leicester in 1977 Dr Peter Sanders, director of the Commission's Equal Opportunity Division, talked of 'encouraging employers, local authorities, estate agents and others to promote equal opportunity so that discrimination does not occur'.

Sanders promised to make full use of 'new powers of investigation' that 'had been shown to be necessary by the experience of the Race Relations Board in operating the weaker 1968 legislation': 'subpoena powers would be available where information was deliberately withheld, and at the end of the investigation the Commission could publish a report making recommendations for change'. [18] These were powers that gave the Commission more leverage over employers and other agencies to enforce compliance.

Sanders announced another proposal, too, which was more positive: 'his Division would be concentrating on producing a Code of Practice for Employment'.

In April 1980 the new Code of Practice[19] was announced: 'The importance of the Code was that it was a model that employers could incorporate into their own policies.'

The Code of Practice

The point of the Code was 'to give practical guidance which will help employers, trade unions, employment agencies and employees to understand not only the provisions of the Race Relations Act and their implications, but also how best they can implement policies to eliminate racial discrimination and to enhance equality of opportunity'.

The important point about the Code was that it was voluntary: 'the Code does not impose any legal obligations itself'. But the appeal to voluntary compliance was made in the context of the Act, since if 'its recommendations are not observed this may result in breaches of the law where the act or omission falls within any of the specific prohibitions of the Act'. And, 'moreover, its provisions are admissible in evidence in any proceedings under the Race Relations Act before an Industrial Tribunal'.

The appeal to employers was that by adopting the voluntary Code of Practice they would get ahead of the policy, and avoid having it imposed upon them, so retaining control of the process. The background to the adoption of the voluntary Code was that 'the Race Relations Act 1976 makes it unlawful to discriminate against any person, directly or indirectly, in the field of employment'. The risks of investigation, or a ruling against them in an Industrial Tribunal, all added up to a lot of potential embarrassment for employers, some of whom preferred to adopt a voluntary code.

As the Commission explained, under the Act of 1976, 'Responsibility for providing equal opportunity for all job applicants and employees rests primarily with employers'. It was to this end that the Commission 'recommended that they should adopt, implement and monitor an equal opportunities policy to ensure that there is no unlawful discrimination and that equal opportunity is generally available'. To make sure that the policy is effective, employers should allocate 'overall responsibility for the policy to a member of senior management'.[20]

The Commission motivated the Code to employers on the grounds that 'many of the Code's provisions show the close link between equal opportunities and good employment practice'. The claim that an employer's adoption of an equal opportunities policy would be good for business would become very important. The idea is that the interests of employers and minorities would be happily reconciled in an equal opportunities policy. Instead of being the villains of the piece, the employers would be the good guys, and it would help their businesses, too.

As well as creating a new responsibility for managers, the Code also had consequences for employees, and for relations between managers and employees. So, 'to assist in preventing racial discrimination and promoting equal opportunity it is recommended that individual employees should... cooperate in measures introduced by management designed to ensure equal opportunity and non-discrimination'. Unions, too, were called upon to 'cooperate in the introduction and implementation of full equal opportunities policies'. As we shall see, this injunction to cooperate with management was made at a time when workers were, on other issues, contesting workplace codes of discipline — and challenging the 'managers' right to manage'.[21] Here, though, obedience to management diktat was justified as being in support of a larger goal of equal opportunity, not the more narrowly-defined interests of managers getting more out of their workforces.

As the Code set it out, employees, by their actions, were cast as a threat to racial equality, and it was demanded that they 'refrain from harassment or intimidation of other employees on racial grounds, for example by attempting to discourage them from continuing employment'. Unions, too, were warned that 'is unlawful for trade unions to discriminate on racial grounds'. On the other hand, the Commission thought that 'trade union officials at national and local level and shopfloor representatives at plant level have an important part to play', and that 'trade unions should encourage and press for equal opportunities policies so that measures to prevent discrimination can be introduced with the clear commitment of both management and unions'. So it was that the Code aimed to draw unions into the implementation of equal opportunities policies, and even to make them into an advanced guard for the same, proposing that:

> although positive action is not legally required, unions should encourage management to take such action where there is underrepresentation of particular racial groups in particular jobs, and where management itself introduces positive action representatives should support it.

There were of course a number of trade unionists on the Commission, such as Bill Keys and Bill Morris. In the years that the Commission for Racial Equality's Code was being taken up, union negotiating rights, and status generally, were under attack. The promulgation of the Code as it was taken up by employers, alongside parallel commitments to women, was a revolution in workplace relations with far-reaching consequences. Some of those changes would challenge aspects of workplace organisation in ways that were resented by workers and their local union leaderships. On the other hand, other union officials welcomed the new policies, and were glad that their own status as agents of change was recognised by the Commission for Racial Equality.

In July 1981 the Code was still under consideration, according to Secretary of State for Employment Jim Prior, who in answer to a question said that both the Confederation of British Industry and the Trades Union Congress 'have suggested a number of detailed amendments'. The MP John Grant was hoping to hear 'whether the Government have objections to the proposals', but the Employment Secretary said that he had not been presented with the final version, at which point, he promised, he would decide whether to agree to it or 'withhold my approval'.[22] Events, though, were moving quite quickly, and it seemed as if the equal opportunities policies would be unequal to the task.

The following year the Commission had better news. In their Annual Report for 1983 they welcomed 'the Secretary of State for Employment's approval and Parliament's acceptance of its Code of Practice on Employment'. 'Looking back,' chair Michael Day thought that it was 'astonishing that the CRE's Code of Practice in Employment was approved by the' very right wing Minister Norman (now Lord) Tebbit.[23] The Commission

> hopes the Code will do for employment what the Highway Code has done for driving and ensure that good practice becomes almost automatic for all but the perverse and dangerously incompetent, the small minority against whom sanctions are appropriate.

It seemed like an optimistic hope. The Conservative government was not known for its progressive stance on race. A leading cadre of police chiefs — Kenneth Oxford in Liverpool, James Anderton in Manchester, and Kenneth Newman in London — did much to harass and criminalise West Indian youths, in a rising campaign of persecution.[24] Immigration law was tightened and its enforcement ramped up. The government's message to the country led most to expect more state-sanctioned race discrimination, rather than any serious mitigation of it.

After David Lane, the Commission chairman Peter Newsam served until 1986, when Michael Day, who had been a senior probation officer, took over. In 1993, the first black chair of the Commission, Herman Ouseley, was appointed by Home Secretary Tom Clarke. Ouseley seemed to be a radical choice (see below) but he had shown himself to be a stabilising force as Chief Executive of the Inner London Education Authority (overseeing its abolition, in fact) and in the same role for the troubled Lambeth Council. The CRE under Michael Day had suffered dissensions with one member of staff accusing the Commission itself of racial discrimination.[25]

Ouseley was knighted in 1997, and handed over the chairmanship to Gurbux Singh. Singh's range of experience was narrower than his predecessor's. He had worked as a policy officer at the Commission, and he had been Chief Executive of Haringey Council. Singh had shown some willingness to criticise the government over its asylum policies. Singh was arrested while drinking at a cricket match, and

David Lane, Peter Newsam

demanded of the policeman 'Do you know who I am?', and then later threatened to get the officer sacked, as he knew the Chief of Police, Ian Blair. The scandal was too great and Singh resigned. The last chair of the Commission for Racial Equality was Trevor Phillips who took over in 2003. Phillips, who had been a television producer and former President of the National Union of Students, was a figure of some stature, a respected campaigner against racism, but also something of a maverick. Phillips served up until the Commission for Racial Equality and the Equal Opportunities Commission were combined as the Equality and Human Rights Commission, and then went on to chair that body.

In 1986 the Commission for Racial Equality under Peter Newsam had a staff of 205 and a budget of £10.5 million — of which a quarter was granted to local Community Relations Councils. By the year 2000 the budget had increased to £16.6 million and the staff complement had hardly changed.

Over its 30 years, the Commission for Racial Equality was often criticised, and even mocked for its bureaucratic tokenism — criticisms that often seemed to have a point. But over those 30 years, public attitudes and policy shifted; they shifted slowly, glacially slowly it seemed, but in the end, pointedly in favour of race equality. Most remarkable of all changes was the change in the country's workplaces in favour of the idea of equality of opportunity. It was not that racism was abolished — far from it. But grounds on which race discrimination could take force from official sanction were pared back further and further. To what extent the Commission was a symptom of those changes, and to what extent it was a cause, is not always clear. When we come to look at the transformation that was taking place in the world of work we can give a better answer to that question. All the same, the curious institutional innovation that was the Commission for Racial Equality would play its part, as well as being a model for that other important body, the Equal Opportunities Commission.

— THREE —

The Equal Opportunities Commission

'Equal pay is the oldest wage claim in the history of the British trade union movement', the TUC President John Newton told its first ever equal pay conference in 1968.[1]

The call for equal pay was first made by matchgirls' strike leader Annie Besant in the 1890s, and raised at trade union congresses many times since. In the Second World War the claims made by Esther Lahr and others in the Transport and General Workers Union were reported in the papers: 'The government was today urged to give women the same pay and conditions as men.'[2] After the war the Trades Union Congress took a traditionalist line, arguing that

> the home is one of the most important spheres for a woman worker and that it would be doing a great injury to the life of the nation if women were persuaded or forced to neglect their domestic duties in order to enter industry particularly where there are young children to cater for.

The TUC agreed to the Labour government's closing wartime nurseries, and said that equal pay was 'inappropriate at the present time' because of 'the continuing need for counter inflationary policies'.[3]

A Civil Service Commission of 1948 tentatively suggested equal pay, while worrying about the 'psychological impact' on men. The women on the Committee, though, put in a minority report saying 'the claims of justice between individuals and the development of national productivity point in the same direction' — equal pay.[4] By 1955 staff unions had negotiated equal pay in the civil service and in the Post Office, though inequality in grades and promotions was untouched.

In the quarter century after the Second World War the economy grew strongly and more women went to work. Between 1964 and 1970 women made up 70% of the growth in trade union membership. The shop workers' union USDAW won the Trades Union Congress to a resolution for equal pay in 1963, leading to an Industrial Charter for women that called for equal pay, equal opportunities for training, re-training facilities for women returning to industry, and special provisions for the health and welfare of women at work.[5] The following year the Labour Party pledged new laws on equal pay.[6] In 1965 the TUC resolved

> its support for the principles of equality of treatment and opportunity for women workers in industry, and call[ed] upon the General Council to request the government to implement the promise of 'the right to equal pay for equal work' as set out in the Labour Party election manifesto.

The unions' attention to equal pay and sex discrimination helped them to recruit more members. Between 1968 and 1978, the number of women in the public employees' union (NUPE) more than trebled, that of the local government officers' union NALGO more than doubled, that of the health service union COHSE quadrupled, and the white-collar workers' union ASTMS multiplied its female membership by seven times.[7]

The changing mood over equal pay spread to the professions, too. Baroness Seear had worked at the Production Efficiency Board at the Ministry of Aircraft Production in the Second World War, having been a personnel officer at Clarks before. Afterwards she taught at the London School of Economics, where she championed women's employment, writing in 1964 that 'if we want to find an unused reserve of potential qualified manpower it is among women that it can most easily be discovered'.[8] More women were going on to higher education courses, where some were founding women's groups, like the London Women's Liberation Workshop, reading Betty Friedan's *The Feminine Mystique* and Germaine Greer's *The Female Eunuch*, and publishing the magazine *Shrew*. In the 1970s, women at Ruskin College organised the first Women's Liberation Movement conference.

The events that led to the two laws on Equal Pay (1970) and Sex Discrimination (1975), creating the Equal Opportunities Commission, can best be understood in the context of the heightened social conflict of the day. The Labour governments of 1964-71 and

Women's Liberation Movement conference, Birmingham, 1978

1974-79 were in the grip of a revolt from below embodied in a number of unofficial strikes. That the focus of sex discrimination law was pay was because of inequality, and also because pay was the issue of the decade.

Women played a big part in the militancy of the late 1960s and '70s. They were active in strikes at Rolls Royce and Rootes in 1968, of the London Night Cleaners over union recognition in 1970, and in the teachers' strikes as well as the Leeds Garment Workers' strike of that year. The following year saw a London telephonists' pay dispute. In 1972 women joined the occupations of Fisher-Bendix on Merseyside and Briant Colour Printing in London. Women at Goodman's, part of Thorn Electrical Industries, successfully struck for equal pay. In 1973 hundreds of thousands of hospital workers, mostly women, went on their first ever national strike. In the same year 200 women in GEC, Coventry, struck for eight weeks over piece rates.[9] Many of these strikes were backed by an umbrella group, the National Joint Action Campaign for Women's Equal Rights. The most important of these conflicts was the strike by women machinists, stitching the upholstery in Ford's works in Dagenham, East London, which is generally credited with changing the law.

The Dagenham strike and the Equal Pay Act

The Labour Minister responsible for employment in the 1964-70 government was Barbara Castle, who would propose the equality legislation. Her main role, though, was to face down the trade union demands of men and women. Some in the government, like Peter Shore and economic adviser Tommy Balogh, came to think that if socialism meant a planned economy, then that should mean that rates of pay should be set by the state, too. Others like Jim Callaghan, who had been a trade union leader before he was a Member of Parliament, argued for 'free collective bargaining' against state intervention in the rights of trade unions to strike their own pay deals. The different sides of the argument were not exactly clear at first, and did not fit with the obvious ideas of 'left' and 'right' in the party. Barbara Castle, having come from the left, was between the two positions, but as the Minister she argued the case for an incomes policy, setting her at odds with the trade unions, usually in the person of their largely male leaders.

The incomes policy that Castle fronted, 'In Place of Strife', hurt her standing in the labour movement, casting her as the mean witch holding down workers' pay. She had to defend government intervention against the trade unions, whittling away at her socialist credentials. The strike at Dagenham was 'the dispute that marked the start of her disenchantment with trade unions'.[10]

The women struck at Ford Dagenham over the way their work had been graded, not specifically about equal pay, though the way that management had not recognised their skills was discriminatory. The strike was a blow to Castle because it came just as Ford and the unions were signing off on a 'no strike' deal that the government had put its weight behind. Castle called the union leaders in to talk about what had gone wrong, and 'asked them what they could do to help get the women back to work'. In her diaries Castle was scathing when the engineering leader Reg Birch told her 'equal pay was the policy of his union'. For Castle, the issue was the agreement with Ford, while Birch insisted that 'new issues have been thrown up since it was signed'. Castle thought 'this, of course, is a recipe for anarchy'.[11]

Though her first thought was to end the Dagenham women's strike, Castle was uneasy. She sent the whole issue back to a Court of Inquiry, but that was taking a long time, while the strikers were getting good press. Seeing that things were moving too slowly, Castle writes, 'I blew my top, saying emphatically, "This is where I intervene".' From her office, she twisted Ford's arm to regrade the women, which, while hard for them, was not as costly as a long strike would have been. Calling the strikers in, Castle saw the public relations boost.

'She herself sat in the middle of the sofa and gathered them around a large, mumsy tea-pot', writes biographer Ann Perkins: 'The photographers came in early, in case the talks went too badly for pictures to be taken later.'[12] As Castle wrote at the time,

> The best part of it from my point of view was the genuine rapport I had established with the women. I think I managed to make Government look again as if it consisted of human beings and not just cold-blooded economists.[13]

Later she bumped into one of her more radical parliamentary colleagues, who had been critical about the 'In Place of Strife' white paper: 'Glowing congratulations from Eric Heffer about the Ford settlement', she writes, as he says: 'This is the kind of intervention I believe in.'[14] Castle found that that the equal pay issue was one where an incomes policy was popular. It was also one where the government had moral authority over the unions, not the other way around.

Soon after the Dagenham strike, another equal pay issue blew up in negotiations between the engineering employers and unions. The women's pay grade had been left to the end of the talks. The employers were not giving much. The engineers were threatening strike action to get the women more pay. In Castle's eyes the extravagant claims of the men were to blame: 'the unions had always understood that there would have to be some concessions by them on the women's differentials if they pushed up the skilled rate'. Instead, the unions hoped she would lean on the employers to give more. She wrote that she 'well and truly blew my top, telling them icily that I had been waiting for a long time to hear when they were going to start talking about the women and was shocked to find that they had left it to the very end'.

Turning on the union side Castle was pleased that she had started a 'ding dong row' between engineers' leader Hugh Scanlon and the only woman on the negotiating team Marion Veitch. She notes that Scanlon was 'clearly nervous at the success of my attempt to turn the tables on him'. Castle boasts that she has stopped a strike in favour of more pay for the women, and persuaded the men to take a smaller rise.[15]

Around this time Barbara Castle was facing the full fury of the unions over the 'In Place of Strife' white paper, with its proposals limiting union action, with a cooling-off period, compulsory strike ballots, and penalty clauses for unofficial strikes. Though some radicals, even Tony Benn, backed the proposals, the campaign against them picked up steam.

In 1969, as the Cabinet prepared policy ahead of the Labour Party Conference, Castle 'said that my paper on the Industrial Relations Bill could wait but could we clear equal pay urgently?' At the conference, Castle was pleased to find Transport and General Workers Union leader Jack Jones livid about 'my announcement about equal pay which robs him not only of a grievance against the Government, but of some of the leadership on industrial issues which, I am now convinced, he wants exclusively concentrated in the hands of the unions'. Staking out new ground on women's pay, she found, played up the union leaders' weakness on the issue. Foundry workers' leader and Labour Party chairman Willie Simpson congratulated Castle on the equal pay proposal, saying 'the equal pay debate at the TUC… made me sick': 'As you say, they've been talking about it ever since 1880 and never done anything about it themselves except criticize.'[16]

In 1969 Castle was talking to a delegation from the TUC, led by Vic Feather. Castle again grabbed the moral high ground by goading the union leaders for leaving women in the lurch: 'talking of job opportunity, when were the unions going to give a lead – on allowing women bus drivers, for instance? It's time we had some militancy, I gibed.'[17] While the incomes policy in the 'In Place of Strife' white paper was made unworkable by union opposition, the more positive incomes policy of equal pay became law in the last months of the Wilson administration. Its provisions were delayed until 1976 to give employers time to phase in the changes.

The Sex Discrimination Act and the Equal Opportunities Commission

On its own the Equal Pay Act would not work. Baroness Seear's research project on the impact of equal pay legislation found that in half of the organisations she surveyed 'action was taken to minimise the employers' obligation': 'Such minimising action included the creation of new all-female grades, the retitling of jobs and undergrading job evaluations exercises.'[18] Equal pay rules meant that women doing 'like work' to men would have to be paid the same. But if men got the promotions, or were put on different grades, employers could dodge equal pay; and if women were not given the chance to get the jobs men did, equal pay would mean nothing. Like the Race Relations Act (1976), the Sex Discrimination Act outlawed direct discrimination in hiring, promotion, training, and treatment, alongside the 'equal pay' clauses of the 1970 Act.

The 1976 Act also set up the Equal Opportunities Commission — again, like the Commission for Racial Equality, an arm's-length independent government agency. The Equal Opportunities Commission had powers to help individuals to seek redress under the Acts at an industrial tribunal. The Commission also had power to investigate organisations, and to issue 'discrimination orders' telling them to fix discriminatory policies, and monitoring them.

For its first ten years the Commission was led by miner's daughter Betty Lockwood, who had studied at Ruskin College before becoming a Labour Party organiser. Her second-in-command was Elspeth Howe, who stood down in 1980 around the time her husband Geoffrey became Chancellor of the Exchequer in the new Conservative administration.

The new organisation started with a modest grant of £850,000, rising to £2.5 million in 1980, when there were 170 people working in its main office in Manchester.[19]

In 1977 the Commission pursued actions against 'W' Ribbons Ltd, where 'the grading structure contained women-only grades which were paid less than any male grade'; the Sealed Motor Construction Ltd, where 'the majority of women were in lowest grade and paid unskilled male rate'; Anderson Mavor Ltd, where 'a new pay structure was rejected by the Department of Employment; James Robertson and Sons, where 'a women-only grade work[ed] 40 hours while the men worked 44½ but the difference in pay was too great to be explained by the extra 4½ hours'; Unbrako Ltd, with its 'completely segregated grading structure with women occupying the lower grades'; Armitage Ware Ltd, where 'the lowest grade [was] all female'; and many more. The actions also named the unions AUEW, TGWU, USDAW, EETPU, ASTMS, ACTS, and others as the negotiating parties that had agreed the rates and grades of pay. One finding was against the APEX union, which 'accepted a new unisex structure'. In almost all cases the parties agreed to make changes before any penalty or finding against them was made.[20] In one case a formal investigation was opened at the Luton site of Electrolux Limited.

Legal coercion was an option but it was not always needed, because employers were on the whole eager to keep within the law, and more often sought advice on how to change things than resisted. Once it had found its feet, the Commission found it 'possible to visit organisations and advise management, employees and trade unions on the legislation and its implications at the place of work'.[21] To try to discover the problems, but also as a way of building bridges, the Commission undertook an investigation, with Baroness Seear and the London School of Economics, into the ways that 500 companies (later expanded to 575) had reacted to the new legislation. In those early days the findings were that not much had been done positively, though most complied with the letter of the law.

Protective legislation

One reform that the Equal Opportunities Commission championed from early on was the repeal of the special protective legislation that barred women from certain jobs and shifts, such as the Mines and

Quarries Act (1954) and the Factories Act (1961). As the *EOC News* explained, 'Legislation embodied in the Factories Act dates from Victorian social reforms that were designed to protect women from the "evils of exploitation by unscrupulous employers."'

But they argued that

> today these restrictions on hours of work not only prevent a woman worker applying for the better paid shift work that her male colleagues can do, but they also mean that in many cases, women are not considered for factory jobs at all.

They commissioned research that showed that 'the majority of working women approved of women being allowed to work evenings and double day shifts'. On the other hand, most women 'do not approve of it being done by women with young children'. The Commission recommended 'lifting the restrictions on nightwork, shiftwork and overtime for women and replacing them with legally enforceable Codes of Practice on hours of work, applicable to both sexes'.[22]

The Commission was supported by the Health and Safety Executive, which had recommended the repeal of Section 20 of the Factories Act 1961 (the section that 'deals with the cleaning of moving machinery and provides for the protection of women and young persons, but not for men'). The Commission 'agreed with the HSE's recommendation that the section should be replaced by regulations ensuring that only trained adults (regardless of sex) should do this work'.[23]

Convincing industry

The early years of the Equal Opportunities Commission were marked by success. Their newsletter was full of reports and photos of women who were the first in their field, like Linette Simms, the first to drive a school bus for the Inner London Education Authority; Claudine

Ecclestone, the first council plumber; Margaret Gardner, the first woman to become a guard on the Underground; Joanne Oxley, David Brown Tractors' first engineering apprentice; Anne Haywood, training to be Britain's first gas-fitter; Debbie Ryan, the first to be taken on as an apprentice painter and decorator under the Construction Industry Training Board schemes; and Jacqueline Abberley, training to be Britain's first train driver.[24] There were firsts for women in the professional world, too: Ellen Winser, the first stockbroker; Geraldine Bridgewater, the first woman to be admitted to London Metal Exchange; and Judith Bell, Marine Broker at Lloyds.[25]

Gwyneth Mitchell, Scotland's first ever female artificial inseminator, joked to the *EOC News* that the 'main qualification for doing the job well was a strong right arm'.

The important innovation in the 1980s was, in parallel with the Commission for Racial Equality, the Equal Opportunity Commission's work to persuade employers to adopt their own equal opportunity codes, mirroring the legislative framework set out by the Equal Pay and Sex Discrimination Acts in company policy. In a booklet *Guidance on Equal Opportunities Policies and Practices in Employment*:

> [T]he Commission believes that equal opportunities will not be achieved principally by enforcing laws against discriminatory practices; they can only be attained by the acceptance by employers, and employees and their trade unions, that the full utilisation of talents and resources of the whole workforce is important in their own interests and in the economic interest of the country.[26]

Baroness Seear's survey, published as *Equality between the sexes in industry: how far have we come?*, helped the Commission to identify good examples. In all, 'Eight firms, Sainsbury's, ICI, Delta Metal, Cadbury's, Wilkinson Match, Lloyds Bank, H J Heinz and Rolls Royce are singled out for praise in a report':

> ICI, for example, who have a widely publicised policy on equality, have instituted an auditing system with a built-in monitoring function: factory management have a checklist for identifying the cause of imbalances, and suggesting a course for remedial action.

And:

> Sainsburys Limited have adopted a particularly positive approach, identifying areas for action, and providing such benefits as a training course for women wishing to return to work, and special training for women to undertake work previously done only by men, for example, in butchery.

In the last case the Commission added that 'in the last three years this policy has resulted in the doubling of women managers from 41 to 89'.[27] Both Rolls Royce and Lloyds Bank had used positive measures to get women into training, in apprenticeships at Rolls Royce, and in a management training scheme at Lloyds Bank.[28] Bringing in equal pay had been done through the employers' federations and the corporate boards that were common at the time:

> National Joint Industrial Councils influenced some employers when the Equal Pay Act was introduced, as in the motor vehicle and repair industry. Others were influenced by their appropriate Federations' recommendations and suggestions. There was an agreement within the chemical and allied industries towards moving towards introducing equal pay four years prior to the effective date of the Equal Pay Act. Central Arbitration Committee Awards were made in respect of at least four employers we contacted.[29]

Moreover, 'a few large companies have made approaches to the Commission for guidance in developing policy in the period of the survey, which indicated that willingness to respond to the issues is beginning to emerge'.

The Commission did worry that 'only a quarter of the companies surveyed by the EOC had written equal opportunities' policies, and that positive measures they proposed were 'seen as low priority compared with other business pressures'. Also, they suspected that 'traditional and attitudinal barriers have been part and parcel of a view that positive action on equal opportunities is unnecessary and costly'.[30]

Under the Sex Discrimination Act, 'the Equal Opportunities Commission has the power to make recommendations to the Secretary of State to lay Codes of Practice before Parliament'. Early on, the Commission prepared a draft Code of Practice to be 'considered by the TUC, the CBI, the Department of Employment and ACAS as well as other interested bodies and individuals'. The draft was published in March 1978.[31]

In 1985 Baroness Writtle, who had taken over as chair of the Commission, could announce that 'last April marked a milestone in the history of the Commission in the approval of our Code of Practice by Parliament, with the wholehearted support of both sides of industry':

> The Commission's Code of Practice on employment came into effect in April 1985, after several years of consultations, and received the forceful and unqualified support of the then Secretary of State for Employment, the Rt. Hon. Tom King, MP.[32]

As well as providing 'far-ranging guidance on the promotion of equal opportunities to give effect to the spirit of the law', the Code now blessed by Parliament meant that it could be used by any employees 'as evidence in an industrial tribunal'. The Code was launched at a meeting with Tom King MP, Judge West-Russell, President of the Industrial Tribunals, Sir Terence Beckett, Director General of the CBI, Mr Norman Willis, General Secretary of the TUC and 'over one hundred employers' representatives from the private and public sector and representatives of the trade unions'.

At the launch the Tory Minister for Employment, Tom King, said:

> I believe passionately, that for Britain to succeed, we do have to make most of all the resources that we have: and one of the most neglected resources that we have as a country is the skill, ability and intelligence of many women in society, which has not had the opportunity that it should in the past, but which can make a significant contribution to the future. That is why I support equal opportunities, quite apart from the equity and fairness of it, because for us to succeed as a nation, we must ensure that the

potential of women in senior management, professional and skilled occupations is properly recognised and more developed than it has been in the past.

King's message was echoed by the Confederation of British Industry which issued its own Code of Practice on Equal Opportunities at the same time. The Equal Opportunities Commission's Code sold 52,000 copies in its first eight months.[33]

Fifteen years later the Commission would report that in 'a survey of senior managers in larger UK organisations in Summer 2000, 68 per cent of organisations claimed to have an Equal Pay policy'. What was more, '40 per cent claimed that they were currently monitoring the relative pay of women and men'.[34] That was a long way off from 1985 though. Looking back, Irene Bruegel and Diane Perrons saw that:

Equal opportunities legislation and in-house equal opportunities policies are generally complementary. The legislation provides a framework for equal opportunities while organisations' policies set out more practical ways of implementing the policy.[35]

Beryl Platt was a scientist before she led the EOC

Baroness Writtle claimed that 'much has changed since the Equal Opportunities Commission came into existence ten years ago, not all of it visible to the public'. Still, she thought that 'in its totality the change amounts to a record of achievement for which the Commission can fairly claim a substantial share of the credit'. How much was due to the Commission and how much due to broader social changes might be argued over, but in any event Writtle was right to say that 'the transformation of the attitude of the press and mass media, from one of flippancy and trivialisation to a genuine understanding of the issues, is the most visible change'. The attitude of the general public was one 'which no longer needs to be convinced'. She highlighted the most lasting change, saying that 'ten years ago the educational establishment regarded the Sex Discrimination Act as at best marginal to its concerns'. 'Today', by contrast, 'equality of opportunity in education between boys and girls is regarded as a central part of a school's business'.[36]

For all that, there was a strong feeling that the early successes of the Equal Pay Act were followed by diminishing returns. So, in the *EOC News*, it was reported that:

Between 1970 and 1975 when firms were preparing for the implementation of the Equal Pay Act women's average gross weekly earnings increased from 54.5 per cent of men's. By 1976 when the Act had come into force they had reached 64.3 per cent. But it looks as if this improvement is tailing off.

The Commission thought that:

It is generally accepted that the Equal Pay Act had a once-for-all effect. There are many other factors contributing to the low pay of women, such as their concentration in low-paid industries, which the Act can have little influence on. The Commission envisages a shift of emphasis over the coming years from ensuring that women are paid equally for equal work to ensuring that the can acquire the skills needed to work in more highly paid occupations...[37]

Again, in 1982, the Commission had a sombre message, saying that 'we must also draw attention once again to the fact that the marked progress towards equal pay between 1970 and 1977 has been effectively halted in the last five years.'[38] Women's gross hourly pay seemed to have plateaued at 74% of men's in the early Eighties.

Outside the Commission, many feminist activists were sceptical. In the magazine *Spare Rib* Jenny Earle and Julia Phillips wrote that 'there is little room for doubt that the impact of the Equal Pay Act is dwindling — not that it was ever that substantial'. The narrowing of the pay differential 'seems to have gone into reverse'.[39]

Development of the Commission

Another issue that was hard for the Commission to make headway on was the provision of nurseries. Already, at the Women's Liberation Conference of 1970, campaigners had connected childcare and women's equality at work. If women were tied down by commitments to raise children, they would not be able to compete fairly with men in the labour market. The WLM Conference called for 'free, 24-hour nurseries'. The demand seemed utopian to many, but it crystallised the structural inequality in women's social position.

The Equal Opportunities Commission took up the argument in 1984, saying that 'Opportunities for women in employment and other areas continue to be restricted by the inadequate provision of childcare services'. As they argued, 'services for the under-fives and school-age dependent children are essential in allowing parents to combine careers and public duties with a responsible family life'.[40] The harsh recession, along with a government committed to resisting public spending commitments, was not a good time to be asking

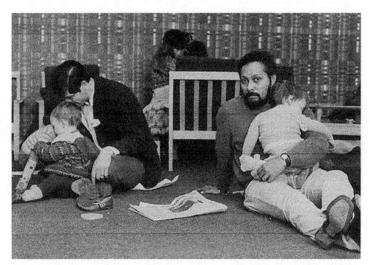

Stuart Hall on duty at the Women's Liberation Movement Creche, 1970

for greater spending. Ideologically, Conservative Prime Minister Thatcher was sharply opposed to women with young children working, and to nurseries for pre-school age children, which she described as 'soviet' in an interview with Radio 4's *Women's Hour*.

Later on the Commission would shift its emphasis toward the questions of 'work-life balance', flexibility in work, childcare for working mothers, and the minimum wage in its efforts to close the gender pay gap — which we will look at later on. But still, at the turn of the new century the Commission was appealing that 'the Government needs to reform the Equal Pay Act which is now 30 years old'.[41]

Betty Lockwood was chair of the Equal Opportunities Commission from 1975 to 1983. Beryl Platt, Baroness Writtle, who had a background in engineering and was a Conservative Party supporter, if a modernising one, served as chair from 1983 to 1988. After Writtle, Joanna Foster was appointed as chair. She had worked in the Conservative Party Press Office in the 1960s, but was also the first chair to have had 'a background in the women's movement'.[42] Beatrix Campbell explains that the Conservative women put in charge of the EOC played a key role relaying the Commission's message back to the party: 'Amongst Conservatives it was left to the Tory leaders of the EOC alone to defend women against their own party and their own government.'[43] Foster was replaced in 1993 by Kamlesh Bahl, who had been on the Law Society executive, and working for British Steel and Texaco on equal opportunities issues. Bahl, though, was a divisive figure among the Commission staff, who saw her as a tyrant, preferring the Chief Executive Valerie Amos, with whom Bahl clashed.[44] In 1999 Julie Mellor was appointed chair. Mellor had worked in senior Human Resource Management positions for Royal Dutch Shell and the Trustee Savings Bank, as well as for Islington Council, the Greater London Council and the Inner London Education Authority. Jenny Watson, who had worked at Liberty and Charter 88, as well as in some private-sector positions, took over from Mellor in 2005 until the two Commissions, Equal Opportunities and Racial Equality, were combined as the Equality and Human Rights Commission.

As we have seen, the Equal Opportunities Commission's budget had been kept down to £3.4 million in 1985, rising to nearly £6 million in 1993, when the Commission employed 171 people. Two years before it was wound up, the Equal Opportunities Commission had a budget of £8.5 million and still a staff of 171. The Equal Opportunities Commission was a little smaller than the Commission for Racial Equality, and spent less, but then the CRE also granted a share of its budget to local Community Relations Councils. The EOC, whose head office was in Manchester, supported sub-offices in Cardiff, Glasgow, and Belfast.

Beyond its own offices, of course, the Equal Opportunities Commission was carried by a lively and intellectually productive women's movement. Women's groups, though they were often short-lived, proved to be a durable form of not-so-formal political organisation for thousands of women, who argued and wrote and protested in all kinds of ways. College campuses and trade unions also sustained strong women's groups and caucuses. There were many feminist newsletters and magazines, of which *Spare Rib* (1972-93) was only the most popular, alongside more short-lived publications like *Red Rag* and *Women's Voice*. Bookshops like Silver Moon (1984-2001), the publishing house Virago (since 1973), and the Fawcett Library sustained many women's groups. Women's Studies courses were developed at many universities, though these found it difficult to thrive.[45] And as we will see, municipal authorities, especially in the larger cities, were the basis of durable women's committees and offices. Less declaredly feminist women's organisations like the Women's Institute, National Association of Women's Clubs, and the Mothers' Union also helped to feed ideas into the Equal Opportunities Commission, as well as promoting the Commission's work.

— FOUR —

Equal Opportunities at Work —

How They Came About

The equal opportunities policies are about changing relations at work. From 1980 to 1990 there was a marked uptake of equal opportunities policies and today they are the norm. But back in the early days of the Equal Opportunities and Race Equality Commissions there were no equal opportunities policies. Here and in the following chapters we look at the adoption of these policies and what they meant for the world of work, and why they were adopted.

What stands out is the timing. Equal opportunities policies were taken up around the same time that the older, corporatist, or 'tripartite' system was being dismantled. As we saw in Chapter One, the older system of workplace relations was built on a bargain between organised labour and employers. That bargain often meant that women and migrant workers were on a lower rung in the pecking order. But when that older system, the 'tripartite' system, was taken apart, a space opened up for a new kind of setup at work. More than that, employers felt they needed to rebuild their relationship to their workforces on a different footing. Surprisingly, given the reactionary tenor of the times, equal opportunities policies featured in the new workplace relations.

Municipal innovators

Among the first employers to adopt equal opportunities policies were London municipal authorities, typically those under Labour Party ruling bodies. As the Commission for Racial Equality reported in 1986:

> The local government sector has generally been more responsive to the recommendations of the Commission's Code of Practice in employment than other sectors, whether public or private. Particular authorities, such as the London boroughs of Lambeth, Lewisham and Wandsworth and the cities of Leicester and Bradford have provided a lead in this respect.

Lambeth, and the Greater London Council were soon followed by other Labour-led London Boroughs (Brent, Camden, Hackney, Haringey, Islington, Newham, and others), and also the Inner London Education Authority. Later they were followed by larger municipal authorities outside London (Birmingham, Manchester, and so on) and, around the same time, by London Tory-controlled authorities like Barnet and Westminster — 'over half of the county councils in the South have introduced elements of equal opportunities policy', said the CRE. By that time equal opportunities policies were also being adopted by larger businesses, like British Telecom, Sainsbury's, Lloyds, Ford, and so on. In 1985 the Commission for Racial Equality held a two-day residential seminar near Oxford for over 50 delegates from private-sector companies: 'Speakers from Austin Rover, Boots Company, Midland Bank, Halifax Building Society, Whitbread, Dixons and Tesco gave accounts of their experiences in implementing and monitoring equal opportunities programmes.'[1]

The reasons that the London local authorities adopted equal opportunities seem to be very political, and they were at the time sharply challenged (we look at the reaction later on). Given that these were politically chosen local leaderships it seems straightforward to look at the adoption of these policies as political acts, which they were. But at the same time local authorities were important and large employers (in the London Borough of Lambeth 10,000 people worked for the Council). Though they seem to have been bending to other winds, the local authorities' equal opportunities policies were the model for all the policies that were later taken on by commercial businesses. As we shall see, the local authorities' motives were not so very far from those of the businesses.

The big hill that local Labour councils had to climb in 1979 was Labour's unpopularity. As the party most closely tied to the corporate society, Labour failed when it failed. Many of its own working-class supporters blamed Labour for the way that the government had failed to back the low-paid workers in the 'winter of discontent'; the middle classes, on the other hand, blamed Labour for being too soft on the unions and encouraging strikes, and many of them backed the new Conservative government's drive to limit union power. The old alliances between trade unions and the Labour Party were weakened by the clashes of the Seventies, by the failure of Jim Callaghan's government to back higher wages, and by the following victory of a stridently anti-union government in 1979.

Labour-led boroughs in the 1980s, especially in London, were not only trying to marshal their forces, but to build new coalitions to hang onto power. The left that came to power in the London Labour Party in the 1980s was often called 'new left', as opposed to an 'old left' that was based on Labour's traditional trade union base. Martin Boddy and Colin Fudge cite Doreen Massey's story of the new left as 'very different politically: the old labourism dominates the regions', but 'new alliances are growing in some cities'; and again they call on the account by labour historian Eric Hobsbawm of how 'a wide and heterogeneous range of discontented voters can be brought together', as a social base for a new Labour vote.[2]

An interview with Ken Livingstone, the Greater London Council leader, finds him telling how Labour's support had changed: 'A Labour Party based in the industrial trade unions in the 1940s and 1950s was credible, but the contraction of the industrial base means [it] isn't an adequate base on its own.' Said Livingstone, 'the Labour Party has to change its own structure so that women's organisations, black organisations, community organisations have a direct input rather than via the trade unions'. At times, and mirroring the rows in the London Labour Party between the right and left, Livingstone could be harsh in his criticism of unions: 'the craft unions grew up as much out of the benefits of colonialism as British capital did', he claimed, unfairly, and 'they're the ones who laugh loudest about gay rights or feminism, the ones who are most reluctant to give a strong lead over racism'.[3] As many saw, Livingstone was trying to reach beyond that shrinking base to appeal to other constituencies. Similar to the model that many Democrats had built in American cities, Livingstone was building a 'rainbow coalition'. He worked hard to win support from London's large Afro-Caribbean minority, and appealed to Bengali and other minorities in London, and to women voters.[4]

In 1982, about 700 ethnic-minority groups in London were written to by Livingston, 'inviting them to assist in shaping the Council's policies as they affect the capital's minority population'. Livingstone took on the role of chairman of the GLC's Ethnic Minorities Committee, saying that they would be 'developing the most extensive programme ever embarked upon by a local government with ethnic minorities in London'.[5] The Labour group's optimism about action on discrimination was part of a wider vision of local Keynesian-style public sector-led growth. The Greater London economic plan foresaw more hiring and more opportunities to take on workers who had been overlooked in the past. Many policy-makers in the early Eighties hoped that governments could kick-start economic growth, as was tried in France and Greece. But in time it became clear that

London was in for a severe recession, and state spending was cut back, undermining the GLC's plan.

In Islington, the skirmishes between the more traditional Labour-right leaders on the Council and the more radical activists came to a head when the Labour councillors all defected to the 'moderate' breakaway Social Democratic Party — only to lose all their seats in the 1982 election. The voters stuck with the Labour Party, but got new councillors drawn from the more radical end of the party, led by Margaret Hodge and the Trotskyist Alan Clinton, who scrabbled to rebuild local support on the basis of the newer constituencies. In their early race-relations literature, the new Council announced that 'we are determined to ensure that this workforce accurately reflects the multicultural make-up of the local community' — it was a statement as much about their hope for popular support as it was about racial justice.[6]

The pioneer of all of the London councils' equal opportunities policies was Lambeth Council's leader from 1978, Ted Knight, who had been on the far left before joining Labour. Lambeth was a borough with a mismatch between its large black minority (around 60,000, or 21%, of 286,000 residents)[7] and a local authority that had recruited its staff from an older, whiter population. When Lambeth's non-manual workforce were surveyed just 8% were Afro-Caribbean, 3% Asian, while 88% were white.[8] Under the old order, an order that had after all been built up over years, councils built up their ties to the traditional working class, which was to say, by and large, the white working class. According to one report on discrimination over in East London, 'neither central nor local government employs a single Asian living in Spitalfields, despite the fact that nearly 20 per cent of the rest of the ward's population are State employees.'[9]

The problem that the London Labour councils were struggling with seemed very special to them. But at its heart it was a problem of their legitimacy, in the eyes of their voters and their staff, which is not that different from the problem that other employers faced, the problem of their legitimacy in the eyes of their customers and their employees. Strange as it might have seemed at the time, the 'extremist experiment' in 'social engineering' of the early Eighties would become the ordinary way of organising workers in the 1990s.

The local councils were struggling with the job of how to hold onto their support in the face of a hostile government. Government hostility was shown in the government trying to cut back on the councils' public spending, meaning that their 'rate support grant' — the extra money they got from central government — would be cut. Councils were in a stronger place where the money they wanted to spend was part of a statutory duty. So it was with spending on race relations. As the Commission for Racial Equality explained,

> Section 71 of the Race Relations Act 1976 obliges local authorities to make sure that their various functions are carried out with due regard to the need to eliminate racial discrimination and to promote equality of opportunity and good relations between people of different racial groups.

On 10 June 1977 the government issued a joint circular to local authorities on the Race Relations Act that drew attention to the provisions of the Act and in particular to the statutory obligations created under Section 71. It said that 'local authorities will need to examine their policies and practices to ensure that these meet the requirements of the Act'. More, the circular urged local authorities to be positive: 'Bare compliance with the provisions of the legislation is not enough.'[10]

The Commission, then, was the council's ally. Spending on race relations would help them to do the right thing, and win support, and do their duty under the law. That was spending that they could justify. The CRE helped them out: 'During the reporting period the CRE consulted the Association of Metropolitan Authorities, the Association of District Councils, the London Boroughs Association, the Association of County Councils and the National Association of Community Relations Council.' All of this consultation led to 'a pamphlet giving specific and detailed guidance on Section 71'. The message from the CRE was this: 'The Commission wants local councils not merely to comply with the letter of the law but also to take steps to ensure that no section of the population in their area is disadvantaged by their actions or omissions.'[11]

In 1978 the Commission for Racial Equality reported that 'Camden council will declare itself to be "an equal opportunity employer" in all of its recruitment advertisements'. The Council's statement said that it 'recognises and welcomes the existence of minority groups in the borough, reflecting a multicultural Britain, and seeks to redress the imbalance of employment opportunities of members of these groups'. Councillor Evans said: 'Camden council has been on its guard against overt or conscious discrimination in its employment policies, and it is fitting that we should be one of the first authorities to implement not only the letter but also the spirit of the new Race Relations Act.' Camden Council was around the

Herman Ouseley in 2014

same time being praised by the Equal Opportunities Commission for its 'policy designed to promote equal opportunities for the men and women it employs'.[12]

Lambeth's Community Relations Council called for 'a small Race Relations Unit by Lambeth Council within one of its departments'. The Unit 'would provide the information necessary for the Council to develop its strategy to eliminate discrimination and disadvantage, thereby promoting racial equality'.[13] In the event, Ted Knight's Race Relations Unit had more powers that were originally proposed. As described by its first head Herman Ouseley, the Unit was made up of 'a Principal Race Relations Adviser with a back-up team… other race advisers would be based in the Directorates of Social Services and Management Services alongside the existing adviser in Housing Services'.[14]

The Unit, and the Council leadership, saw themselves at odds with an entrenched management and workforce. Council leader Ted Knight saw a struggle against 'the inertia of the bureaucracy':

> The establishment of the Race Relations Unit, for example, a very significant development, demonstrated, and still demonstrates, that whilst you can take all the policy decisions you like, it is a continuous battle against the bureaucracy to make a change.

For Knight, the struggle over the Race Relations Unit was a sign of a broader fight with the Council officers, whom he saw as 'very conservative, and probably so politically, as well as just in general attitudes — so, it's a fight'.[15]

Ted Knight's time as leader of Lambeth Council was cut short when he was disbarred from office for failing to set a 'rate' — that is the local property tax from which councils then raised part of their income — after the Conservative Cabinet cut the central government subsidy to rein in local spending (discussed later). After Knight the radical policy was carried on by the new council leader Linda Bellos, but the authority was increasingly embattled in its conflict with central government.

Though Lambeth's adventures seemed outlandish at the time, much of what they did became mainstream later on. One clear continuity was that the Lambeth Race Relations Unit was the model for another, at the Greater London Council.

In 1983 the Greater London Council launched its Code of Practice, 'on advice from the Commission for Racial Equality', and sent it to 'all staff with managerial and supervisory responsibilities' in a booklet called *Towards Equal Opportunities*. Others could pick up a copy from the new Equal Opportunities Unit, a part of the Personnel Department. To showcase the policy, the GLC started a new internal paper called *Equals*, 'a new avenue for publicising developing opportunities and rights for all employees', said John

Valerie Wise, Ken Livingstone, Charlie Ross, and John McDonnell, outside the GLC, 1981

Carr, chair of the GLC Staff Committee. It would, he wrote in the first issue of *Equals*, make 'a reality of the phrase "the GLC is an Equal Opportunities Employer"'.[16] *Equals* was edited by Judith Hunt, who had been active on the left and published on women's rights (she went on to be Chief Executive of Ealing Council). Though the Staff Committee chair was put up to announce the policy, Livingstone recalled that 'here in the GLC, the staff association is deeply reactionary, whilst maintaining that it is apolitical'.[17]

The GLC was not only an innovator in race relations. Its equal opportunities policy covered sex discrimination as well as race discrimination. In 1981 the GLC voted to set up a women's sub-committee, and a women's unit, with a budget of £6.9 million (twice that of the Equal Opportunities Commission) and 18 staff. A series of open meetings gathered activists, many of whom were co-opted onto the Committee. The model of a women's committee and women's unit was taken up in Lewisham, Camden, Islington, Southwark, and Hackney.[18] The equality unit set out the scale of the challenge, with the example of Sue Batten, 'the GLC's only female firefighter' out of 6,706; more, the 'GLC employs only one woman electrician and only one craftswoman among 294 engineering craftsmen'.[19] On 10 June 1983 the Staff Committee held the GLC to the view that 'it is just as much against the law to discriminate *in favour* of women and ethnic minorities as it is to discriminate against them', and that, therefore, 'quotas are unfair, unlawful and unhelpful'. In the absence of quotas, County Hall adopted targets, as a 'yardstick for measuring the success of the equal opportunities policy': 'an agreed proportion of women and ethnic minorities which may realistically be achieved within a certain period of time is a specified area of work'. They went on to say that 'the eventual aim is that the makeup of the workforce mirrors the population of the GLC's catchment area as closely as possible', thereby tying employment to representation.[20]

It was not that women did not work for the GLC, the newssheet explained, 'GLC workers are fed and cleaned up after by an army of women: mums at home as well as at work'.[21] The GLC adopted a far-sighted view of the sphere of domestic work, when Ken Livingstone said that he would aim 'to treat childcare and other areas of housework as an economic sector'.[22] That was rather different from the mainstream view on the left, which in adopting its own 'Alternative Economic Strategy' focused largely on industry, and on the workplace.[23] In 1983 the GLC and the Inner London Education Authority announced that 'it would be opening Day Nurseries at County Hall and the former Bellenden School' for its own workers.[24]

The Greater London Council had quite a hill to climb. Its first survey found that 'the proportion of ethnic minority and women employees stands at 9% and 20% respectively'. Worse, '75% of white males are at grade MG10 (earning over £7500 per annum) compared with 40% of ethnic minorities and only 30% of women'. As it seemed to Livingstone's team in 1983 'there is a clear pattern of occupational segregation which covers both women and ethnic minorities and ensures that they are over-represented in low paid areas and under-represented or completely absent from a broad range of senior positions'.[25]

The Town Hall equal opportunities programmes had definite limits. They were dependent on a rate support grant from central government that was not sympathetic to the Labour groups' empire building, and trying to hold down spending anyway. Town hall workforces were already in post, and however sympathetic they were to change, would not be willing to lose their jobs over it. In a tight economic climate turnover was low, and councils found it much more difficult to restructure and turn over their workforces than private industry did. The rate at which new jobs could be created was slow. A survey in May 1986 found that only two councils, Hackney and Lambeth, even had a workforce that matched the local ethnic mix; and in any event, in all councils surveyed, black employees were concentrated in the lower grades.[26] The Greater London Council claimed in 1985 that it had increased its black workforce from 7% to 11% of the total since 1981, and the proportion of women had risen to 21%. The Council tended to blame the workforce for the slow pace of change, saying that '"Newcomers" can be forced to deal with the worst excesses of racist and sexist behaviour from those who are threatened by a woman or a black person clearly capable of doing the same job as them', and promised disciplinary codes to 'protect them'.[27] Even the success in the London Fire Brigade turned out to be oversold. The '30% increase' in black recruits turned out to be an increase from 1.2% to 1.6% of the total. 'There were fewer black firemen in London at the time of the abolition of the GLC than there had been under the old London County Council in 1948.'[28] The County Hall nursery was turned into an aquarium, though it only ever catered for a small number of children.[29]

The municipal pioneers of equal opportunities policies were to see their project bogged down in controversy and in-fighting. As we explore in greater depth in Chapter Five, the reaction on the part of the government to the local authorities that pioneered these policies was harsh. And yet surprisingly the self-same equal opportunities policies that were reviled and mocked when they were first trialled by the local councils were widely taken up by all kinds of employers in the private sector.

The private sector

In October 1984 Barclays Bank appointed Tina Boyden, formerly a branch manager and manager of Barclays International, as Equal Opportunities manager at their London Head Office, 'to ensure that the bank's policy of treating all applicants equally regardless of racial group, sex or marital status, is effectively carried out'. The previous November, all Area Officers were sent the bank's Code of Practice, and from 1 January 1985 all applicants were asked to record their ethnic origins using a six-category classification. Around the same time British Petroleum's 29,500 UK employees were subject to a new

Code of Practice. In March 1984 the Group Personnel Department was briefing groups of managers in personnel in a series of seminars as part of their Awareness Programme, with the chairman telling them 'that for the policy to be effective there was a need for managers and staff… to be aware of what constitutes discrimination, and to be conscious that discrimination can be the result of attitudes as well as employment practices'. Also in 1984 the 10,900 employees of the Halifax Building Society came under its new equal opportunities policy, agreed with the Staff Association, and issued to all who worked for the company. Managers in recruitment were to be trained and the workforce monitored by ethnicity. Imperial Chemicals Industry's 50,000 employees, too, were brought under a similar code, incorporating 'the equal opportunity statement and an ethnic origin question on all application forms'. Other companies that adopted equal opportunities codes included Midland Bank (which had a published equal opportunities policy from 1977), Safeway Food Stores, W H Smiths, Smiths Industries, and many more. [30]

In September of 1985 the Confederation of British Industry held a conference at Centre Point in London on equality at work. The point of the conference was to inform members of the Confederation about the Equal Pay (Amendment) Regulations of 1983, which came into force in 1984 after a European Economic Community ruling. The new rule made the equal pay law more precise. For the most part the CBI treated the new rules as simply part of legislative ground on which members worked, and most of the papers circulated were on the technicalities of compliance, though the CBI was promoting its own draft code of conduct at the same time.[31] There were some arch comments among accounts of cases brought that expressed a little cynicism. More forward-thinking employers, though, were proactive on women's opportunities at work as they were on those of ethnic minorities. In October of 1986 employers and personnel managers were instrumental in setting up the organisation Equality Exchange — 'an information network of organisations interested in promoting equal opportunities for women in employment' that was formally launched on 1 January 1987. By the end of the year 269 organisations had joined.[32] The companies that were actively working with the Equal Opportunities Commission to address inequality at work at that time included British Gas, the Halifax Building Society, and the Metropolitan Police. Also, Tate and Lyle were working with the Commission to address the problem of sex segregation in their workplaces, while Esso was getting advice on 'a series of short awareness-raising seminars on race and gender issues.[33]

In 1992 a group of researchers at Leicester University asked employers about their experiences and motivations for introducing equal opportunities policies for ethnic minorities (specifically about ethnic monitoring, but the reasoning is broader, covering all facets). The researchers ordered the different reasons that employers gave for adopting the policy.

In the first case, employers said that the equal opportunities policy was a case of justice and morality: 'both personnel and line managers frequently emphasised that monitoring was the right and proper thing to do'. Also, 'the good employer, it was sometimes suggested,

Norwell Roberts was one of few black officers in the Metropolitan Police

was not merely driven by the threat of legal sanction but voluntarily responded to the climate of the times with respect to such matters'. Public-sector employers in particular put 'an emphasis on the provision of public service and care for the community was seen to entail an active involvement in the provision of equal opportunities'.

On the other hand, equal opportunities policies were often 'developed in response to a variety of external pressures such as Head Office demands; CRE investigations; political lobbying; anticipated legal risks'. Similarly, 'it was commonly recognised that the possession of an equal opportunities policy and monitoring system could be an advantage in the event of complaints of discrimination or tribunal proceedings'. To some managers the policy would be a kind of legal protection, 'to keep the buggers away from our door'. In 1987 the Commission for Racial Equality reported not only that 'the number of individual complainants who came to us for assistance rose by a quarter', but that 'in the employment cases we took up the success rate doubled, and there was a similar increase in the number of cases settled on terms'. So too did the size of award rise considerably. To the Commission these changes pointed to 'a growing confidence in bringing complaints as well as a greater awareness of the nature of the racial discrimination by industrial tribunals and the courts'.[34]

Earlier on legal enforcement was a strong motivation. In 1985 an Industrial Tribunal reprimanded British Telecom when they heard that it was 'unable to point to any document setting out the ingredients of the policy and what practical measures it was thought appropriate to take' towards equal opportunities. In April 1986 an industrial tribunal found that British Rail had not discriminated against an Asian applicant for a senior position, but all the same reprimanded BR for its lack of an equal opportunities training policy. The tribunal wrote to chairman Sir Robert Reid who agreed to make the change.[35] As important as observing the law was to employers as a motive for bringing in equal opportunities policies, these legal norms were quite quickly internalised by those employers who adopted them as their own. As many of the managers interviewed by Nick Jewson and the researcher at Leicester University said, 'the publication of the Codes of Practice by the CRE and the EOC had had a decisive influence on management thinking'.[36]

An argument of growing importance was that equal opportunities policies were, in any event, good for business. For the Leicester University researchers, the gain from equal opportunities policies had lots of sides to it. So ethnic monitoring was seen 'as an aspect of the rational recruitment, use and management of labour was a key theme in the reasoning of managers' who were interviewed by the Leicester University team. It was also the case that 'equal opportunities policies... were seen to confer market advantages'. Many thought that equal opportunities policies would contribute to 'a positive corporate image'.[37]

Attitudes to equal opportunities among employers were changing. By 1996 Confederation of British Industry Director General Adair Turner was saying 'our goal as wealth creators must be to give individuals opportunities, prospects and participation in the economy's success'. Like many, he thought that it made perfect sense that an equal opportunities policy was good for business:

> There is sound commercial sense in lifting the barriers to equal opportunities to achieve an employment meritocracy: and there is no case for unjustified discrimination based on characteristics which bear no relation to an individual's ability to do the job.

To Turner equal opportunities were good because they let business:

- Access a wider and higher skilled labour pool
- Gain a diverse workforce which reflects the composition of the wider community
- Achieve increased flexibility and competitiveness
- Eliminate unjustified and unlawful discriminatory practices
- Increase morale at work and beyond

Turner's speech was made into a booklet by the CBI, who commissioned the militant anarchist designer Clifford Harper to draw the cover, giving it the look of a left-wing pamphlet, titled *A Winning Strategy — The Business Case For Equal Opportunities*.[38] Researcher and activist Cynthia Cockburn pointed out that 'we are now seeing companies, whose managers would not so long ago have castigated [London local authorities] as "loony leftists"… announcing similar provisions'.[39]

Hearing the managers' claim to be on the side of justice and the good naturally draws a lot of cynicism from a lot of people. The 'business case for equal opportunities' sounds to many like a contradiction in terms. It would be a mistake, though, to think that managers act in a vacuum. They respond to social pressures like other people. The hard thing to understand is what pressure employers were under that made them feel that they had to do good things.

The best way to understand the employers' position is to look at the character of industrial relations in the period that the equal opportunities policies were taken on board, the Eighties and early Nineties. By all accounts this was a difficult time. Many managers made many harsh choices that hurt people's living standards, working conditions, and security. Many of them downsized, contracted out, delayered, and laid off workers; many imposed new contracts with worse hours and conditions. Importantly, many employers junked the old bond that tied workers and managers together, the negotiated agreements with union representatives. These changes, they thought, were needed to restructure business to make it competitive. Some who were interviewed by the Institute of Personnel Management 'were found to have been very unhappy with the previous accommodation to trade unions which their organisation had to make for one reason or another in the past'. In the survey, taken in 1984, managers were asked if their attitude to labour was more bullish: '61 per cent affirmed that it was, while a further 10 per cent said their approach had always been bullish.' One personnel manager in a food-processing plant explained:

I think we've also been affected by the current atmosphere of imposing the right to manage… so we've made quite a few changes which you could say diminish the conditions of employment.

Another said 'we (management) want total autonomy on this site'. The logic of the market seemed to demand that the corporate partnership of managers and employees should be broken up. The idea that we were all in it together, backing Britain, was put to one side; now everyone was in it for themselves. But in the chill wind of Thatcherite individualism, the gulf between managers and their employees was great. The workplace reforms had taken away many of the mediating links between workers and bosses. The 1984 survey also found that 'some personnel respondents were concerned about "rubbing the unions' noses too much into the ground"'. [40]

It was not just that there was antagonism in the relationship, but that the employees were strangers to their employers. More and more they became preoccupied with the problems of recruitment and retention and of employee loyalty to the firm. After years of breaking down the traditional ties between managers and employees, firms started to talk about their Corporate Social Responsibilities. One clue to Barclays' motives for its equal opportunities code was that at the same time as the equal opportunities post was created, a 'Social Responsibility Unit' was set up under Colin Dyer, with responsibility for the bank's 'inner city and community improvement'. [41] Barclays had a bad reputation in the early Eighties, boycotted by many students and black people for its policy of investment in South Africa. Later in the decade it was trying to repair that reputation.

The business case for equal opportunities has been criticised. But the important thing is that it is understood. The core claim of the business case for equal opportunities is that there is a community of interests between employer and employee. As one manager told researchers at the University of Leicester, equal opportunities policies were 'in the interests of their own business and therefore

in the interests of everyone who works there.'[42] Both are served by the policy of equal opportunities at work. To understand why such policies have been adopted you only have to ask why it was that firms felt the need to assert such a community of interests. The reason was that they had gotten rid of the older idea of a community of interest, which was corporate or social democratic in character. Under the older idea of community, a deal between workers, who were seen largely as English and male, had been struck through workplace negotiation: 'British jobs for British workers.' In place of that older ideal, a newer claim, the claim to be an 'equal opportunities employer', was being made.

One employer whose reputation was seriously hurt by the way it managed its workplace relations was the Ford Motor Company (UK). As we have seen, Ford was right in the middle of the argument over equal pay for women; it also had a bad reputation for its race relations (see Chapter One) with black workers on the assembly line overseen by white managers, and kept away from the more skilled jobs in the tool shop.

Ford were, however, early adopters of equal opportunities policies. Their first outline race policy was adopted in 1970. When they talked to the researchers from Leicester University, Ford told them that 'seminars on the cultural background of ethnic minority employees (including case studies), intended for managers and supervisors had been established in the 1970s'; then, 'in 1982, a new course on avoiding unfair discrimination in selection interviewing had been started, designed for supervisors and managers responsible for recruitment and selection decisions'; and 'in 1987 a training seminar was launched for more senior managers who were responsible for implementing the equal opportunities strategy'.[43] Given the way that black workers at Ford told their own stories to the *Race Today* Collective (see Chapter One), you have to wonder what was being said in those earlier management seminars. And as we shall see, Ford's later experience on the question of race relations at work was far from harmonious. On the other hand, the company did set up a National Working Party in 1986 that led to 'a Joint Statement on Equal Opportunity' issued by the company and all the trade unions in 1988. Copies of the Joint Statement 'were circulated to all employees in the form of a pocket-sized laminated guide'. Then that same year the company 'set up a small Equal Opportunities Department, directly responsible to the Executive Director of Personnel', under an experienced and senior manager.[44]

Ford also made a big push to get black recruits, and to give them a fair chance in interview. At one of its sites, 'to increase ethnic minority participation, the apprenticeship training school had put on a careers conference for youngsters, parents, teachers and careers officers in the work-force catchment area'. When they struggled to keep the new black recruits they were getting, Ford set out 'to improve the pass rate of ethnic minority applicants by developing access courses' in association with a College of Further Education, and offering bursaries to help.[45]

One reason that Ford was keen to improve its relations with the local community was that there 'had been a substantial reduction in the size of the Company's UK workforce'. Moreover, there had been intense conflict at the plant. In 1988 new working practices that broke down job demarcations in the name of 'flexibility' provoked a nation-wide strike.[46]

Throughout the 1980s and early 1990s employers were developing new ways of relating to their employees, and to the public. Though the municipal authorities that modelled the first equal opportunities policies seemed to be doing it for different reasons — political reasons — than the other private-sector employers, their motives were more similar than they appeared. In both cases, large employers were trying to remotivate their moral purpose, and in that, their relationship to their employees, first, and to their customers. The old order of corporatism, working through union agreements, was being dissolved by a new individualistic approach. Strange as it may seem at first, the growing importance of 'equal opportunities at work' was a part of that shift. Certainly 'equal opportunities' was a more attractive side to the drive to labour market liberalisation, and for many women and black people, the greater openness was a boon. What it did not do, though, was to bring about equality between employers and employed. Later we will look at the way the new equal opportunities revolution helped to reorder relations at work.

In the next chapter, though, we must look at the reaction that the policies provoked.

— FIVE —

Reactions

L ooking back at the growing influence of equal opportunities policies in the 1980s, one might think that this was a markedly progressive or radical decade. Anyone who was there will tell you
it was not. Massive changes were underway in society, but these were
not obviously favourable to women or black people. The Conservative
governments of the 1980s are known for their social conservatism.

Two headline messages from the Conservative leader, Margaret
Thatcher, set out the boundaries of the party's attitudes on equal
opportunities. The first was in an interview she gave to the TV show
World in Action shortly before she was elected Prime Minister.
There she said:

> [I]f we went on as we are then by the end of the century there would
> be four million people of the new Commonwealth or Pakistan here.
> Now, that is an awful lot and I think it means that people are really
> rather afraid that this country might be rather swamped by people
> with a different culture and, you know, the British character has done
> so much for democracy, for law and done so much throughout the
> world that if there is any fear that it might be swamped people are
> going to react and be rather hostile to those coming in.[1]

Though it was put forward as worry over others' reactions, the headline for the papers the next day was the word 'swamped', and Thatcher's
fear that immigration would threaten the British way of life.

The second headline message was also given in an interview, five years later when the Prime Minister talked about the 'Victorian values' of thrift and self-help (the words were interviewer Brian Walden's, but she happily took them up). Thatcher had already said, 'I feel very strongly that women should not leave their children to come home to an empty house'.[2]

The Conservatives' ideas about equal opportunities can be seen in the 1982 Cabinet talks on policies for the approaching election. The Cabinet's Central Policy Review team put together papers outlining their ideas. The first was to 'encourage mothers to stay at home'. Behind their thinking was not just traditional attitudes, but a hope that the family — women, that is — would take on the extra work that the government was trying to get out of, as a kind of bulwark against the recession. The team asked 'what more can be done to encourage families to resume the responsibilities taken on by the state, for example, responsibility for the disabled, elderly, unemployed 16 year olds'. (Later on, benefits for younger people were cut, on the understanding that unemployed youngsters would have to rely on their families into their twenties.) The Cabinet wanted parents to take on more responsibility for schooling, and for the care of the elderly. On race, the Cabinet team thought that it would be good to 'publicise success stories of immigrants who have made good', in 'accordance with philosophy of self-reliance, e.g. Asian corner shops' (as patronising and tokenistic as these proposals were, they would later on become quite important). While they were looking for success in the private sector, the Cabinet looked askance at the work of the quangos their Labour predecessors had set up to push for equal opportunities, arguing that they should 'Review the effectiveness of the Commission for Racial Equality and the Equal Opportunities Commission'. A question they asked of the CRE was 'how far present institutional arrangements in this field, most of which were introduced primarily to settle immigrants, are appropriate for dealing with problems faced by a largely British-born ethnic community'. It sounded as if, behind closed doors anyway, the government wanted to get rid of the two Commissions, and that their idea of equality of opportunity was met without any special measures, but through the market. At the same time cuts in welfare services to the elderly and the young, at a time when unemployment was rising sharply and incomes were under pressure, put a greater burden on families, enlarging women's duties at home.[3]

The message from the government was for 'liberalisation' of financial markets and labour markets, but they were very illiberal in other ways — often about sex and race. The 1981 immigration law drew up the drawbridge around the UK, against black and brown migrants — and the immigration police raided, detained, and deported people they called 'illegal'. Young black men, who were much more likely to be unemployed than their white counterparts, were targeted by the police who regularly searched them 'on suspicion', talking about them as a problem of 'street crime'. Many were beaten, like Trevor Monerville, left with brain injuries after a police attack, or killed, like Clinton McCurbin, strangled by arresting officers in Wolverhampton. When young blacks reacted to these provocations by fighting back, as they did in the summer of 1981, in Brixton and then in Southall, Toxteth, and St Paul's, Margaret Thatcher saw the fault lying first with 'young men, whose high animal spirits' had been 'unleashed' in a 'virtual saturnalia', 'a fiesta of crime, looting and rioting in the guise of social protest'. While some of the ripples from the 1981 riots would lead to social programmes to deal with race discrimination, the headline was what Thatcher told the police: 'I promised them every support.' When fighting broke out again between the police and black youth at the Broadwater Farm estate in Tottenham, Tory policy advisor Oliver Letwin dismissed calls for spending to encourage social stability and a black middle class, saying that the money would only go to 'subsidise Rastafarian arts and crafts workshops' or to people who 'will set up in the disco and drug trade'.[4]

Margaret Thatcher and Oliver Letwin

The family, and sexuality too, were the focus of a lot of legislation. The 1989 Children Act opened up family life to much greater scrutiny by the police and social services. The changes were argued for by pointing to the supposed problem of broken homes and bad mothers who neglected their children. An amendment to the 1988 local government act, 'Clause 28', put by Dame Jill Knight, banned schools from holding up homosexuality as a 'pretended family relation'.

In the summer of 1981, after the inner-city riots, the chair of the Commission for Racial Equality David Lane talked about his plans to meet the problem of black unemployment. In parliament, the government was asked over and again whether it would talk to Lane. The riots 'were of course', said Thatcher, 'a godsend' to 'the government's critics in general': 'Here was the long-awaited evidence that our economic policy was causing social breakdown and violence'.[5] 'Does the Secretary of State agree with the Commission for Racial Equality', Hackney MP Clinton Davis demanded of Michael Heseltine, 'that effective measures to tackle racial disadvantage have been frustrated by the shift of resources from the inner cities for which he has been responsible?'[6] In turn, Tory backbenchers, led by Nicholas Winterton, attacked the Commission for Racial Equality.

In November 1981 a Select Committee Report into the Commission found that it was amateurish and ineffective. The criticisms may have come because the Commission had been critical of the government's 1981 Nationality Bill. At that time there were doubts among Tories whether there really ought to be social engineering of race equality. In the House of Lords Max Beloff asked whether it was true to say that 'we accept the fact that Britain is now a multiracial or multicultural society', arguing that the laws against discrimination were not to be taken as seriously as 'the laws about larceny, divorce or whatever it may be': 'they are quasi laws'.[7] In the Select Committee Report it was the Commission's grant-making that came in for criticism, as overreaching. In the press, '"Failure of a Commission", "Lady Bountiful race board attacked", and "Rocket for Race Chief", were just some of the headlines'.[8]

The Home Affairs Committee hauled the Commission and its chairman David Lane over the coals. The Tory backbenchers, and their friends in the press, made fun of the names of the groups that got grants from the Commission — 'the Dominican Joy Spreaders, Women in Dialogue, for example' — and the report argued that the grant-making powers be taken away. In Parliament Nicholas Winterton asked whether 'following the First Report from the Home Affairs Committee... on the Commission for Racial Equality, he will review existing race relations legislation, with a view to seeking the repeal of the Race Relations Act 1976'. But the outright call for abolition was not taken on by the Home Affairs Committee, which instead of calling for it to stop its actions, attacked it for the slow pace at which it was dealing with race discrimination claims — in effect they were demanding it prosecute the law more efficiently, a demand that the Commission took on board. In answer to Nicholas Winterton, the Home Office Minister Timothy Raison said that the government had 'no plans to abolish the Commission for Racial Equality or for the repeal of the Race Relations Act 1976'.[9] All the same, Chairman David Lane was made to stand down, and Peter Newsam took his place. Less was heard of the CRE in Parliament after that, but Newsam, who came from a municipal background, working in the Inner London Education Authority, was more proactive behind the scenes.

The Commission's model code of conduct for employers was at last signed off by the government, after the Home Affairs Committee's attack. A Commission that upheld the rule of law, and encouraged a voluntary approach by employers to equal opportunities, was preferable to the government than one which was voicing criticisms over the inner cities. The Commission complained that their 'statutory responsibilities give us a plain duty to diagnose their particular problems and to draw public attention to them', but they had effectively been told to rein it in.[10]

As well as losing its chairman, the Commission was starved off funds. Money was tight anyway, and the government had little feeling for quangos that attacked them. According to the Commission:

> Early in 1979, the Government's Staff Inspectors suggested that the size of our task justified an increase of about 40 per cent in our staff complement, including more staff for law enforcement work, but the Home Office could not agree and our complement was reduced.

The Equal Opportunities Commission was similarly out of step with government thinking. While the Cabinet was planning that women should spend more time in the home, the Equal Opportunities Commission was arguing that 'services for the under-fives and school-age dependent children are essential in allowing parents to combine careers and public duties with a responsible family life'.[11] It was a message that won little support from the governing party. The Equal Opportunities Commission, too, found that 'resources, both in terms of staff and in terms of finance, [were] far more slender than it was led to expect when it was first established'.[12] All the same, radical journalist Martin Wainwright was relieved that there had been 'no moves to abolish the Commission for Racial Equality or the Equal Opportunities Commission'.[13]

Assault on the 'loony left'

The early experiments in equal opportunities policies by Labour-controlled local authority employers were targeted by the Conservative government and its supporters in the 1980s. Local government was, in Thatcher's view, one of the places in which the 'hard left was entrenched'. She was sure that the public 'knew that Labour's "loony left" had a hidden agenda of social engineering and sexual liberation'.[14] To right-wingers schooled in the thinking of Frederick Hayek and Karl Popper, policies designed to redress discrimination seemed like an example of 'social engineering'. For the Centre for Policy Studies, David Regan wrote a pamphlet about the *The Local Left*, which analysed their supposed methods:

> Social engineering is the deliberation manipulation of people's attitudes and behaviour to produce predetermined types of society as opposed to allowing natural social evolution... seeking to create a radically changed society according to some ideological blueprint.

And, thought Regan, 'perhaps the most distinctive feature of the new approach is an obsession with "discrimination"'.[15] In Camden, Tory councillor Julian Tobin said the decision to keep ethnic records was 'one of the most retrograde steps this council has taken'.[16]

Sometimes employers dug in their heels. Mrs Jean Jenkins, a part-time machinist at the Kingsgate Clothing Company in Harlow, complained that she ought to have been paid the same hourly rate as a full-timer. Though she lost the case at an industrial tribunal, the Equal

Opportunities Commission helped her take the case all the way to the European Court of Justice, which found for Mrs Jenkins. 'All the politicians bend their knee to the Equal Opportunities Commission, the most powerful quango in the land', fumed the company director Bernard Clayman.[17]

The press took its cue from the Tory right and looked for stories to show how the left-wing council leaders were using public money for eccentric causes. Some of these instances of 'loony left' policies were invented and others elaborated. It was also true, though, that unable to effect a substantial increase in jobs for women and ethnic minorities, the local authorities had supported token projects which, while unexceptional to the funders, were at odds with the ideas of the public. Particularly alarming were the advisers in schools and councils that the press labelled 'race spies', whose actions struck many as dictatorial and extreme. The 'loony left' label hurt the Labour Party in local elections because they had not always won the public over to support the reforms that they thought had to be made.[18]

For the Tory government, though, it was important to make sure that the left did not succeed in securing a social base by taking the credit for counter-cyclical spending programmes at the local level. In the lead-up to the 1983 election the Cabinet set out plans to limit municipal spending (by putting a cap on the 'rate support grant', central government's subsidy to local government) and also the abolition of the Greater London Council. A war council of the Labour-left-controlled authorities decided to take a stand, and agreed that they would refuse to set a rate or publish a budget, but go into illegality, rather than implement the cuts. But in the event, only Lambeth and Liverpool Council held to the agreement. Lambeth leader Ted Knight and his councillors, along with the Liverpool Labour group councillors, were removed from office (and landed with enormous fines). Seeing which way the wind was blowing, the other councils stood down and agreed to set a budget and rate within the government's agreed limits.

The outcome was misery for the many council workers who lost their jobs, and for residents who were relying on council services that were cut back; and it was humiliation for those council leaders, and the senior officers that they had put in place. 'We're trying to find a way of ensuring that the misery is shared out equally and fairly', said Hackney councillor John Bloom in 1984.[19] Better a dented shield than none at all, said that master of lowering expectations, Neil Kinnock. In Haringey Council, where I worked in the 1980s, many new staff had been taken on in an expansion that was funded through borrowing on the financial markets. The Council's solicitors told them that the new staff had to be on temporary contracts, because the spending commitments could not be secured. When the government told the Council that they had to cut back expenditure, those on temporary contracts were all sacked. Since they were also the staff that were recruited under the new equal opportunities policy, many were black or Asian, and yet these were the people that were being singled out for sacking. Among the new senior officers employed by the Education Offices at Haringey was the feminist historian Carole Adams. School secretaries, who were made to take on great stacks of extra work to cover for the sacked staff, protested at a seminar Adams was giving about the exploitation of women workers in the nineteenth century. Adams had taken the job in the hope that she might do good, but instead found she was the person making working women's lives worse.

One of the reasons that the Labour-left councils were humiliated by the government is that the Conservative Party nursed a lot of resentment against the equal opportunities policies that they were pioneering. That was the sub-text of a lot of the criticisms of the 'loony left', the alarm of 'race spies in the classroom', 'lesbian workshops', and so on. These criticisms played on prejudices that were grounded in more traditional ideas of race and family. But they also played on the idea that equal opportunities policies would penalise white working-class men. It was, thought Anna Coote, a zero-sum game: 'If women had more power, more opportunity, more pay, more time, more choice, men would have less', she wrote: 'It is rare for any group or class of human beings to give up power voluntarily.'[20] The Labour-left councils lost support among some working-class voters because they did not think that the newer policies were aimed at them.

The sharpest blow to the equal opportunities strategy in local government was the abolition of the Greater London Council. The Commission for Racial Equality announced 'a general investigation into the effects of the abolition of the GLC on ethnic minority employment in local authorities and related areas'.[21] The GLC had been in many ways the laboratory in which equal opportunities policies and practices had been developed. Along with the surcharging of Lambeth councillors, the champions of equal opportunities in local government seemed to have been delivered a knock-out blow, but in the event, things turned out differently. After David Lane, the Labourist and educationalist Peter Newsam, too, was replaced at the Commission for Racial Equality by a senior probation officer and church-goer, Michael Day. Day worked with the government, and Newsam's investigation 'into the effects of the abolition of the GLC on black employment' was 'discontinued'.[22]

Just as the government was targeting the 'loony left' councils and pulling the plug on their social engineering, they were, more quietly, taking up the cause of 'equal opportunities'. The House of Commons Employment Committee's report on discrimination in employment 'strongly endorsed the importance of positive action and also recommended a form of targeting', reported the Commission for Racial Equality, under its new chair. The report fully endorsed 'the adoption of equal opportunities policies by employers'. 'In particular', the Employment Committee 'mentioned the importance of ethnic record keeping and monitoring'.[23] The Employment Committee also 'recommended that wider use should be made by employers of schemes which would help suitable black candidates to acquire the required qualifications', and suggested that the civil service should give these 'in its training programme'.[24]

Challenged by the Tottenham MP Bernie Grant in Parliament a spokesman insisted that 'the Government are firmly committed to the elimination of all unlawful discrimination and to the promotion of equal opportunities in employment for all workers regardless of race'.[25] A proposal to stop local authorities from using their buying power to persuade contractors to adopt equal opportunities policies had been floated by the Government, but they backed down after lobbying from the Commission for Racial Equality and the Equal Opportunities Commission. In Parliament the Tory back-bencher Tony Marlow complained that 'our heroic Government have been got at by the moral blackmail of the race relations industry'.[26]

Once the issue had been prized out of the hands of the left-wing Labour councils, the government felt much more at ease with the idea of equality of opportunity. The ideological leadership of the government in the 1980s was at odds with the idea, but the pragmatists in the Ministries, helped by the civil service, promoted equality of opportunity as a policy that was all about modernising industry and increasing competition. In the first place, the civil service itself took on the equal opportunities policy, as well as ethnic monitoring. Since 1978 the government had been pressed to introduce equal opportunities policies, but had resisted.[27] From 1986, though, the civil service had begun monitoring its staff and adopted an equal opportunities policy. The Commission for Racial Equality welcomed 'the decision of the civil service to strengthen the central unit responsible for equal opportunities policy'. They were pleased, too, to note that the Equal Employment Opportunities branch 'has now been enhanced to divisional status and is now part of the Personnel Management Group of the Cabinet Office' — a sign that the changes were being taken seriously.[28]

Around the same time the Minister of Health, Barney Hayhoe, lent his support to a big push to reform the Health Service. The London Association of Community Relations Councils (LACRC), had published a survey of equal opportunities policies in London health authorities, *In a Critical Condition*, funded by the CRE. The work was the basis for a special project set up by Hayhoe called the 'Kings Fund Task Force', 'because health authorities were putting equal opportunities policies into practice too slowly'.[29] According to the Tory Minister, 'every health authority in the land should subscribe to the principle of equality of opportunity, but most would agree they were a long way from achieving it'; 'Lack of equal opportunities in promotion is one of the major issues in the NHS'.[30] According to the Kings Fund's report: 'Racial inequalities between managers and staff in the service are glaring.' 'When the Task Force was set up in 1986 a minority of health authorities had formally adopted an equal opportunities policy', they noted in 1990: 'Most have done so now.'[31]

Most importantly of all, the Department of Employment got behind the adoption of equal opportunities policies, as did the Confederation of British Industry. Even the abolition of the Greater London Council had an unanticipated consequence quite at odds with the hopes of the ideologues that pushed for it. The GLC worked as a laboratory, and a training school for experts in equal opportunities policies. As the organisation was shut down, a surprising number of its officers went on to become chief executives, Human Resource managers, and managers in other municipal authorities and the private sector. Many set up as private consultants advising companies on the adoption of equal opportunities policies.

In spite of all the noises coming from the Prime Minister and the Tory backbenches, the equal opportunities revolution was underway. Indeed, the greatest take-up and expansion of such policies took place while Thatcher was in office, between 1979 and 1990. The revolution was not really from the bottom up, as revolutions are supposed to be. There were important popular protests and movements around the issues of sex and race equality, but these were largely confronted and demobilised over the Eighties. Nor was the revolution from the top down, if the top is 10 Downing Street. The revolution was a molecular change, which reproduced itself through the adoption of Codes of Conduct, recruitment, training, workplace review, and monitoring policies. Its foot-soldiers were Human Resource managers, volunteers in workplace reorganisations, civil servants, quango-crats, consultants, trainers, and local government officers.

The radical reaction

Radical activists played a big role in giving the equal opportunities revolution its first push around 1980. But that was only after a debate within the left over the way forward. Initially, many radicals were sceptical of the more committee-room approach of the champions of equal opportunities. The first critique of official anti-discrimination came from the left. In 1972, in the pages of the *Red Mole*, the 'Race Relations Industry' was sharply criticised, both the 'various strands within the State machinery, which constitute a good part of the race-relations industry', and also 'those independent bodies like the Institute of Race Relations[32] and the Runnymede Trust'. These liberal Christian lobbies were influenced by their South African and Portuguese paymasters, according to the *Red Mole*'s correspondent, 'S. C.'.[33]

The radicals and the Commission for Racial Equality

Under the well-meaning Etonian David Lane's leadership, the Commission for Racial Equality was widely mocked. Writing in *Race Today*, Mala Sen (later known for the screenplay for *India's Bandit Queen*) was caustic about the 'recently appointed chairman designate of the Commission for Racial Equality', leading a procession of 'elders, all of them professional community relations wallahs', but without being able to 'restore confidence in the platform'.[34] The radical *Black Voice* newspaper included among its 'Short Term Demands', 'the scrapping of

Mala Sen

the Commission for Racial Equality and the 1976 Race Relations Act'. It was 'merely a tool for the purpose of maintaining the status quo'.[35]

In *Race Today*, a column signed 'Tic Tac Toe', probably by Darcus Howe, made the point that the Commission had failed match up to the events of that year — when the police operations in Brixton, Manchester's Moss Side, and Liverpool 8 provoked wholesale rioting. That was the background to the CRE's public humiliation: 'the public trouncing inflicted by the Parliamentary Select Committee and there is no way that David Lane and Co could continue to justify the use of public funds to finance their whims and fantasies'. 'Exit Chairman Lane, not without a firm prod from the Home Office', said Howe. According to *Race Today*'s leader writer: 'Pleased I am to note that Newsam intends to leave the black community alone, and to concentrate all of his forces on the white community. Many of us are breathing sighs of relief.'

Howe had some advice for the David Lane's replacement, Peter Newsam, 'the bureaucrat from the Inner London Education Authority':

[F]ire the entire staff. No single quango in the UK boasts such incompetence in the middle and upper echelons. Time servers they all are. Step number two relates to the funding of self-help groups. That programme ought to be abandoned. Whatever else they are a cursory glance at their income would reveal that they are not self-help at all, but state-propped organisations.[36]

Race Today was only echoing the criticisms that came from the government. From them, the new Commissioner sought a promise that the CRE was not going to be hamstrung. After consultations, the Commission reported that 'The Government backs the promotional and educational work of the CRE', and that 'They feel that the CRE could make an important contribution to the public debate on racial disadvantage in information, education and advice'.[37]

The reason that radicals were sceptical about official anti-racism was that they saw their movement as a popular, grassroots campaign. As we have seen, many black radicals dismissed the Race Relations Act and the Commission for Racial Equality as a top-down manoeuvre to divert activists. Even the Greater London Council's attempts to reach out to black organisations were treated at first with scepticism. In *Race Today*, Farrukh Dhondy wrote scathingly about the 'celebrated grandees of anti-racism, amongst them Ken Livingstone himself, A. Sivanandan who needed no introduction, Cecil Gutzmore who needed no microphone and Paul Boateng who needed only a seat in Parliament'. Dhondy saw it as 'the GLC's placemen in charge of the event, led by the polite and irreplaceable Mr Herman Ouseley'. To Dhondy it seemed that the event was a gathering of 'Livingstone's lost tribes, the beneficiaries or the hopeful, future beneficiaries of the limited largesse of the Greater London Council earmarked for blacks'. Among them 'the no longer young Bengalis, erstwhile street fighters, now turned leaders of projects and makers of films about Bengaliness and anti-racism for the fourth channel'.[38] Leonora Brito wrote up her bad experience of going for an interview for a special training post to promote black journalists at the Polytechnic of London's School of Communications, under the title 'Positive Discrimination: who needs it?' To Brito it seemed that to 'enable black people to compete for jobs in the media on an equal footing with whites' was a 'familiar litany' that meant finding token black candidates who would adopt the professional values of the mainstream.[39]

Not just the *Race Today* Collective, but the Institute of Race Relations was sceptical about the municipal approach to anti-racism. In a review of a book in the Institute's journal *Race and Class* in 1987, Rashid Mufti dismissed the arguments laid against Liverpool Council that it had not done enough for the city's black population: 'The rapid growth of municipal "anti-racism" during the past five years has been a key feature of the local state's response to the rebellions of 1981', Mufti framed the argument, 'Yet there is little evidence to suggest that this has made any significant impact in dismantling racist structures and practices.' Pointedly, Mufti went on to decry the fact that 'the campaign for the city council to adopt an equal opportunities policy is seen as the most important development during this six-year period'. Much more important to this writer were the 'the ways in which the community organised itself politically'. Also in *Race and Class*, Lee Bridges argued that the 'official organs', the 'Commission for Racial Equality and local community relations councils, have proved so ineffective'.[40]

The head of the Institute of Race Relations, A. Sivanandan, was invited to speak at the Greater London Council's meeting. Sivanandan announced 'I come as a heretic, as a disbeliever in the efficacy of ethnic policies and programmes to alter, by one iota, the monumental and endemic racism of this society'. But this doubting Thomas had seen a small chink of light: 'there is room for manoeuvre here, for a war of position if you like'. Sivanandan was sceptical, but he did not want to be left out. Anti-racists he thought, shouldn't be purists and stand outside:

We can't fight the system bare-handed. We don't have the tools, brothers and sisters; we've got to get the tools from the system itself and hope that in the process five out of ten of us don't become corrupt.[41]

Sivanandan's rhetorical scepticism gave way to practical compromise. The background was that the wave of protest of the 1970s was dying back, and the opportunities for militant activism were narrower, making the local government-left look sexier than it really was.

At a trade union meeting organised at the end of 1984, Bernie Grant spoke for the Black Trade Unionists Solidarity Movement. The meeting was very radical, and already speakers had argued that 'the English working class had become a "labour aristocracy" due to the indirect benefits it accrued from the super-exploitation of the under-developed countries', and that 'there was a legacy of cultural imperialism inherited by the labour movement in this country'. Grant spoke carefully, pitching his talk as critical of ameliorative social programmes, saying that there was

a very real danger that many fine sounding initiatives — for improved training, equal opportunities policies, less racist council services, support for independent groups like B.T.U.S.M. and local Women's Units — would become tokens only without real substance.

What he meant, though, was that these would become tokenistic if the Conservative government succeeded in cutting back the funding, not the radicals' criticism of the 1970s that they were inherently tokenistic. Grant's conclusion, like Sivanandan's, was that black groups should lend their support to the equal opportunities and grant-giving powers of the local authorities, and defend them from the attacks that the government were making.[42]

Feminist scepticism about the business case for equal opportunities

Amongst feminists there were some misgivings about the embrace of the Greater London Council and municipal socialism, but not many. Some thought that the drift into the corridors of power would lead to the bureaucratisation of the movement, and even called the new women's officers and committee members 'femocrats'. But these complaints were not typical.

Cynthia Cockburn does look at the conundrum that 'equal opportunities' is a policy 'introduced into organizations by owners and managers "on behalf of women"'. Further she says that when they do so 'it is organisational ends they have primarily in mind', such as 'to improve recruitment' or 'they just want a good image'.[43]

As the equal opportunities agenda developed and was taken up by private industry there were more openly expressed doubts about the 'business case for equal opportunities'. Linda Dickens in particular worried that 'In recent years the promotion of equality action appears to have rested primarily on one strategy — getting employers to see that equality is in the interests of the business, the so-called business case for equality'. Dickens quotes an argument made by Forbes that 'support for equal opportunities becomes associated with a set of values unrelated to equality, difference, justice or diversity', and, going further, suggests that this set of values 'is potentially as much in conflict with, as supportive of' equal opportunities.[44] Dickens argues that relying on the claim that good business practice leads to equal opportunities is a mistake because it might be the case that it was good business practice to discriminate. She points out that the 'business case' has 'greater salience for some organisations than others' — that some employers might have less interest in promoting equality of opportunity; further, Dickens argues that 'the appeal of particular business case arguments may vary over time as labour or product markets change, giving rise to "fair weather" equality action'.[45]

Irene Bruegel and Diana Perrons make a similar point about the limitations of the business case for equal opportunities. They set it out that 'in the late 1980s there was also concern about the demographic time bomb' — a predicted labour shortage — 'and efforts made to tap into new labour reserves, especially women and ethnic minorities'. It was because of this labour shortage that 'measures associated with being an equal opportunities employer were consistent with commercial self-interest' and 'a business case for equality could be defined'. 'However', argue Bruegel and Perrons, 'the labour market forecasts were invalidated by the recession of the early 1990s and some of the enthusiasm for enhancing the role of women in organisations evaporated'.[46]

So too does Dickens say that 'the defusing of the demographic time bomb in the recession of the early 1990s, for example, led to some backsliding in the detail and extent of equality provisions in response to market pressure'.[47] These are the same sentiments expressed in the Equal Opportunities Commission report for 1992:

> There was tremendous optimism and hope in the late 1980s and early 1990s. We were set to see a skills revolution and the proper recognition and valuing of women's contribution to society brought about by what was described as the 'demographic time bomb'. Much of that optimism receded with the onset of the recession and the continued concentration of women in low paid, low status jobs.[48]

Bruegel and Perrons conclude from the experience of the 1990s that 'the business case is in reality associated with cyclical economic change', that is that the British Industry will prove to be a 'fair weather friend' of women's equality. Cynthia Cockburn sees employers 'increasingly alarmed by the "demographic time bomb"' — which is to say, the coming labour shortage.[49] The suspicion that a downturn in the economic cycle would be bound to de-rail progress towards equality was strong. The Equal Opportunities Commission painted a depressing picture of the impact of the recession of the early 1980s on women's employment and on equal pay: 'The impact of growing unemployment has fallen heavily on women', and 'women have borne a disproportionate share of the increased rate of unemployment'. Moreover, 'the severe increase in unemployment has meant a drastic reduction in opportunities for women to enter into paid employment' and also arrested the move towards equal pay.[50]

The scepticism of feminists towards the business case for equal opportunities was an important expression of doubt over the direction of the policy. Still, in its assessment of the impact of the economic cycle on women's employment and on equality at work, it proved to be too pessimistic — at least about parity between women and men. The record is that in the recessions of 1980-81, 1990-91, and 2009-10 the comparative position saw women increase their share of jobs, while pay parity either plateaued or improved — as we shall see in Chapter Seven.

Where radicals had expressed their doubts about the bureaucratisation of the movements for radical change, and their incorporation into the official, top-down structures of municipal socialism, those doubts were muted. Because of the government attacks on the GLC and the 'loony left' councils, and their radical policies on race and gender, activists tended to set aside their doubts, and instead rally to the defence of the policies under attack.

Radical criticisms of equal opportunities policies have generally been that they have not gone far enough, or that they have remained paper policies, not seriously put into action. Radicals shared the goals of equality of the sexes and the races to which the policies appealed. What was less often noticed was that while the purported content of the policies was equality, the form they took was an enhanced authority of the employers over the employees. Considered as process rather than as outcome, the operation of equal opportunities was a streamlining of recruitment, the management of diversity at work, and a common set of values enshrined in company policy.

Doubts over the worth of equal opportunities policies shape our perceptions of policy change. The headline attacks on equal opportunities policies from Tory backbenchers, the tabloid press, and ministers all lead to an assessment of the 1980s as a decade in

Beatrix Campbell

which progress was put into reverse. Looking back, Beatrix Campbell said that in the 1970s 'we won new laws on equal pay, marital status, reproduction, sexuality' but 'when Margaret Thatcher and the neoliberal Conservatives won the election of 1979 all that was threatened.'[51] According to Herman Ouseley, 'the government at that time was focused on promoting individualism, about people being competitive, and about no real sense of shared society'; for that reason 'the agenda of "race" was limited in terms of how far we could push on'.[52] Those are understandable reactions to the ideological onslaught against 'social engineering' for 'Victorian values', alleging black criminality and fecklessness. The irony is, however, that changes were put in place in the 1980s that would make the equal opportunities revolution unstoppable.

— SIX —

Human Resource Management

With the propagation of firm-based equal opportunities codes, the day-to-day work of making them happen passed from the two government Commissions, the CRE and the EOC, into the hands of managers in firms. In particular, it was the personnel department, or, as it came to be called, the Human Resource Department, that carried through the policies. The change of name to Human Resource, or just HR, was itself a marker of a new agenda, of which equal opportunities would be an intimate part.

In the later twentieth century, business theory set out two main strands. The first was the need for restructuring. In the 1980s management gurus Peter Drucker, Tom Peters, and Charles Handy all made the case that managers must be constantly changing. They had to become change agents, restructuring their organisations. Their slogan was from the Greek philosopher, Heraclitus, for whom there was 'nothing permanent but change'. In his book *Thriving on Chaos*, Peters wrote that you 'have to learn to love change', and argued against those who could not see the point of reform, that 'if it ain't broke you just haven't looked hard enough': 'fix it anyway'.[1] With the new business gurus 'outsourcing' took off. First it was a matter of shedding non-essential functions, like the canteen, plant security, or deliveries, by contracting them out to business service companies. The goal was a lean firm, agile enough to adapt to changing market conditions. But later on it was not just the non-essential functions that were outsourced. Increasingly managerial and strategic decision making were bought in, in the form of consultancy firms that specialised in re-engineering companies, like McKinsey and Accenture.

The second major innovation in business theory in the Eighties was called Human Resource Management, and it was a reaction to the problems created by the craze for downsizing, contracting out, and delayering. All told, this was a bruising time for employers and for managers. Downsizing, delayering, restructuring, and repurposing came to feel like unending misery. According to business professors Ronald J. Burke and Cary Cooper, firms suffer a 'downward performance spiral as organisations address real performance problems such as low profits, high costs, poor customer service, and low stock prices'. Faced with these 'typical organizational responses include staff layoffs, greater use of part-time and contract staff, a restriction on hiring and promotions, freezes or cutbacks, and reduced investment in training and employee development'. The trouble, explain Burke and Cooper, is that 'employees respond, in turn, by reducing their job involvement, exhibiting lower job satisfaction, decreasing their effort, increased accidents, and greater turnover'. On top of that, 'these individual behaviours have the effect of increasing the performance problems that led to the organizational responses in the first place': 'Thus the downward spiral continues.'

The point of Burke and Cooper's telling of the story is that there is a different way that will break the vicious circle. They are arguing for the new Human Resource Management, the next major innovation in business theory, in their book *The Human Resources Revolution*. There is, they claim, 'considerable empirical evidence that the use of effective human resource management practices increase firm performance'. 'Performance increases because employees work both harder and smarter', he says:

Employees work harder because of greater job involvement, greater peer pressure for results, and the economic gains based on high performance. Employees work smarter because they can use their knowledge and skill acquired through training and development.[2]

Burke and Cooper are not on their own. 'Human Resource Management is a growing field with an increasing influence on organizational strategy and practice', the Catholic University of America assures prospective students: 'In its Occupational Outlook Handbook, the U.S. Bureau of Labor Statistics projects a robust 17% job growth in human resource management between 2006 and 2016.'[3] 'In recent years human resource management (HRM) has firmly become embedded within a business mindset', writes Tom Short of the University of South Australia, who notes 'two decades of rapid growth in human resource management practices'.[4] Tom Keenoy says that 'over the last twenty years "HRM" has emerged as a global discourse'. He explains that HRM 'developed slowly in the US where it was seamlessly incorporated into management thought'. However, it 'appeared in British universities almost overnight in the mid-1980s and, by the early 1990s, its introduction had effectively transformed the language deployed to analyse employment relations'.[5]

HRM is put forward as an alternative to aggressive management, and also an alternative to workers pushing their interests collectively, through unions. The Workplace Industrial Relations Survey that has been running since 1980 over time has recorded first the decline of unions, and of union recognition, to the point that just 26% of the workforce were in unions by 2011. Even where there was high membership, this was so 'in workplaces where managers are in favour of membership' — meaning that those workplaces that are unionised are so because management wants it that way.[6] Second, the Survey has identified the growth in specialist Employment Relations managers. This was identified in the 1998 Survey, and there was 'increasing specialisation in personnel... in workplace level in the late 1990s and early 2000s'.[7] There were doubts about how to understand the changes that were taking place: 'Some argued that a new style of management was emerging which, in some cases, amounted to a more integrated, strategic, people-centred version of personnel management, labelled "human resource management" or HRM'; but 'Others said that, in practice, developments were more in keeping with the cost-reduction or "macho-management" approach of the early 1980s'.[8] The ambiguity was understandable. On the one hand managers remained as dominant in regard to organised labour as before; on the other, the mood music had changed, with employers addressing workers' presumed needs and interests more solicitously. Some of the changes that took place, the shift away from national pay awards, and further, towards individual contracts and rates, towards individual performance reviews, and towards flexible working hours, could be represented either way: as the domination of labour by disaggregating collectivities, or as liberating individuals with a more personalised approach. To achieve these ends, personnel departments did indeed grow, and often changed their names to 'Human Resources'. The Standard Chartered Bank, for example, has 6000 people in its Human Resources department serving a workforce of 88,000.[9]

Stephen Machin and Stephen Wood at the London School of Economics argued that HRM departments were not replacing unions. They marshalled some good statistics to show that, in fact, larger HRM departments tended to correlate positively, rather than negatively, with recognised unions.[10] Still, the influence of unions is clearly declining, and also the HRM function clearly increased up to the mid-Noughties. More to the point, the style of personnel management plainly had changed, in ways that were better summed up by the 'Human Resources' model than the Industrial Relations one.

What was the idea behind Human Resources?

The rhetoric of Human Resource Management is very much drawn from motivational seminars and therapeutic ideas of self-growth.

The core proposition in Human Resource Management is not so remarkable. It is that 'people are our most valuable resource'. Human Resource Management is 'people-centric'. The phrase 'human resources' was probably coined by Peter Drucker in 1954, but it was not really developed to mean what it means today until the Eighties, by Mike Beer and his colleagues at the Harvard Business School. David Guest summarised that 'HRM comprises a set of policies designed to maximise organisational integration, employee commitment, flexibility and quality of work'. Tom Keenoy highlights that in the account of HRM there is not 'any space for trade unions or joint decision-making'. Keenoy picks through the HRM literature to show how it is preoccupied with 'high commitment', 'high performance', added value, and 'sustained competitive advantage for the organisation', and he paraphrases it as 'what is the best way to more effectively exploit the labour resource?'[11]

According to Bogdan Costea and his colleagues at Lancaster University's Department of Organization, Work, and Technology:

> Put simply, human subjects are exhorted to expand and intensify their contribution as selves (as 'human resources') in order to enhance production, maximize value, thus leading the organization to success.

They go on to explain how with the slogan 'people are our most important asset', 'subjectivity is broken down in multiple aspects, and how it is reassembled around an idealized "better self" created by a variety of "therapeutic" techniques and tactics'.[12] In all of this, according to academics Graham Hollinshead and Mike Leat, 'the position of the individual employee is in fact quite precarious, with a high degree of dependency on the benevolence of employers'.[13]

Looking at HRM as ideology as well as organisation, we can go further, and say that it is an assertion of a community of interest between employer and employee. Coming at the end of many

years of workplace strife, it is easy to see why managers might be thinking about workers' commitment. Many of the campaigns of cost reduction and 'macho management' left managers anxious that they had undermined their employees' loyalty to the company, so they were willing to invest in new personnel managers to cope with the fall-out. The growth of HR departments suggested some differences between the ways that companies related to their employees. The enhanced HR side was in some ways at odds with the more day-to-day discipline of line managers. Human Resource managers were more likely to be at specific sites, got greater independence, and were more likely to be represented on the board.[14] These HR departments were needed to oversee some of the new ways that companies were relating to workers. Performance review, performance-related pay, and job assessments are all things that might be difficult for line managers to do without losing objectivity. The separation of the two aspects of line manager/Human Resource manager opened up some conflicts in management function. Commanding workers in a given task has its own order and logic, which can shade into bullying and personal domination. The Human Resources department on the other hand is generally aloof from the immediate work process, dealing for the most part with routine tasks of payroll and staffing levels.

But in managing the workforce as Human Resources, rather than technical command, the personnel department can pull in different directions, dictating caution and consideration to line managers, and handling employees' concerns. So, while Human Resources have only an occasional and even tangential relation to most employees and most workplaces most of the time, they still can set the parameters of what is and what is not acceptable at work. HR departments that intervene into day-to-day organisational questions, such as workplace discipline, recruitment, or workload, may have a large impact, and do a great deal to set down the boundaries of acceptability. Though it might seem that Human Resources departments are on the side of the employers, that is not really the case. While line managers can be bullies, Human Resources departments drop their own kind of misery on employees. Performance reviews and disciplinary hearings are often relentlessly oppressive experiences which are marked by an inhuman and unreflective process, unchecked by common sense.

Considering the drive to innovate work processes it is always worth bearing in mind just how conservative UK managers really are. Michael Porter looked at the British economy for the DTI. He found that British business was good at setting people to work hard, but invested much less in capital stock than America, Germany, or France. Corresponding to the low levels of investment in new technology, Britain's investment in R&D was lower too, and would be much lower were it not for the exceptional amounts of research done by the bio-technology sector, in which Britain enjoys a world-leading position. Another DTI investigation blamed the UK's 'risk-averse approach' for low levels of entrepreneurial activity and for frustrating the early adoption of new technology and new products.[15] According to the Design Council's National Survey of Firms, 58% 'neither developed nor introduced any new products or services in three years'.[16] For the most part employers plan to do next year what they did last year. Still, the language of innovation was important for motivating the case for industry.

Human Resource Management and equal opportunities

It should be clear from the outline of the Human Resources Management paradigm that HR and equal opportunities policies are fairly close — or that a Venn diagram of both would show mostly overlap.[17] The Human Resources revolution (Burke and Cooper) is the equal opportunities revolution (Hakim) — largely two accounts of the same process. Where the equal opportunities revolution is more profound than HR, is that equal opportunities yokes a remotivation and reordering of workplace discipline to two (and more) substantial movements for social justice, the Women's Movement and the Anti-Racist Movement (and more latterly those for lesbian and gay rights, and more). Many newer and younger additions to the workforce identified with the greater opportunities that the policies represented. Millions of women and black people were being recruited, many of whom saw the equal opportunities policies as working in their favour. By contrast, the Human Resources revolution always lacked a strong sense of purpose, and was easily parodied, as for example in *The LEGO Movie*'s parody of a company song, 'Everything is Awesome'. In industry, these methods were readily mocked by employees when they were associated with Japanese management methods, as an alien imposition. But equal opportunities policies had a much stronger moral call on workforces, substantial numbers of whom identified with the advances that they represented.

Equal opportunities policies help employers in several ways. The first, and most important, is that opening up the employment market to more potential workers reinforces the authority of the employers. Second, equal opportunities policies serve as a motivation for restructuring workplace relations and reconstituting the workforce. Fourth, they serve to motivate workplace discipline and as an important framework within which employees are socialised into a set of values that are enshrined in company policy. Third, an equal opportunities policy enhances the authority of employers over employees, by disaggregating working collectivities.

Restructuring the workforce

To open the workforce up to greater competition was the point of labour market liberalisation. More market entrants meant more competition. More barriers to employment meant less competition. The point of labour market liberalisation was to keep wages competitive — which is to say lower.

This is an argument that understandably makes a lot of people uncomfortable. It seems to say that it is women and migrants who are pushing down wages. Employees have at different times taken on a strategy of limiting access to their trade to keep wages high. At times they have tried to exclude women and immigrants. These are self-defeating strategies. A class of employees divided against each other is not really in a strong position to defend its jobs, wages, or conditions. On the other hand, it would be naïve to imagine that employers would open up their employees to greater competition out of a sense of justice for women or minorities alone. Employers want to be able to recruit from a large pool so that they can find the talents they need without paying too much for them.

That early champion of equal opportunities for women, Baroness Seear, made her case for their recruitment in contrast to labour market rigidities in 1976: 'monopolistic and protectionist devices have grown up at every level to render rigid an economy whose only hope of survival lies in flexibility'. As she explained,

the 'right to work' has been interpreted as 'my right to continue in the particular job in which I find myself at a given moment of time'. This belief has been strengthened by such notions as the 'property

of the job' which, by a subtle abuse of language reinforced the idea
that a man has an entrenched right to a particular job.[18]

Seear hoped to undermine workers' security and open them up to
more competition.

Later on, Human Resource Management theory was saying that
the workforce was much more diverse than managers were used to,
and employment practices had to change to take advantage of that.
Under the heading 'Adapting to Change in the Work Force', Dennis
Kravetz says that the US workforce 'has changed greatly' since it was
'dominated for many years by white male employees' — but that
now they are the minority. 'Women now make up 45 per cent of
the workforce', and more, 'members of minority groups now make
up 15 per cent of the workforce'. Soon a fifth of all workers will be
immigrants, says Kravetz, and 'Human resources and line managers
need to plan for this event now'. Of those more established workers,
Kravetz has a different message. He says that the workforce is getting
older, a change which has a 'negative side': 'Employees entering the
work force now will find a large group of baby boomers ahead of
them', and 'Younger employers will find it difficult to advance into
management'.[19]

Human Resource managers are committed to the idea of diversity
in the workforce because they have greater authority over a divided
workforce. Divide and rule, said the Romans. But just as managers
talk up diversity in the workforce, they also want to believe, and want
their employees to believe, that workers and managers alike are all in
it together. An equal opportunities policy is an assertion of a common
interest between employer and employee. When organisations say
that they are 'an equal opportunities employer', they are saying that
they have the interests of the workforce at heart. 'Equality', that slogan
of the nineteenth-century labour movement, had been taken over by
employers at the end of the twentieth century. But just as the policy
foregrounds the value of 'equality', it also emphasises difference

Managing Diversity

— indeed later versions of the policy often use the title 'managing diversity' over 'equal opportunities', with the implication that diversity is a fact of life to be managed, rather than an inequality to be overcome. Nick Jewson and his colleagues at Leicester University found that 'it was not uncommon for [ethnic] monitoring to be opposed on the grounds that it both encouraged and facilitated discrimination rather than eliminating it'. They were surprised to find that 'this view was expressed by both ethnic minority and white respondents'.[20] It is not often noticed that 'managing difference' is the Roman policy of *divide et impera*, divide and rule. The authority of the Human Resource manager stems from the need to manage difference in the workforce.

Companies confronted with staid and unimaginative leaders often hope to reorganise and lose the dead wood. When firms adopted equal opportunities policies in the 1980s and 1990s, they challenged the outlook of their older managers and employees. In the summer of 1992 the police service agreed to monitoring after a tribunal ruled that Senior Police Chief Alison Halford had been discriminated against when she was not short-listed for a post with the Merseyside Police Force. In 1999, after the public inquiry into the death of Stephen Lawrence, and the police failure to prosecute the perpetrators, Police Commissioner Sir Paul Condon gave his support to the fast-tracking of minority officers in the senior officer training programme. Many of the early candidates, like Ali Dizaei and Tariq Ghaffur became the target of sustained campaigns of abuse and allegations of impropriety by long-standing officers. 'Let me be unequivocal from the outset', said the new Commissioner Sir John Stevens, 'there is no place in the Metropolitan Police for racists'. Those who could not get used to the new conditions should 'get out of the Met now'.[21] A good job, too, you might well agree. Still, the fall-out from the Lawrence Inquiry and the discrimination hearings was a marked turnover of staff. In 2014 a Freedom of Information request showed that more than 800 police service employees had been investigated over racist, homophobic, and threatening comments on social media. Many were disciplined, but many more simply left before the cases could be considered. 'More than 70 have retired, resigned or been sacked over the past five years'.[22] The reform process accelerated staff turnover in the police forces across the United Kingdom. According to one report, 'some 50% of officers faced with a misconduct hearing choose to resign', and as the author makes clear, resignations ahead of hearings are thought of as advantageous both to the officers investigated, and to the police. Another report by the Independent Police Complaints Commission noted that investigations of race discrimination could end in resignations.[23] In Parliament, questions were raised about the way that many officers seemed to have evaded disciplinary hearings in discrimination cases by taking early retirement.[24] Many more, older officers heard the message that the force they had trained in had changed, and left, leaving the way for a new generation of career officers like Cressida Dick and Bernard Hogan-Howe.

Herman Ouseley and Usha Prashar explained that Lambeth's new Race Relations Unit would cut across traditional management structures. Race officers would 'have direct access to their appropriate committee chairmen, and their reports would appear at respective committees unaltered, but with appropriate comments from chief officers, if necessary'. 'These innovative reporting arrangements', they added, 'made the function and role of the Race Relations Unit quite unique':

> Thus the advisers were given an independent role with access to power. The Unit also had access to the Leader of the Council to generate speedy intervention on any issues of great concern.[25]

Council leader Ted Knight saw the senior council officers in post as a self-serving bureaucracy, and a barrier to change. The Race Relations Unit and the Race Officers were a lever to prise open the Council, and change it in the image of the Labour administration. The Race Officers were called 'Race Tsars' by a hostile press, though, suggestively, the model was widely adopted in government in the 2000s. Special officers to deal with social problems were created like the 'Social Mobility Tsar' (Alan Milburn), the 'Respect Tsar' (Louise Casey), and more recently a 'High Street Tsar' (Mary Portas). In management theory the goal that Tom Peters and Peter Drucker identified of innovation was given an added moral foundation with the equal opportunities revolution that was taking place in the town halls, and would soon migrate into private industry.

In the way that the workplace was organised, the union had less authority, and the Human Resources department, more. Senior union representatives looked at in the Workplace Employment Relations Survey were three fifths male, whereas 'around three quarters of HR managers and almost two thirds of personnel managers were women'. HR departments and HR managers were much more likely to be female. [26]

All across the world of work, from Lambeth Council to Lever Brothers and the Metropolitan Police, older employees who had been recruited in different times and under different social mores either learned to change, or took early retirement. In the early 1990s black employees of the London Underground pushed hard for representation in senior grades. Since then the Tory London Mayor from 2008-16, Boris Johnson, gave out surprisingly generous payments for early retirement. The effect has been that there are many more black managers and drivers, while older white union members, many of whom were active in earlier labour disputes, are leaving — just as the Underground is closing ticket offices and arguing for a 24-hour service and driverless trains. 'The lean, "streamlined", "slimmed-down" firm has lost most of its hierarchical grades', write Luc Boltanski and Eve Chiapello, 'consigning whole layers of hierarchy to unemployment'.[27] With the way opened up, younger aspirant managers who identified with the changes would advance their careers by learning the new mantras. One woman, a manager in the civil service, told Cynthia Cockburn, that 'we see ourselves as one of the agents of change, the "managers of tomorrow"'. On the other hand, 'there is no room in this scenario for fetishized masculine careers', according to Cockburn — echoing the Thatcherite slogan, 'no more job for life'.[28] Those who were promoted were more beholden to the newer style of management. As one recruiter in television explained to me, they were appointing more women as producers and assistant producers because they were more eager to prove themselves, while the men were more reluctant to put themselves out and prone to clock off at six. These small adjustments in the relative positions of men and women, and of white and black, were at the same time substantial adjustments in the position of employee and employer — in the latter's favour, as managers gained greater authority over a diverse workforce — and got rid of a lot of older, male, and perhaps less motivated and more cynical hands.

Socialising the workforce

Brand strategists decided in the 1990s that the company's ethos would drive the workforce. Brands and company catechisms were all the rage. Loyalty to the company brand, it was hoped, would bind employees to the company. Chuck Pettis said that workers should recite the corporate catechism, to remind them of their higher purpose:

> Employees should have the positioning statement and the associations posted at a visible spot near their telephones so that they can refer to them when communicating with any of the companies' publics, including prospects, customers and suppliers.[29]

When the supermarket Asda was in trouble in 1996, they raised emergency funds, selling shares to the workforce. Their strategy for re-branding was directed at the staff, as chairman Archie Norman insists: 'central to the Asda proposition is straight talking'. For Asda employees that meant 'living the legend' — and 36,000 were made to buy shares.[30] Company brands are important, and the hope that employers would identify with the success of the company is not irrational, but perhaps too naked an appeal to succeed. Another feature of business in the 1990s was the 'mission statement', which would put the company's unique selling proposition into a grander and more benevolent-sounding frame. With a lot of scepticism towards 'fat cat' city traders and bankers, many companies took on the goals of 'corporate social responsibility', and not a few took on mentoring and other social work in wider society. Reports by committees under Adrian Cadbury (in 1992) and then under Sir Richard Greenbury for the CBI (1995) investigated the public perception that big business and chief executives in particular were dishonest and overpaid. British Petroleum, mindful of the criticisms of the carbon economy, went to the self-abnegating extreme of branding itself 'Beyond Petroleum', expressing a commitment to invest in alternative energy sources.

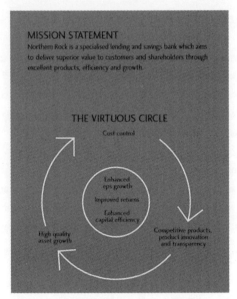

Northern Rock mission statement, 2006

The guilty secret behind a lot of the attempts to re-motivate the moral standing of business was that it was not just the wider public that did not trust bosses. In 2003 Mercer Human Resources Consulting found that 'only four in 10 employees trusted their managements or thought their behaviour was consistent with company values', while 'fewer than half thought their company was well managed'. Worse, trust in management fell the longer people had been working there.[31]

Before the words 'mission statement' had ever been used by a British company, thousands had adopted equal opportunities policies. The great advantage of the policies to managers was that it cast the company's purpose in a positive light, enjoining workers to support the cause. Employers could demand acceptance of the equal opportunities policy.

When Lambeth Council published its equal opportunities policy in a Code of Practice in March 1981, it 'became the responsibility of all council employees', and 'failure to operate or comply with the Equal Opportunities Policy' was made punishable as a gross misconduct. In recruitment, 'the equal rights dimension of service provision should be included in the personnel specification', with the clause: 'It is essential that the post-holder exhibits a clear understanding of the social background and problems of Lambeth's community and in particular of the disadvantaged black, female and disabled groups.' In the new code of conduct, 'failure to do so should be considered as an excluding factor'. In interview, 'a candidate's expressed opposition to the operation of the Equal Opportunities Policy should represent sufficient grounds for non-selection'. On appointment, staff were to sign a declaration:

> I have read and understood the Council's Equal Opportunities Policy, and acknowledge that the offer of employment is made subject to my agreement to pursue actively that policy during the course of my employment and to undergo any training associated with this.[32]

Justified by the moral exigency of 'equal opportunities', the employer, Lambeth Council, was demanding a remarkable degree of loyalty. They were saying that not only should employees follow company policy, but that they should believe in it, too. Some people were sacked for acting against the equal opportunities policy. More took the lesson to heart that the values of the employer had changed, and changed their own behaviour, and perhaps their beliefs, accordingly. Whether a belief that the equal opportunities policy was tokenistic, or that the 'business case for equal opportunities' was doubtful, would have proved an 'excluding factor' we do not know.

In her book *The Managed Heart*, University of California sociologist Airlie Russell Hochschild explains how employers demand 'emotional labour' from 'nannies, daycare workers, eldercare workers, nurses, teachers, therapists, bill collectors, policemen, workers in call centers'.[33] At the Prêt À Manger sandwich chain, the *Daily Mail* reports:

> bizarre 'emotional labour' rules mean employees of the popular sandwich chain are expected to be 'charming', to 'have presence', and to 'care about other people's happiness', and should never be 'moody', or 'just here for the money'.

What is more, 'mystery shoppers visit branches every week to ensure all staff are displaying "Prêt perfect" behaviour.'[34]

What seems exploitative in retail, emotional engagement with management policy, appears not to be so when the outcome is generally understood to be a social good; the demand that employees believe in the equal opportunities policy does not seem to cross a line, where the goal is social justice rather than sales.

Even though the explicit outcome was a social good, employees' active adoption of the equal opportunities policy had advantages for employers. By upholding the policy, and expecting employees to do the same, managers were socialising their workforce in shared norms. It was, after all, the company's equal opportunities policy that the workforce was expected to observe. Policies were generally negotiated with unions, but once adopted were enforced by management — by HR in a larger company. The disciplinary process was in the hands of the management, which would lodge the original complaint, prepare the charges, and organise the initial hearings, under the terms of the policy. At one North London school a teaching assistant was being managed for poor attendance, and let slip in an informal hearing that she had become depressed when her daughter started dating a Turkish man. The school promptly dropped the investigation of her work, and sacked her instead for discrimination, though there was no evidence that she had discriminated against any schoolchild or teacher. Her union representative sympathised with her plight, but agreed with the enforcement of the policy. The disciplinary process enhanced the authority of the employers over the employees.

To reinforce the common norms of the equal opportunities policy, employers can train staff in procedures laid down in the policy, and even in the motivation and attitudes behind the policy. From 1985 the Equal Opportunities Commission offered companies training in the application of the code of conduct it published that year. The Commission took note of 'the Awareness Training Programme launched by Esso UK Ltd', which, they explained, 'is an important initiative, structured around a series of short awareness-raising seminars on race and gender issues'. In 1986 the Ford Motor Co Ltd gave training to managers involved in interviewing and the same year Woolworths started a training programme with the advice of the Commission for Racial Equality.[35]

At the Greater London Council, in April 1983, 'the first 4-day course for GLC employees on multicultural ways of working' was held. The courses were run by Linda King, a black community worker and trainer. 'It made me think in ways I'd never thought before', said one participant: 'I'll never tell a black person in future they're being "too sensitive" about racism.' Another taking part said that she had thought of herself as a 'non-racist' before the course, but 'now I describe myself as an "anti-racist" — actively opposed to racism'.[36]

Training on equality policies suited companies who were thereby taking control of an issue that had caused them difficulties in the past. Training programmes generally have a tendency to reinforce company authority. They are a way of communicating with employees that is didactic, not negotiated. The Institute of Personnel Management's 1986 survey found that managers were less interested in negotiation, more interested in 'information-giving exercises such as briefing groups', because 'such exercises strengthen the 'line' authority of management': 'The majority of personnel managers are enthusiastic advocates of this type of communication exercise — they are devotees of employee involvement rather than industrial democracy'.[37]

Staff training fits well into the ideal of top-down communication; training in equal opportunities has the advantage that the content of the training is egalitarian while the process gone through would tend to reinforce the authority of the trainer, and therefore the employer. The Transport and General Workers' Union branch chair at Ford's Dagenham plant, Jim Brinklow, remembered one confidence-building exercise: 'the garage steward was there with a magazine and a pair of scissors and he was cutting out pictures'. Brinklow demanded 'what the fuck are you doing?' and then threatened 'I am going back to the plant, and I'm going to tell your members what you're doing': 'Pack it up and get a bit of dignity inside you.' As Brinklow saw it, the exercise was demeaning for a workplace representative, and also a means of covering up the real conflict between the employers and the workforce.[38]

The Commission for Racial Equality thought that training in race would have the advantage of 'increasing awareness of racism and prejudice, both at an individual and an institutional level'. There were two approaches, they thought: 'race-related training is the subject of a debate about whether the focus should be on attitudes or behaviour'. The Commission was sympathetic to courses developed by Judy Katz in the United States based on behavioural therapy, which they said would:

- Facilitate the process whereby whites 'own' the problem of racism, i.e. acknowledge and accept responsibility for it
- Facilitate acceptance by whites of their individual role in sustaining or removing racism

Reluctant to commit to the idea that employers could tell their workers what to think, the Commission concluded that 'there can be little quarrel with the view that employers have the right to expect a certain code of conduct from their staff, consistent with the law and fair employment practice'.[39] Of course, no manager wanted to engage in a quarrel over equal opportunities, but rather to dictate how such relations would be carried on at work. Equal opportunities training would help to socialise employees in the kind of conduct they could expect from staff.

Rationalisation of labour

Early on, the laws on sex discrimination were used to modernise labour contracts and personnel management. When Barbara Castle looked at equal pay legislation, she was advised by a civil servant John Locke (he went on to be the first Director of the Health and Safety Executive). Locke, who 'did an excellent job on the Bill', argued 'that "equal value" should be linked to job evaluation schemes and firms' pay structures'.[40] A survey on the impact of equal pay legislation noted that:

Other than narrowing differentials, the main effect of the Equal Pay Act, has been a greater degree of systematization in pay structures: equal pay was a factor in the introduction of job evaluation in nine organizations.[41]

The Equal Opportunities Commission paid special interest to the promotion of job evaluation schemes, and helped to draft guidelines for these, because 'there is no provision in the Equal Pay Act for a woman to claim equal pay for work of equal value if a job evaluation scheme has not been carried out'.[42]

Equal opportunities policies also helped employers to systematise their monitoring of their workers. Employees were often hostile to companies keeping personnel records in the post-war order. 'Company spies' were hated amongst shop-floor militants, and the records kept by the Economic League were the basis of a blacklist of many of them.[43] When it was first brought in, ethnic monitoring alarmed many workers, some of whom told Nick Jewson and the researchers at Leicester University that 'ethnic identity was a personal and private matter that was not of relevance to the public world of work'.[44] When Islington Council introduced ethnic monitoring they felt they had to say that 'while mindful of the understandable fears and anxieties of individual employees, the Council will attempt to introduce a manageable monitoring and recording system, which fundamentally safeguards the confidentiality of individuals at all times'.[45] Employees' scepticism about ethnic monitoring was not unfounded. The private company with the oldest ethnic monitoring policy was Ford UK, a policy they had adopted from their parent company in America which had long held records on the race of their employees, and in Britain first 'monitored the ethnic composition of its hourly paid workforce in 1969'. Back then workers' cards were marked 'white' or 'coloured': 'when new employees entered the Company, ethnic origin was incorporated into their personnel records'. When Ford first started writing down the race of their workers they did not tell them, but 'by using data in personnel records it was possible to obtain a detailed picture of the ethnic minority composition of the workforce in all parts of the Company'. Given that Ford was known for the racial hierarchy it introduced into the organisation of the production line, the ethnic monitoring was not really there to stop discrimination, but to help it. Later Ford used ethnic monitoring as a part of its 'equal opportunities' policy so that 'computerised systems enabled the Company to identify the proportions of women and ethnic minority employees by plant, Department, grade, age and years of service'. Whether these were truly working in the interests of employees is debatable.[46]

Irene Bruegel and Diane Perrons at the London School of Economics raised doubts over the way that market rationalisation and labour market flexibility were helping women. In particular they argued that after job evaluation, the introduction of performance-related pay might mean that 'discretionary elements may be reintroduced into previously formal pay structures which could allow "gendered stereotyped imagery and evaluation to come into play"'. The evidence, though, was mixed. Some evaluations of performance-related pay did show gender bias. There were, though, counter examples: 'Boots the Chemists found that an increasing proportion of women were obtaining management roles as a consequence of the introduction of individualised appraisal systems'. What was also clear was that pay differences *between women* were growing with these reforms of pay structures: 'Although in some respects gender inequalities have narrowed there is also evidence of widening inequalities between women.' When these schemes were introduced they were opposed by between one fifth and a quarter of workers, and many had to be abandoned. [47]

Rationalisation of employment contracts and labour management associated with the introduction of equal opportunities policies may have adjusted the balance amongst the workforce, but most of all they helped managers and companies to get the most out of their employees.

From the point that individual employers adopt an equal opportunities policy, they own and control the process. There are, without doubt, compromises and substantial reforms of past practices involved, but these do not lead to a loss of managerial authority over the workforce; on the contrary, they lead to an enhancement of that authority. Surveyed by the Institute of Personnel Management, more than two thirds of those employers who had adopted an equal opportunities policy thought it was a success.[48] It is available to employees to challenge individual managers, and even long-standing managerial prerogatives, but only in an appeal to company policy, as enforced by senior management, and operated day-to-day by the Human Resources department. Though companies often adopted such policies with the intent of getting ahead of the issue, and to avoid being forced by the external authority of the Equal Opportunities Commission, the Commission for Racial Equality, and the employment or industrial tribunal, there is always potential for the enforcement of equal opportunities policies to be taken out of their hands. Still, even then, the process only ever restored the lines of authority that rested on management prerogative. Equal opportunities policies had costs for managers, but they also belonged to companies, however much employees identified with, or invested hope in them.

— SEVEN —

The Policy and the Working Class

Equal opportunities legislation was introduced in Britain around the time that the corporatist labour organisation was in crisis. The determination of employers and the government to limit union power — and a marked fall in union membership — in the 1980s coincides with the growth of equal opportunities policies at work.

Unions supported the legislation for equal pay and against discrimination on grounds of sex and colour. As they did so, they also accepted a new framework of legislation on pay that they had resisted. All through the Sixties and Seventies, unions had resisted legal restraints on pay. They defended the right of unions to freely negotiate contracts with employers.

The legislation that they had fought against was designed to limit pay awards by government rules. The laws on pay discrimination were different. They aimed to increase pay. Still, the movement towards government regulation was a novelty.

'In 1961, the Trades Union Congress, traditionally devoted to voluntary methods of achieving change for its members, called on the Government to ratify the International Labour Organisation (ILO) Convention 100 on equal pay', noted two researchers at the Department of Employment. They saw that the TUC, 'in doing this, recognized that as a last resort this might mean that legislation would have to be introduced to enforce equal pay.'[1]

When the Equal Pay Act of 1970 was tightened up in 1985, the *Financial Times*' labour correspondent John Lloyd noted that the Equal Pay (Amendment) Act 'carries with it further large implications — for the unions'. The laws on sex discrimination, explained Lloyd, offered 'a large number of workers redress through industrial tribunals (and ultimately the courts)'. Lloyd saw that the question that was troubling many trade unionists was 'if the law can give workers what they want, will they want us?' Lloyd looked back at the tradition that the unions had defended of 'collective laissez faire' — which is to say that governments did not override the agreements between employers and unions. As Lloyd saw it, two different forces were changing workplace relations: on the one hand there was a growing individualism, and a government withdrawal from the role of negotiator between capital and labour; but on the other hand there was, in the shape of the legislation on equal pay, a growing regulation of labour contracts: 'British collective bargaining is bit by bit ceasing to be collective laissez faire', wrote Lloyd.[2]

Unions had, of course, supported the legislation on race equality and sex discrimination that ushered in firms' equal opportunities policies. Still there were many points at which unions might clash with the Commissions for Racial Equality and Equal Opportunities. In 1979 the Trades Union Congress spoke out against the Equal Opportunities Commission's 'proposals to reduce the levels of protective legislation for women workers':

> The effect of what the EOC proposes is that in many circumstances, employers would have a free hand to decide the hours of employment of women. This is not a step towards the equality of women. It opens the door to their greater exploitation.

Perhaps what provoked the TUC most was the fact that 'the Commission makes no reference to the work of trade unions in preventing exploitation'.[3] For, the Commission Baroness Lockwood explained, where there is a genuine difference in the points of view of the TUC and the Commission, as there has been in the matter of the reform of protective legislation, I am afraid we shall have to present our own distinctive point of view to the public without fear or favour, and let the public choose.[4]

Given that the Commission was fending off allegations of interfering in management's prerogatives at the time, the disagreement with the TUC was not such a problem. The Equal Opportunities Commission often positioned itself as somewhere between the unions on the one hand, and the employers on the other. The Commission's claim that 'there is no room for doubt that the momentum towards equality will be lost unless Government and both sides of industry take steps to see that it is maintained' very much situated it as a 'tripartite' institution, which is indeed where its origins lie, though it would become a model of the kind of workplace regulation that displaced the old tripartite system later on.[5] In its early days its investigations were often of industry agreements so that the judgments it made were often against both sides of the industry, employer and union, equally.

In the early days of the Commission, Baroness Seear pointed to evidence that:

Shopfloor and local trade union resistance to breaking down segregation is regarded by many employers in printing, chemical process and packaging and pharmaceutical production as a substantial barrier to progress.[6]

The *EOC News* reported APEX general secretary Roy Grantham's complaints that 'complacency and lack of interest reigned supreme on the Trades Unions General Council's attitude towards women': 'Only 5 per cent of the council's seats were allocated for the 27 per cent of the movement's members who were women and they had been "fobbed off for years."'[7]

Later the Equal Opportunities Commission would support the activism of women trade unionists, like Patricia Turner, Equal Rights Officer for the General and Municipal Workers Union. Turner wrote in *Equal Opportunities News* about the growing number of women who were joining unions, contrasted with their less active participation, adding that 'many men still regard trade unionism as essentially men's business, to which women are not expected to be committed'. She outlined a number of special measures, including courses and a women's conference to encourage participation.[8] Encouraged by the Equal Opportunities Commission, and knowing that they were recruiting more women than men, the Trades Union Congress published a ten-point charter to press its members to act in 1979. Five years later 40 unions had set up women's or equality committees, and 25 had appointed equality officers. Some, like the General Municipal and Boiler Makers Union, had provisions for equality officers at branch level.[9]

Trade unions took up the cause of race equality, too, and the Commission for Racial Equality was more enthusiastic towards them than the Equal Opportunities Commission. In 1980 the Trades Union Congress announced a 'black equality charter'. The headline point was to 'get equality of opportunity written into all national and local union agreements with employers', which was one of the pressures that moved the advance towards equal opportunities from national legislation to the adoption of firm-wide equal opportunities policies. Interestingly, John Monks, for the TUC, highlighted the claim that 'we are seeking not a legal approach but voluntary self-regulation in the tradition of British trade unionism'.[10] The Commission for Racial Equality worked with a number of trade unions, like the NUJ, AUEW, ASTMS, Council of Civil Service Unions, Barclays Group Staff Union, CPSA, and TGWU. The Commission organised fringe meetings at the Trades Union Congress, worked with the TUC's Race Relations Advisory Committee, and helped to develop the Black Workers Charter that was published in 1987.[11] Bill Morris, the Transport and General Workers

Union leader, who went on to become TUC president, was a member of the Commission for Racial Equality in the late 1970s.

As part of 'its training programme for lay persons and lawyers to present cases in industrial tribunals', the Commission for Racial Equality 'began training trade union officials'.[12] Around the same time, the Equal Opportunities Commission also began training trade union officials to follow cases under the Sex Discrimination and Equal Pay Acts. 'The majority of applications to Industrial Tribunals', the Equal Opportunities Commission acknowledged, 'were from groups of women supported by their unions'. So it was that in 1985, 'a number of unions including NALGO and APEX asked the Commission to collaborate in the design of training programmes to enable their own officers to identify and pursue test claims'.[13]

The two Commissions encouraged the equal opportunities cause in trade unions and they helped union officials and representatives to pursue complaints under the laws against employers. As they were doing so they were helping to reform the unions. Beatrix Campbell once called the unions 'the Men's movement', arguing that they had become part of the 'patriarchal system'. In her view industrial tribunals are to this day 'congested with equal pay claims, the cause of which is those differentials and bonuses' that macho trade unionism imposed in the 1970s. Later on, Campbell argues, the unions were reformed by the women's movement to become altogether more woman-friendly institutions.[14] The substantial change was that the unions had reoriented themselves to the new terrain of workplace relations. Instead of collective action, union officials today are more likely to represent their members' individual claims in tribunals, and with the HR department, often on the basis of the equal opportunities policies that they had negotiated with the management. A more courtroom-style model of union work in committees and tribunals had replaced the earlier parliamentary style of rank-and-file mass meetings. The unions were playing their part in the new regime of equal opportunity workplace organisation.

To drive home the reform of industrial relations that was being put in place, John Major's Conservative government folded reforms asked for by the Equal Opportunities Commission into legislation that limited trade union power. The Equal Opportunities Commission was glad to note 'a stated commitment to "equality proofing" of new legislation'.[15] The 1993 Trade Union Reform and Employment Rights Act got rid of the 'length of service' restrictions on maternity rights, so that 'every woman who becomes pregnant will be able to take a minimum of 14 weeks' maternity leave and will be fully protected against losing her job because of her pregnancy'. The Act also included 'the confirmation of the EOC's power to draw up a draft Code of Practice on the Equal Pay Act 1970'.

For trade unions, though, the Act had definite downsides. Unions who wanted to take strike action would have to hold a postal ballot (bringing an end to the mass meeting vote on industrial action) and also to give advance notice to employers of any such action. The Act was, according to Labour peer Bill Wedderburn, the end of a campaign whereby unions were 'regulated, harried, battered, fined and sequestrated, step by step by step, in Act after Act in pursuit of the aim of decollectivising the workplace'. 'Is not the world of tripartism', summarised Lord Skidelsky approvingly, 'completely out of date'.[16] Some reforms directly linked advances in equal opportunities with dismantling the older model of collective bargaining, such as 'the right for individuals affected by discriminatory rule in collective agreements to ask an industrial tribunal to declare the rule null and void'.[17] The Equal Opportunities Commission of course supported the Act, Baroness Writtle speaking in its favour, and its main provisions welcomed in the Annual Report as a positive step forward for women, as it was at the same time a reform of industrial relations. Under this new regime, workplace relations were both more individuated, and also more regulated.

More recently the rules governing Employment Tribunals have changed to prioritise claims under discrimination legislation. As it stands, an employee can bring a case against his or her employer if they have been working there for two years. That threshold is lower if the claim is made on the grounds of sex or race discrimination (as well as a few other exceptions). More, an employee who is making a claim for unfair dismissal can be compensated, but only up to the sum of £76,574, or one year's full pay, whichever is lower. There is no such limit on cases that are brought under the laws on sex or race discrimination. Understandably, employees and their representatives, often trade union officers, have worked out that they have more rights to pursue cases that can be understood as race or sex discrimination. A great many grievances people have against their employers do have some element of sex or race discrimination, and complainants are more likely to frame their complaints in that way if they can. The consequence is that in 2014 fully 55% of all cases were brought under sex discrimination law, a marked rise since just 2012, when the percentage was 38.[18]

Though the Equal Opportunities Commission took to working with the trade unions, they were still ready to investigate cases where unions might be discriminating. In 1986 the Commission reported Diana Robbins' investigation into widespread discrimination against women in British Rail, and the railway unions' collaboration in it. Local managers who were in charge of recruitment, found Robbins, 'were largely hostile to employing women', and a wide range of 'indirectly discriminatory recruitment criteria and processes were used including age bars, mobility requirements and word-of-mouth recruitment'. Damningly, Robbins 'found the railway unions uninterested in equal opportunities'.[19]

SOGAT '82

The most pointed investigation of a union that the Equal Opportunities Commission undertook, however, was that of SOGAT '82, the printers' union, between 1984 and 1986. The case against the Society of Graphical and Allied Trades was pretty clear cut. As the descendant of the centuries-old printers' guilds, print unions had much more say over work than most unions do. For many years they had controlled access to their trade and jealously guarded the skilled craft against the introduction of new technologies that might undermine their power. Work was allocated through the union branch. The print unions had been and still were organised around a male monopoly over work, 'the historical demarcation between "men's work" and "women's work"'. In SOGAT '82 that was clear in the division between 'the London Central Branch (the LCB) and the London Women's Branch (the LWB; this branch later became known as the Greater London Branch)': 'The Commission found that… specific practices resulted in LWB members either remaining ignorant of or being denied access to the higher paid and higher status vacancies controlled by the LCB.' One instance flagged up was that of

> threats made by an LCB Chapel to take industrial action if a woman
> were employed as a binder at a craft bindery [which] amounted to
> an attempt to induce the management of that firm to discriminate
> against the woman contrary to… the Act.

The Equal Opportunities Commission's investigation of SOGAT coincided with the publication of Cynthia Cockburn's book *Brothers: Male Dominance and Technological Change* in 1983. *Brothers* is a brilliantly researched account of the print industry in Britain which highlights the way that the jealous defence of craft skills served to secure men's domination of the industry. Cockburn's account also echoes some of the employers' criticisms of the printers' 'phenomenal earnings', that the compositors' 'wage levels were indeed staggeringly high', and that the linotype operators were 'virtually writing their own pay cheque'.[20]

When the Commission first talked to them in 1984, 'SOGAT and the Branches were unwilling to put an end to this serious and continuing discrimination'. The union 'maintained that their practices were justifiable and that alterations to these arrangements were both impracticable and incompatible with the Union's democratic organisation'. At that time the Equal Opportunities Commission 'decided therefore that it would have to enforce the necessary changes, and in June 1984 the Commission informed SOGAT and the Branches, in accordance to the Act, that it was minded to serve on them non-discrimination notices requiring to change their call room and seniority practices'. At this 'the two Branches asked the Commission to defer the final decision on the issue of the non-discrimination notices, so as to give them time to amalgamate', and a ballot was held which 'returned majorities in favour of amalgamating the LCB with the LWB'. Welcoming that decision, the Commission heard that 'owing to a series of internal and external difficulties the Branches were unable to complete the amalgamation'. For that reason, the Commission served its notice of discrimination at the end of 1984.[21]

They reviewed the case in 1986 and found that 'the parties continued to experience difficulties'. When they met with SOGAT that year, they thought 'it was apparent that the impetus for change had been lost': 'In September the Commission accordingly issued non-discrimination notices in a form almost unchanged from those prepared in 1984.'[22]

What the Equal Opportunities Commission did not explain in its reports was that the external difficulty that the union was experiencing was a dispute over the introduction of new technologies that would lead to the destruction of their trade and the end of their union. News International, which owned the *Times* and the *Sun* newspapers, moved the whole operation from Fleet Street to Wapping, sacking 6000 print and clerical staff, and introducing a new computer graphics system called ATEX. Already, Times Newspapers Limited, under its previous management, had faced down a year-long strike in 1978-79 over manning levels, at the end of which the new technology had been brought in, but still operated by the printers. As Cockburn wrote in 1983 just before the change, 'often a new labour process implies a new labour force', as 'a company sacks one lot of workers and engages others'. But in the aftermath of the 1978-79 strike the employers' side was 'forced to convert its existing craftsmen', which was, Cockburn thought, 'an unusual situation'.[23]

The Wapping dispute

In 1984 the General Secretary of the SOGAT union was Brenda Dean, who had just taken over from Bill Keys. Before going ahead with his move Murdoch had secretly negotiated with Dean who offered a reduction of manning levels at News International. What Murdoch wanted to know from Dean 'was whether I could assert my new authority over the London members of SOGAT'. In her memoirs, Dean felt she had to explain how it was that she had secretly met with Murdoch and his chief executive Bruce Matthews. People would be surprised, she thought, to know how many such meetings 'have littered industrial history and to find that quite often, when harsh words are being hurled across the headlines, remarkable trust and complete confidentiality can co-exist between the two sides'.

Explaining her willingness to push Murdoch's line, Dean explained that 'I was looking at the wider picture and wondering how I could break the logjam of the Fleet Street workers' attitude', adding that 'change, like it or not, was coming fast'. Murdoch was impressed by Dean but had his doubts about her ability to deliver the traditionally militant print workers: 'I looked him straight in the eye and told him I did not know but I was going to have a bloody good shot at it.'[24] But while he was talking to Dean, Murdoch had secretly arranged a 'sweetheart' deal with the electricians' union, the EETPU, and its leader Eric Hammond, to replace the print workers with their recruits.

Gender was key in both Brenda Dean's relation to the London print workers and also to the Wapping dispute. When Dean won the vote for General Secretary she became the first woman to lead a trade union. Dean saw union militancy as intrinsically male, writing about the 'left-wing macho clique' that opposed her. Her base of support was outside London, where more women worked in the trade. She was facing down the 'London Central branch who ran the union and where the power lay', trying to rein in the 'bloody-mindedness and strong-arm tactics for which the London print workers were infamous', as she saw it. When the conflict with Murdoch came, 'the testosterone amongst London print workers, who loved a fight, convinced them that they would win it'. In Dean's mind, if only the London Central Branch had been faced down earlier, the union 'might have avoided the ultimate disaster of Wapping'.[25] Dean's charge of testosterone-fuelled, macho militants echoed the allegations of 'picket line bullies' that could be heard from the Tory backbenches and in the tabloid press. Feminist Beatrix Campbell wrote of the characterisations of trade union 'Barons' and 'bully boys', that 'trade unionism is constantly represented in Tory women's discourse as the unacceptable face of masculinity'.[26]

The dispute was very bitter, and the sacked workers protested outside the Wapping print works for a year. Though you might not have known it from the press reports, hundreds of women, mostly clerical workers, were also laid off and took part in the campaign, as did many of the male print workers' wives. The violence was intense, with mounted police baton charges made in narrow streets against strikers and protestors, and one 17-year-old protestor, Mike Delaney, was run over and killed by a News International lorry. The strikers fought hard too.

It was generally a miserable time in Britain in the winter of 1986, when one of the most popular television shows was the darts, where a top score would be greeted with the chant 'ONE HUN-dred and EIGHT-ee'. On one of the many protests held outside the Wapping plant, I saw protestors pull up iron railings to throw at the police. A rail sailed over my head like a javelin and hit a policeman's shield, sending him sprawling on the floor. Behind me were a row of women in fur coats who, like a Greek chorus, called out, 'ONE HUN-dred and EIGHT-ee'.

One protestor, Deirdre, told John Lang and Graham Dodkins that she had often attacked the trucks: 'peaceful demos were hopeless. It sounds terrible, but I really think we should have done more damage. I think it was war, I really think it was.' Another, Joyce, took issue with the tenor of the SOGAT leadership's campaign:

There was a Women's march at Christmas time… [A] girl at the front next to Brenda started singing 'Little Donkey' through the loud hailer. I couldn't believe it, I thought, 'this is a farce'… [T]hat was the idea, that it should project the usual symbol of women as the Earth Mother. But I said, 'what is this, peace and love and make the sandwiches, is this what we are reduced to after all these months? Peace and love and light me a candle sister: Come on.' But I can see that Brenda would think it was a good image: women the peace-makers instead of big, macho pickets beating up the Old Bill and chucking smoke bombs.[27]

Writing in *Spare Rib*, another striker Liz Jones saw the struggle as:

> [A] war where the people who were called out to fight for their union, find their union reluctant to fight for them, and stand accused of being 'wreckers' when they tiresomely persist in fighting on for reinstatement and union recognition long after their leaders have decided the fight is unwinnable. [28]

Eventually Dean announced that despite successive votes against, the union would abandon the print workers, to save the union office: 'This has been a very difficult decision for the executive to take', she said, 'but what they were faced with was the sequestration of our total union and a fine'.[29] In any event the union did not survive. Once the print workers at New International had been defeated, all the other newspapers adopted the new technology and the jobs of compositors and other metal-type print workers came to an end. With the union wound up in 1992, the difference between the London Central and Greater London Branches of SOGAT was no longer an issue.

Racism at Ford

Even more than the Equal Opportunities Commission's intervention in SOGAT, the Commission for Racial Equality's at Ford UK Limited had a lasting impact on the firm. Ford UK's website today boasts: 'Ford is a leader in the practices of diversity and inclusion and established a formal equal opportunities policy more than 30 years ago.' In 1978 Ford UK's Industrial Relations manager Bob Ramsay became a member of the Commission for Racial Equality, beginning decades of collaboration between the company and the Commission. 'We believe that a key ingredient to business success is the diversity of our workforce where differences are valued and everyone is included', Ford UK says today.[30] The company has also supported a wide range of community activity with large donations, from sponsoring 80 young black students at the Eastside Young Leaders Academy, to contributing to Gay Pride. Ford UK have worked closely with the former Commission for Racial Equality chair, Herman Ouseley, and are active sponsors of his Kick Racism Out of Football campaign.

In 2011, for the sixth year running, Ford hosted the Kick Racism Out of Football campaign event in East London. Mitra Janes, Diversity and Inclusion manager for Ford of Britain, said: 'We are delighted to continue our support for Kick It Out. Football is diverse and inclusive and is a great platform for our involvement.'

Lord Herman Ouseley, Kick It Out chairman, said:

> Ford has once again put on a fantastically engaging event. We are very proud to be working with Ford, and partners in the Dagenham area, on an initiative that will have a lasting impact on young people. Ford is to be congratulated for an enlightened approach to issues that impact on its local communities.[31]

As we have seen, Ford has often been accused of discrimination, and used a racial hierarchy between overseers, skilled, and unskilled workers into the 1980s. In the mid-Eighties Ford workers at the Dagenham car plant walked out after two supervisors were seen handing out racist leaflets, shutting down the production line (one of the supervisors, Tony Lecomber, had long been active on the far right). Afterwards the company worked closely with the Commission for Racial Equality, and with the unions, to try to repair its reputation and its equal opportunities policy.

In November 1985 Dagenham management wrote to workers to say 'how seriously the Company takes its commitment to Equal Opportunities'. With the Joint Workers Committee, managers set up the Joint Equal Opportunities Committee. At that time 38% of Dagenham's 12,000 workers were black, though they were mostly in the lower grades.[32]

The Paint, Trim, and Assembly plant at Dagenham

Despite the paper commitments, race troubles kept on coming up. In 1988 union stewards took up the case of a black applicant for the truck fleet at Dagenham, who was turned down because informally the drivers were all white.[33] Nine years later Ford payed out over £70,000 to eight Asians who had been refused work on the truck fleet.

The background to the rising tensions was Ford's continuing push to dismantle the strong shop steward movement, and rank-and-file activism at its Dagenham and other plants. The company brought in new arrangements where people worked in teams under a leader. What management called 'flexibility' meant mostly working much faster. Managers put a mean pay offer in 1987 of just 5% over three years, but they misjudged the mood and the workforce voted overwhelmingly to strike in 1988. The deal that the union eventually agreed, though, was not much better in pay, and was still to be phased in over two years. More importantly the agreement demanded more 'flexibility' from the workforce. In all of these agreements the company went over the heads of its more militant shop stewards to deal with the union head office.[34]

At the same time as management were side-lining the local union, they were putting in place the system of group leaders 'to encourage production workers to share management's viewpoint', as one worker commented, and also to cut staff by laying off more than half of the supervisors. A 'Memorandum of Understanding' in September 1988 set out a more 'constructive way of doing business together' and set down that 'the Trade Unions have affirmed their commitment that employees will not be involved in unconstitutional action'. Two years later Ford brought in its Employee Development and Assistance Programme, its own kind of Human Resource Management package, that drew individuals into tailored training and assessment. Ford manager John Houghton said that 'EDAP was seen as an enormous catalyst in changing Industrial Relations in Ford because it was non-confrontational'. EDAP, of course, was an extension of the equal opportunities agreement, with managers taking control of relations with employees on an individual basis, with the collective action of the union playing less of a role.[35]

Despite the EDAP and the equal opportunities policy, racial persecution of workers by managers kept reoccurring. As well as the embarrassment of the 'whites only' Truck Fleet, Ford shot themselves in the foot when a publicity shoot of the workforce was weirdly doctored around 1995. Those that had modelled the part of themselves in this evocation of a multicultural workforce were astonished when they saw a version of the shot where all the black workers had been photo-shopped into white people. What few saw at the time was that the shot was doctored for publicity for a recruitment drive in Poland, where the black population is negligible. It was a crass decision by a designer who had not thought through what would happen when the Dagenham models saw themselves whited out. The episode seemed to show up the insincerity of the equality drive to many cynical workers. A walk-out was narrowly avoided and Ford compensated the insulted participants.[36]

The Dagenham workers' distrust of the equal opportunities policy seemed to be confirmed in the hazing of Engine plant worker Sukhjit Parmar. Parmar recalled that the bullying went on for four years, led by the 'foremen and the Group leaders'. He was dragged across the shop floor by a man shouting 'You Paki bastard'; his food was kicked out of his hand into his face; and on one occasion he was sent into an oil mistifier unit, without the needed face protection, and locked in while people were laughing. 'The company were aware of what was going on and they did absolutely nothing to prevent it', said union representative Steve Turner. When Engine plant foreman Joe Hawthorn and group leader Mick Lambert were disciplined, they rallied white workers in the Engine plant to refuse to work with Asians. Around the same time Shinder Nagra took action against Ford after similar attacks. Long-time union activist Berlyne Hamilton argued that discrimination and racial bullying 'has been going on for years'; 'It is enshrined in the system.' More than 1000 workers at the Paint, Trim, and Assembly Plant walked out, protesting against racist bullying.[37]

Around the time of the Parmar scandal, Ford's global CEO, Lebanese-born Jacques Nasser, visited England. By one account he 'was absolutely livid when his company was accused of being racist'. His conclusion, though, was chilling for the Ford workers, white and black: 'I've had enough of Britain', he said, 'I've had enough of this plant — all I hear about is problems'. From the point of view of the global CEO of Ford that might have made sense. But from the point of view of the employees it seemed as if they were to be blamed — and punished — for the race discrimination that was coming from their line managers.[38]

In March 2000, 'nominated CRE commissioners heard oral representations from a Ford delegation... to help them decide whether to embark on a formal investigation'. Later that summer the Commission for Racial Equality suspended the investigation 'following assurances by Ford senior management that the company would comply with stringent conditions for improvement', and 'representatives met regularly with Ford throughout 2001 to review progress' under a Diversity Equality Assessment Review (DEAR).[39]

A special 'Equal Opportunities Meeting' between union and management representatives heard plant manager Jeff Body say that as far as racism went, 'the company needed to take on the Trade Union's issues and respond', but that 'the culture change needed to be within the Modern Operating Agreement'. Body led the unions to believe that Nasser had said that he could fix the problem by closing the plant if they did not agree. In disbelief, union representative Steve Riley had to ask whether 'Nasser was saying that the plant was under threat due to Equal Opportunities issues'. Car production at the Ford Dagenham plant was stopped in 2002. Though 5000 were still working on diesel engine production, the rebellious Paint, Trim, and Assembly plant was closed. In 2013 the remaining jobs (related to production at Southampton) were lost and the plant closed.[40]

Sheila Cohen interviewed activists in the Transport and General Workers Union branch for the Paint, Trim, and Assembly plant at Dagenham. One, Roger Dillon, won a discrimination case against Ford for the effective racial segregation of the plant (between its north and south estates). He was largely unimpressed by the Commission for Racial Equality, though: 'the CRE was in bed with the Ford Motor Company — they were wined and dined'. Dillon went on to say that 'the company spent millions on Equal Opportunities — but they never changed... they were just ticking the box... The policy documents are used as a cover.' In 2003 Ford UK Ltd 'came fourth in Race for Opportunity's (RfO's) diversity benchmarking survey of private companies' — the year after it closed car production at Dagenham.[41]

In the case of the SOGAT '82 investigation and the equal opportunities policy at Ford Dagenham, paper equal opportunities policies were doing nothing for industrial workers under attack. If anything, the new way of talking about workplace relations cast these employers as out-of-date dinosaurs, who would have to make way for change. It was not that the policies were responsible for the changes that were taking place. But they did add to a perception by managers, and by union leaders, that collective action and workplace militancy was outdated, or 'macho'. The top-down equal opportunities policies were a part of the way that management, government, and union leaders were reordering life at work, which was at once more individuated, but also more regulated.

The economic cycle and the working class

The British economy often seems to go through a cycle of strong growth, followed by a recession or even a crash, slowly recovering again. The metaphor of the economic cycle, though, covers up a marked change in the way that labour was and is rewarded. When organised labour was strong workers got back around 58% of what they made, giving up the rest to the employers' profits. From 1983 workers' share of output fell back to under half, while the employers' share rose accordingly. The cycle had a big impact on employment and the make-up of the workforce, but the reforms of the 1980s decisively shifted the share of income in favour of capital. One way that re-division of the spoils was hidden from view was that overall output grew, so that while workers' share was less, the absolute amount they got was more.

In the long trend, Britain's economic output grew from £874 billion to £1.8 trillion between 1971 and 2014. That growth was punctuated by recessions in 1974-75, 1980-82, 1991, and 2009. Recessions often led to people being put out of work — though the long trend is for a growth in employment from 25 to 30 million.

After the spring of 1975, 150,000 jobs were lost from a total just short of 25 million, and not recovered until 1979. This recovery was

Source: ONS

brief, and between 1980 and 1983 the numbers in work fell from 25,225,000 to 23,630,000 — a loss of 1.5 million jobs. Not until 1987 did employment return to the 1980 level.

As we have seen, it was feared that recessions would hurt the advances that women had enjoyed in periods of economic growth.

The impact of the recessions on the numbers of men and women in work were different. Male employment fell from 1973 to 1978 by half a million to 15.16 million. Over the same period women's employment grew by half a million to 9.6 million.

Between 1980 and 1983 women's employment fell from 10 million by 300,000. In July 1980 the Equal Opportunities Commission warned a House of Lords Committee that unemployment was rising faster for women than men. A more likely explanation was 'the increased tendency of women to register as unemployed as compared with previous years'. Men's employment started to fall the year before, in 1979, and 1.3 million jobs were lost to men up to the spring of 1983, when the numbers in work fell below 14 million. Not until 1989 did male employment return to its 1979 peak, whereas women's jobs were back at 10 million in 1984 and continued to climb to more than 11.75 million in 1990.[42] The Equal Opportunities Commission highlighted the demand for labour to make the case for more nursery provision, writing that 'the dip in the number of school leavers combined with the growing skill shortages requires a major national effort to get the work family balance right and make it easier for working parents to be effective at work and at home'.[43]

Between 1991 and 1994 overall employment fell again, from 26,871,000 to 25,303,000, more than 1.5 million jobs lost. Not until 1997 were those jobs recovered, and the numbers in work carried on climbing until 2009. In 2009 half a million jobs were lost, though these were recovered in three years. In the recession of 1991 around 300,000 women employees' jobs were lost while more than a million men's jobs were lost. In 2012 men made up 53% of all those in work — around two thirds of all women of working age work, while three quarters of all men of working age work. One important qualification is that many more women work part-time — about three sevenths of the total, while only one eighth of men work part-time.

It is worth trying to unpick what has happened. The metaphor of the 'economic cycle' is not as good as it seems.[44] The idea of the cycle is that things go up and down and that we get back to the point that we were in before. The metaphor of the cycle is a way of reconciling change with the prejudice that things do not change.

The theory of the economic cycle, as far as the employment of women and ethnic minorities goes, suggested that they would be a 'reserve army of labour' — put to work in flush times, and then laid off again when times were leaner. Marian Ramelson first suggested that this might not quite be what was happening with women in the labour market, when she anticipated that 'even if the economy goes into a slump or crisis the evidence is that the relative role of women at work does not decline'.[45] What was more, the way that the employers and the government had dealt with organised labour in the 1980s had changed the way that the labour market worked. It was true that there had been a contraction in employment in 1980 and another followed in 1990. But overall the tendency was towards an expansion of the numbers in work. From 1995 onwards the numbers in work grew, not just in Britain, but across the developed world, at a higher rate than the population. The International Monetary Fund called it 'job-rich growth', noting that it was a reversal of the preceding period of capital-intensive growth that followed the Second World War, and ran up to the late Seventies. Most recently, the recovery from the 2008 recession saw a sharper increase in both full-time and part-time employment for women, and an increase in part-time jobs for men, but almost no new full-time work for men, according to the Resolution Foundation's 2015 survey.

A surprising feature of the 'job-rich growth' from the mid-Nineties was that it did not provoke wage inflation, as the economists expected. The reason was that something had changed in the labour market. The organisational and ideological defeats suffered by the labour movement meant that even when the recovery came, they were in no position to take advantage of it. Employment gains, concluded the EC's Directorate-General for Economic and Financial Affairs, reflect 'the effects of several years of wage moderation'.[46] With wages constrained, it was cheaper for employers to expand their businesses by taking on new workers, than by investing in new machinery. The United States and Holland expanded their workforces by inward migration; Germany, by assimilating East Germany into its modern economy; Britain did allow more migrants to come in the 2000s, but largely expanded its workforce by putting more women to work.

The process of recruiting women into the workplace was not planned exactly. Indeed, many senior government figures were saying that the opposite should be happening. The Equal Opportunities Commission said it was 'suggested in an increasing number of places that one solution to the problem of unemployment is for women to return to the traditional role in the kitchen'.[47] But that was not what happened. The change in the gender make-up of the workforce went the other way, as the economy was restructured. Older industries were downsized or broken up. More jobs were created in the service sector. The older jobs were often in unionised firms, the newer jobs more often not; the older jobs were more highly paid, the newer jobs were often not; the older jobs were full-time; many of the newer jobs were part-time, or had irregular hours; the older jobs were permanent, but more of the newer were on temporary contracts. More of the newer jobs went to women, less to men. Men who were used to higher wages and better conditions had to think twice about taking these service-sector jobs on, while they might be a step up for women used to earning less; older men were often demoralised by the collapse of traditional industries. The President of the Society for Population Studies, David Endersley, thought that 'in traditional areas like the North East unemployment has forced changes in family work patterns and whereas men are losing jobs by their thousands, women are finding more work'. 'There's a very sharp increase in the number of households where the women's earnings are predominant and the larger part of the household income,' he added.[48] Where there was a deliberate choice to employ more women, and also ethnic minorities, was in the adoption of equal opportunities policies by employers.

The position of women relative to men improved, but men still had more jobs than women. It does not follow that women's position improved absolutely. It changed. Some things were better. Some were less so. One decisively positive change was that many more women at least had the chance of economic independence. Nearly half of all driving licenses issued are to women, and nearly 4 million women live alone. Economic dependence on men put many women in a vulnerable position in the 1960s, whereas today the possibilities of leaving a difficult relationship are a great deal easier, and since 1991 rates of domestic violence have fallen markedly.

Whether we think women were better off over all depends on what you think of employment – certainly they were working more. Looking at what had happened to men and women in relation to their employers, the picture is different.

Schematically you might say that in 1970 15 million men and 9 million women made goods and services to the value of £830 billion (in 2016 pounds). So perhaps 6 million women worked full-time raising children and keeping home, while another 3 million did that for part of the time, while working for the other part.

By 2015 16.5 million men and 14.5 million women made goods to the value of £1.8 trillion. Six million of the women were working part-time, so were most likely raising children or keeping house in the rest of the time. Two million of the men were also working part-time. Perhaps another 2 million women were raising children full-time.

The workforce increased by 5 million, which means 5 million more pay packets — an increase mostly down to the increase in women working, and largely possible because of a fall in the time spent on housework (which we consider in the next chapter). Double-income households were better off in cash, but time-poor.

If we look at the share of the billions of pounds of output that fell to the workforce as pay we see that as we have moved in the direction of gender equality at work, employers did better relative to employees (see graph above). Between 1948 and 1979 employees' compensation — wages — made up 58%, on average; from 1983 to now, workers' share of output dropped to 49%. Women improved their position relative to men, but employers did best of all. They spent £888 billion setting 30 million people to work to make goods to the value of £1.8 trillion, earning £930 billion for themselves. In 1961 they spent (the equivalent of) £342 billion to put 25 million people to work, to make goods to the value of £583 billion earning just £241 billion for themselves. Those 5 million new workers were making a fortune for British business.

Equal opportunities policies had costs. It would cost to pay equal wages. Beatrix Campbell estimated that 'if women in the banking system in Britain were paid the same wage as men for work of equal value the banks would have to find an estimated £17 billion to cover the cost'.[49] As it happened the costs were not so great since the women were often taken on at lower grades and less pay, while at the same time the men's wages were being held down. The horizon of equal pay approaches not just on the basis of raising women's wages, but also on the basis of holding down men's.

The idea of the 'family wage', according to many of the feminist critics of the old order, was archaic — and they were right. The idea that men were breadwinners and women's earnings were just 'pin-money' reinforced the authority of husbands over wives. Unfortunately, the end of the family wage was really just a limit on wages that meant that both partners had to work just to earn enough to live on, and women's hours were annexed to the office, shop, or factory, putting great strain on families that became work-rich and time-poor.[50]

Manchester council workers demonstrate against the threat to deport George Roucou, 1987

Government also spent more on nursery places. But overall the business case for equal opportunities looks pretty solid.

The relation of black workers to the economic cycle was different. As we have seen, the two largest non-white minorities in the UK in the 1970s, Afro-Caribbeans and Asians, were both hit disproportionately hard by the recessions of the 1970s and the early '80s. Overrepresented in industry, black and Asian workers suffered as industry was downsized. They were hurt, too, by their concentration/ segregation into certain kinds of factory work (like textiles in West Yorkshire or the furniture trade in Tottenham) that were declining. Official oversight on the part of police and immigration services made black workers less secure and opened them to discrimination by employers and workmates alike. The demand that black workers show their passports to employers fixed the idea that they were second-class workers as they were second-class citizens. Most importantly of all immigration from the black commonwealth was

slowed by the 1981 Immigration Act and the many subsequent acts to 'close loopholes'. The impact on work and pay was clear: 'The ethnic wage gap increased from 7.3 in the 1970s to 12 per cent in the 1980s, whilst the unemployment differential increased from 2.6 percentage points to 10.9 percentage points.'[51]

In the 1980s, the non-white share of the population of Britain rose more slowly, through secondary migration (wives and families joining men who had moved in the Seventies and Sixties), or through natural growth. The recession at the start of the 1990s did not see much of a difference in the ethnic pay gap. Black earnings were 11% lower than whites', while unemployment was 9.8% higher.[52] There were some differences emerging though. Indians were doing better relative to Afro-Caribbeans and Pakistanis.

From the mid-1990s a second wave of migration came to Britain. Political conflict and dislocation in a number of developing countries led to a resurgence of movement to Britain by asylum-seekers. Between 2000 and 2010 around 7000 Somalis were granted British citizenship every year, and the 2011 census identified 101,370 Somali-born residents in England and Wales. Other African migrants came as asylum seekers from Algeria in the early '00s, from the Congo and from Zimbabwe (in 2003 the production line at Cowley, where a mostly white workforce had been employed 20 years earlier, had a team of Zimbabweans assembling cars for BMW, under a Mozambican supervisor). There were 201,184 Nigerian-born and 95,666 Ghanaian-born people living in in Britain in 2011. One important shift is that there are now more ethnic Africans than Afro-Caribbeans in Britain. Another important source of inward migration was from Poland, the Polish population of Britain doubling to reach 1.1 million between 2001 and 2011.

The way migrant labour was curbed and then encouraged has led many to see race as tied closely to the economic cycle. Some have argued a direct relation between the economic cycle and the liberality or otherwise of the immigration law. On this view when the economy is expanding the tap is opened to recruit more migrants to work in British industry — as it was in 1948 when the economy was expanding post-war. Later, when growth faltered and employment prospects were poor, immigration was restricted.

This view of immigration law as a response to labour needs seems compelling. But a closer reading of the record of legislators' decision-making shows that far more ideological concerns about national identity, the loyalty of indigenous white populations, and fears over international standing all played a part — and in particular the raft of anti-immigrant measures passed in the 1980s were without much practical rationale, but rather expressions of a fear of loss of national identity, and an assertion of control on the part of the elite.[53]

Towards the end of the 1980s the punitive attitude of the authorities towards black people was mitigated by a growing official recognition of discrimination. Where Lord Scarman's report into the Brixton riots in 1981 fell on stony ground, the police started monitoring racially motivated attacks around 1989, and these were criminalised in 1998, shortly before Sir William Macpherson's report into the killing of Stephen Lawrence put 'institutional discrimination' into the public eye.[54] The official outlook on race was changing, holding up a good ideal of the loyal black Briton, contrasted with the illegal migrant. A Conservative election poster in 1983 had a picture of a smartly-dressed Afro-Caribbean man, with the slogan, 'Labour says he's black. Tories say he's British.' The adoption of equal opportunities policies is a part of that transition in attitudes to race. Settled and accepted ethnic communities have seen their positions improved. Those who are more recent arrivals, or are Muslim, have done less well. So Indians' earnings are not less than those of their white counterparts, and Afro-Caribbeans' only very slightly, whereas Bangladeshis, Pakistanis, and Africans earn around four fifths of the white earnings.

One way of looking at the working class has been the model of the 'segmented labour market'. Charles Leadbeater saw a workforce 'radically divided' between a core of permanent workers, skilled at its centre, along with unskilled; around them he saw a peripheral workforce that is in temporary or part-time work; then there are the recently unemployed, and then a layer of long-term unemployed. It was 'a strategy to legitimise a society where roughly two thirds have done, and will continue to do, quite well while the other third languish in unemployment or perpetual insecurity'.[55] Luc Boltanski and Eve Chiapello highlight these changes as part of the 'New Spirit of Capitalism':

> Casualization has led to a segmentation of the wage-earning class and a fragmentation of the labour market, with the formation of a dual market: on one side, a stable, qualified workforce, enjoying a relatively high wage level and invariably unionised in large firms; on the other, an unstable, minimally qualified, underpaid and weakly protected labour force in small firms, dispensing subsidiary services.[56]

The segmented labour market is clearly an important way to understand inequality between sexes and races. Gill Kirton and Anne-Marie Greene look at the idea of dual labour markets where jobs in the primary sector are better paid, full-time, with better promotion prospects and more job security: 'the primary labour market holds mainly "male" and "white" jobs, and the secondary sector "female", "older worker" and "ethnic" jobs'.[57] This is a similar model to that of the 'reserve army of labour', only fuller perhaps. As Kirton and Greene state, the model is not perfect, and does not explain the advance of women's status at work. The model has explanatory power, but its weakness is that it tends to fix in time a snapshot of what is in fact a changing social and economic landscape. So, for example, many skilled industrial workers of the 1970s, like car or print workers, who would have certainly been reckoned among the core workforce, quickly discovered that they were no longer needed and were pushed out into the ranks of the unemployed. Moreover, the ideal of the 'job for life' was rarely met: some at the Cowley car plant in Oxford were laid off and then taken on again six or seven times, as the market rose and fell, and the plant changed hands from Pressed Steel, to Morris Motors, and then British Leyland. For our purposes here, the problem with the market segmentation model is that it tends to minimise the real changes that have taken place, and reinforce the idea that things are pretty much as they have always been.

Equal opportunity downsizing

In the early '00s British Airways began to lose customers, stalling a planned expansion. The company employed 57,000 people, four fifths in the UK. Needing to find cost cuts of £650 million over two years, BA planned to cut 13,000 jobs. Another company, at another time, might well have used the principle 'last in, first out', meaning that those with the shorter length of service would go first. Such informal agreements often discriminate against black people, and against women, as they tend to have shorter job tenure. British Airways had a workforce that was 'very diverse, with a high proportion of women and different cultures, religions, races, ages and abilities' — though that was less true of its management.[58]

British Airways was self-conscious about the need to avoid what they called a 'knee-jerk' response to cost-cutting that would cause problems. They were also very committed to equal opportunities and 'diversity management', and had been for many years. Not only did BA avoid the 'last in, first out' approach, but they also were wary of trying to meet the problem through voluntary redundancies, fearing that this would jeopardise the work that they had put into recruiting a diverse workforce. They were conscious, too, that it is easier to address equal opportunities 'in the context of a company that is growing', but that 'downsizing makes it more difficult to make progress on the representation issues'. According to one manager: 'we wanted to check we had not got rid of disproportionately more women, or more disabled, or people with different ethnic backgrounds'. Overall, the job losses were borne equitably between men and women, and between black and white — 17,395 women were laid off, and 24,102 men; or, looked at in terms of race, 31,798 white people, and 4,679 black and Asian people lost their jobs.[59]

British Airways' progressive approach to diversity did not save the 37,000 jobs, but it did make sure that the losses were evenly shared. Managers took pride in their approach. But it was little comfort to the workforce. Union leader Roger Lyons said that 'this is a devastating body blow to staff, who have acted impeccably in responding to the needs of the company to safeguard jobs over recent months'. But framing the losses as 'equal opportunity' job cuts caused union leaders some difficulty framing their opposition. 'We will not be rushing to the barricades, but rushing to the negotiating table', said TGWU leader Bill Morris: 'On the basis of no compulsory redundancies and no attacks on our members' terms and conditions, we will help to achieve a managed reduction.'

The unions' commitment to British Airways' 'managed reduction' denied workers an avenue for opposing the losses. Pointedly, a number of peripheral disputes flared up over seemingly unconnected changes, which were nonetheless a knock-on effect of the job losses, managed or not. In the summer of 2003, 2,500 check-in workers struck over the bringing in of a new computerised time-recording system, which they feared would lead to greater flexibilisation (read: irregular shifts). The check-in workers were mostly women, many of whom had taken on part-time work to meet domestic tasks, and were particularly angry about the disruption the system threatened.

In 2005 Gate Gourmet, a catering company at Heathrow that supplied British Airways' meals, announced that it would sack 670 of its workforce, many of whom were Sikh women living in nearby Southall. A bitter strike followed that highlighted the oppressive working conditions of the South Asian workforce. In their eagerness to bring in equitable cost-cutting, British Airways had forgotten that it depended on less enlightened management amongst its contracted-out suppliers.

British Airways' equal opportunity job cuts were a success for the company, but not really for the workforce. In years gone by an employer might well have leant on the racist and sexist thinking of the day to create a moral justification for the kind of cutbacks that they were making. But in 2002-03 British Airways sought to dress up their job-cutting exercise in rather different clothes. Opening up a discussion about the right way to lose jobs, they made it clear that the question of whether jobs would go was not on the table. These were equal opportunity redundancies, but they hurt, all the same.

A new working class

Looking at the impact of the 1980s overall we can say that the working class has been unmade and remade. As left-wing commentator Richard Seymour says, it is 'not your grandfather's working class'. In 2013, one tenth of the labour force was made up of black and Asian people,[60] and 46% were women. The recruitment of these additional workers has greatly enlarged the labour force. All told, these are profound changes.

As profound are the qualitative changes in the way the class of employees are organised. Trade union membership in Britain declined as the numbers in work have — over the long trend — increased. Union membership fell from its highest point of 13.2 million in 1979 to just over 7 million in 2013, from one half to one quarter of the workforce. The nature of union membership has been turned right around. Unionisation is most common where employers favour it. Most pay awards today are imposed, not negotiated. Unions act more often as advocates on behalf of individual members than they do as representatives of a collective will.

Running alongside those changes has been the growing acceptance of equal opportunities at work. The greater number of women and black people in the workforce has come as organised labour has had less influence. Equal opportunities policies have been extended just as the organisation of employment is less collective, and workplace negotiation has given way to a quasi-juridical relationship between employer and employee.

The marginalisation of the trade union movement is more than a sociological question. It says something about the existence of the working class as a class. In the 1980s, the ideology of socialism as a class outlook was effectively defeated, in the electoral and the industrial arenas. That outlook was core to working-class self-identity. Today some 60% of the population think of themselves as 'working-class'.[61] But today the identification does not mean identification with the labour movement, and is not allied to any social project. An appeal to 'working families' is a part of the rhetoric of all major parties, whether of the left or the right.

The greatest material consequence of the remaking of the labour force is the great increase in social inequality, as wages have failed to keep pace with the growth in output. In companies that are badged as 'equal opportunities employers', working people have seen their share of the nation's wealth fall.

— EIGHT —

Sources of Discrimination

Outside the Workplace

The movement in the direction of parity in pay, for women and minorities, has been painfully slow, and the goal is still not won. Reforms in the law, and reforms in company policy, have over the last 20 years levelled the playing field, but inequality persists. Activists, policy makers, and scholars have turned their focus to the discrimination that takes place outside the workplace, in wider society, as the anchor which makes equality at work so elusive.

Critics have pointed to the limitations of civil freedom *outside* or *beyond* civil society, limitations which make the freedoms within civil society into a mask for unfreedom. Carole Pateman explains that modern society is divided between two spheres, public and private, so that 'the private sphere is typically presupposed as a necessary, natural foundation for civil, i.e., public life' ('but treated as irrelevant to the concerns of political theorists and political activists', she points out). At the same time, she says, there is 'the subjection of women within the private sphere'.[1] Catharine Mackinnon makes a similar point when she says that 'Women are oppressed socially, prior to law, without express state acts, often in intimate contexts', adding that 'the negative state' — that is a liberal, hands-off state — 'cannot address their situation'.[2]

Usha Prashar, Daniel Silverstone, and Herman Ouseley make a comparable argument when they say that 'the view "treat them all the same" is quite discriminatory in its effects on different racial and cultural groups'. As they see it, 'the notion of assumed equal opportunity for all has contributed greatly to the relative disadvantaged position of many black people'. More, 'the "same for all" and "treat them all the same" approaches are major obstacles to achieving equality of opportunity, fair treatment and social justice'. They outline what they call 'The System', by which they mean 'the organizational arrangements within large companies or institutions which determine how jobs are offered'. Their judgment is that 'these bodies treat black people less favourably on racial grounds, because racism is an integral feature of organizational structures and individual attitudes'.[3]

These ways of looking at the question of equal opportunities make the case for positive action, over and above an 'equal playing field', because they identify forces that are outside of the ordinary considerations of who is best for the job as a persistent barrier to equality. The ideal of equality in the labour market is sabotaged before the position is advertised, they are saying.

The ways that the extra-economic foundations of discrimination are characterised are many. Many feminists have highlighted a patriarchal system in which power over women is defended and extended by men. Anti-racist activists have outlined what they see as a persistent institutional racism. These are explanations for the way that progress on equality at work has been so difficult.

Identifying the social factors that have stood in the way of equality has been a way of addressing those barriers. For some, though, talking up the limits to equality has turned from a positive programme of change to an excuse for its absence, or even a dogmatic insistence that change is not happening.

Without dealing with all the theoretical questions, we can identify the main barriers outside of work to equal opportunities at work. In this chapter first we will look at the trends in unpaid domestic work at home and its knock-on impact upon opportunities at work for women; second we consider the fraught question of national identity and the entrenched idea of a white indigenous people differentiated from the black other.

In both of these areas the course of events over the last 20 years suggests that many of the non-work bases of discrimination at work are in transition, and greatly diminished.

1. Work-Life Balance

In 1985 the Equal Opportunities Commission explained why it saw the question of equality at work closely tied to that of the burden of housework: 'The Commission has recognised from the outset, a decade ago, that work and the family were inextricably linked', stated the Equal Opportunities Commission in its 10th Annual Report: 'inequality in the labour market was caused by, and in turn reinforced, an unequal burden of domestic responsibilities'. They were lobbying for extended parental leave and childcare, as a way of stopping job losses through pregnancy.[4]

A decade later they were making the point again, under the title 'Reconciling Work and Family Life — Why Equality is Important'. 'The difficulties of working parents and carers in balancing work and family responsibilities are major barriers to equality between men and women', they wrote. Once again, they had in mind the weightiest family responsibility, childcare:

> In dual-earner households, both partners need access to child-care, as may both partners in non-earning households. For couples with children, training or a return to the labour market is made more difficult by the absence of local childcare facilities.[5]

Childcare, as we have seen, was the main point that divided the Equal Opportunities Commission from the Conservative administrations between 1979 and 1991. There had indeed been a reduction in publicly funded nursery places.[6] At that time many people thought that women with young children ought not to work — especially other women. It was a view echoed by the Prime Minister. Widening the question of equal pay to include social provision of childcare was a bold step beyond the Commission's immediate responsibility for tackling discrimination at work.

One avenue that had been looked at was workplace nurseries. There had been some workplace nurseries in the Second World War, and the Greater London Council experimented with these. The Equal Opportunities Commission thought that workplace nurseries were 'one form of childcare provision which both assist working parents and enable employers to recruited and retain qualified and trained staff'. They protested that these ought not to be a taxable benefit, backing a 'workplace nurseries campaign' which did win tax exemption. Workplace nurseries were opened at the Royal Mail's Mount Pleasant Sorting Office, and at Goldsmith's College, University of London. They tended to struggle to fill places, and these have now closed.[7]

The Commission kept up childcare on the public agenda. They commissioned and published a report, *The Under-utilisation of Women in the Labour Market*, written by Hilary Metcalf and Patricia Leighton, economists with the Institute of Manpower Studies. Identifying an untapped reserve of 6 million women not yet in the labour market, the authors found a major 'constraint on those women who actually wish to work' was 'the cost and shortage of available quality childcare'. That was an issue 'which is now at the forefront of national debate', said the Commission:[8] 'Our message — that women and men should be encouraged to be effective and responsible employers and family members — has been disseminated far and wide round the country.' Pointing out that that demand for labour was tighter, as the economy recovered towards the end of the Eighties, the Commission reported that 'there has been heightened interest and awareness from all these quarters, notably employers wanting to know what is the best way forward on childcare'. It was at this point that the Commission raised the goal of a national framework for childcare — a formulation that put the case for government action without it sounding like town-hall socialism. 'We see major contradictions in the Government policy in this area', wrote the Commission: 'the Government is keen to bring women into the workforce, but is unwilling to provide a national framework for childcare'. They welcomed the government's giving childcare payments to lone parents on training courses, but demanded, why not 'to women living with their husbands'?[9]

Commission chair Joanna Foster set out the position in a keynote speech:

> Social policies are needed which reflect the changed reality of women's lives, and of their families' needs and experiences. A co-ordinated system of community-based childcare provision, both for under-fives and older school-aged children, is a pre-requisite for equality of opportunity.

She went on to say that:

> Only when such support is available will women feel free to choose fulfilment from work as well as home, and men feel free to see themselves as participating fathers, husbands, family members as well as breadwinners.[10]

The Commission's advice, drawing on a report titled *Parents, Employment Rights and Childcare* by Sally Holtermann and Karen Clarke, was that 'the cost to government of a phased expansion of subsidized child-care — including out of school care as well as nursery places — would be more than outweighed by savings in social security and increased tax revenue'.[11]

In 1996 the EOC, having 'worked on the issue of childcare for many years', broadened the campaign: 'we decided that it was time to try to establish a consensus on the need for a national strategy on childcare'. They set up 'a working group to discuss the issues around childcare, a partnership of 21 organisations representing a wide spectrum of interests and expertise'. The working group argued that 'expansion in childcare provision' will 'bring major benefits to employers by helping widen the pool of skills which are available and by retaining the investment in the skills of their existing workforce'. For the government Cheryl Gillan at the Department of Education and Employment listened sympathetically. They told her that the 'the benefits to employers of a childcare policy' would include 'the recruitment and retention of committed and experienced staff', 'recouping more of their investment in training', 'reduced absenteeism', and 'improvements in employee productivity'.[12]

The Commission's efforts on childcare did have some impact on even a Conservative government. As Julia Somerville wrote 'in the context of anxieties about labour shortages, positive support came from the CBI, a number of large employers and House of Commons Committees': 'government responded with a number of initiatives, including expanding under-5 places in primary schools, sponsoring voluntary sector provisions, improving regulation of child-minding, encouraging employers to provide workplace nurseries... and introducing a childcare tax allowance'.[13] The number of children under five attending pre-school education in state schools grew from 646,657 in 1989 to 768,112 in 1991. But that was not the only way that families were meeting their childcare needs. Sally Holtermann highlighted an 'impressive growth in day care facilities for young children in the last few years', in her 1995 report. She added that 'the growth of nursery education in the maintained sector has been relatively modest' and that growth had been almost 'entirely in the independent sector'.[14] Apart from any help from the government, women and men were making their own arrangements, creating a new demand for private nursery places and child-minders, so that 'the decade saw a dramatic rise in the provision of under-five childcare in Britain'.[15] In fact the 'percentage of three and four year olds in maintained nursery and primary schools in England has increased from 44 per cent in 1987 to 56 per cent in 1997'.[16]

The policy that was developed by the Equal Opportunities Commission, and only partly yielded to by the Conservative administration under John Major, was the basis of the Labour government's National Family Strategy from 1998. A marked expansion of childcare places was backed with government cash. Government paid for 17.5 hours of nursery provision for three to five year-olds, and many parents paid the extra. By 2001 there were 1,053,000 places for children, with day nurseries, childminders, play-groups and pre-schools.[17] By 1999 three quarters of three to four year-olds were in a formal childcare setting, rising to 94% by 2004.[18] Though there were good reasons to think that the Conservative-Liberal Democrat government that was elected in 2009 would cut back nursery provision, there were still in 2013 '273,814 childminder places and 1,023,404 nursery places'.[19]

From a very unpromising beginning, the case for an expansion of early-years childcare took off in the 1990s. By taking on greater responsibility for looking after children, the government was trying to lessen the domestic burden to help women into the workplace. To see how much of an impact it had, we have to look at what was happening to the way that men and women shared their time between work and housework, and between each other.

The domestic workshare overall

The BBC measured people's time use since 1949, through questionnaires, a study which would have been abandoned if Essex University had not taken it over. The rough story is that in 1961

women did five times as much housework as men, whereas in 2005 women did two thirds of the housework. The time that men spend on housework has hardly changed, up from one and a half hours to one hour and 40 minutes; but the time that women spend on domestic work has fallen sharply from six hours and 15 minutes a day to just under three.[20]

The fall in women's housework, then, is largely due to the fall in time spent on housework overall. Cutting back the time spent on housework is the condition for women to enter the workforce. The main change is due to the increase in childcare places — the responsibility that it is most pressing. Once the share of childcare shifted, so that young children spent more time in nurseries, women spent more time in paid work. For both sexes, the balance of paid employment and domestic work is directly inverse, the more you do of one the less you do of the other. Women and men do roughly the same amount of work, if you add paid and unpaid together.[21]

In the 1970s sociologists looked at the impact that labour-saving devices, like the vacuum cleaner, washing machine, and food mixer, had had on domestic chores. They were surprised to find that there was no apparent fall in the time that women spent on domestic chores. All that happened was that these gadgets soaked up more time in more activities. With hindsight we can see that the impact of labour-saving technologies on the home was limited by the sexual division of labour. Women who were largely excluded from the labour market used the gadgets to do more domestic work, not to reduce the time they spent on it. Today, the sexual division of labour has been altered, with women spending much more time in paid work. The potential impact of white goods on domestic work is realised in the fall in hours spent on it.[22]

Flexibility to make workplaces woman-friendly?

One argument that weighed on the question of women's responsibilities outside work was that of flexibility. The idea was that conventional labour contracts, with long, fixed hours, were a barrier to women with other commitments, like dropping off and picking up children from school. More flexible work patterns might be better for women. In her book *About Time*, Patricia Hewitt sets out some of the main ways that the standard working day has been adapted, such as part-time work and flexible hours — and the 'zero-hours' contract, job sharing, 'term-time' jobs (running alongside the school term), flexi-time, as well as weekend work and work in unsocial hours. All of these non-standard working-hour jobs have been taken up by people, mostly women, who need to meet responsibilities at home. From 1989 the civil service agreed with unions alternative working patterns with guarantees to protect part-timers from discrimination — within two years the number of women working part-time had grown from 5 to 14 per cent. Boots and B&Q have both offered 'term-time' working and other non-traditional hours for many years.[23]

The idea that flexible working is good for women is open to a pointed objection. If it can be argued that the world of work is made more amenable to women with family commitments, are those women not also being trapped in peripheral working environments? So it was that in 1992 the Equal Opportunities Commission recalled that it 'has repeatedly voiced its concerns that the changes we have seen in the labour market and in particular increasing casualization and fragmentation will have a disproportionate impact on women'. Their question was: 'Flexibility has been achieved but at what price?'[24]

Just four years later, though, the Commission was talking up the positive side of flexible working. 'Both businesses and employees can benefit from the introduction of family-friendly employment policies which help the recruitment and retention of staff', they said. Now it was argued that 'Employers need to recognise the different working patterns of women and men in order to achieve the benefits of the flexible labour market'.[25]

Julie Mellor, chair of the Commission in 2000, argued that 'forward-thinking employers realise they do not have a choice — without flexible working policies they will not attract and retain the best people'. In her vision non-traditional hours were important for all parents, because 'work/life balance' is a 'critical issue for fathers as well as mothers'. Social historian Hugh Cunningham is more sceptical, judging that 'however flexible work hours become they're unlikely to produce a situation where women (and men) feel anything other than pressed for time'.[26]

The argument was about whether flexibility was helping women, or helping employers push them into a ghetto. 'Women and men have very different attitudes to working time', argues Patricia Hewitt, 'a difference which directly reflects women's double responsibility in the home as well as in the workplace'.[27] Employers might make the workplace more 'woman-friendly' by scheduling work to fit women's availability, or moulding work to women's other commitments, but to do so was to reconcile women working with their disadvantage in the labour market. The problem can be seen in the Commission's treatment of the question of the most straight-forward adaptation to family responsibilities, the growth of part-time work.

Part-time work

Back in 1978 the Baroness Seear was cautiously optimistic that 'that flexible working hours are reasonably common among male and female white collar workers, but part-time working', which she took as a positive for women, was not widespread. Seear said that 'British industry can only benefit by using the full talents of the country's workforce'. But even as she argued the case for more part-time work, the Baroness was well aware that 'segregation of jobs into men's and women's work is still widespread in industry, and is one of the major obstacles to promoting real equality'.[28]

Lady Elspeth Howe, a former deputy chair of the Commission, gave a speech the following year at Brunel University, where she argued that:

> [P]art-time work is a central issue in progress towards equality for women because it is one of the main ways in which women choose to work and because more and more people (men and women) are realising the usefulness of working hours which allow time for family or other responsibilities.[29]

The following year the Equal Opportunities Commission News carried a double-page spread, written up by journalist Judi Goodwin, 'Scandal of the Low Paid Workers'. In it she argued that 'though part-time work is often considered an easy option that suits a large number of married women, the pay and conditions of part-time workers invariably amount to slave labour!' As Goodwin said, 'the most striking change in the labour market has been the increase in part-time working, a trend which has been described as "The Part-Time Revolution," and one in which women have played a major part'. Goodwin was drawing on a survey, written by Jennifer Hurstfield and published by the Low Pay Unit, *The Part-Time Trap*. As Goodwin explained:

> With inadequate day care facilities for children, and the prevailing attitude of society that still expected a woman to take responsibility for household chores, three-and-a-half million women who want to work have little option but to take a low-paid part-time job.[30]

According to Goodwin, the Low Pay Unit and Dame Howe equal pay laws and other legal guarantees should bring part-timers' hourly pay up to the level of full-timers.

The Commission was still highlighting, in 1991, that '4.6 million women work part-time, 2 million of whom earn less than the National Insurance lower earnings limit (£52 in December 1991)'.[31] Britain's deregulated labour markets had favoured the growth of part-time working, so that 'in 1990, of the 13 million women in the European Community who were employed part-time, one third worked in the UK'. 'Our economy is especially dependent on the part-timer', explained the Commission, adding '83 per cent of whom in this country are female'.[32]

Though part-time work helped women to rejoin the labour force, it was not on equal terms. The gender pay 'differential is even more marked for the many low-paid women who work part-time', noted the Commission:

> They are caught in the trap of doing 'typical' women's work, which is traditionally seen as being of low value and gives fewer rights to the pay benefits and special allowances available to full-time workers.[33]

KFC job advert, 2016

The Commission again emphasised that part-time work was key for women who wanted a chance to earn in their own right. 'Research shows that at a number of points in the life cycle, women would prefer to work part-time in order to cope with caring responsibilities, and many women and some men will continue to prefer part-time work for part of their working lives', said the Commission:

> Their dilemma is that in order to do so, many have to accept working in lower status occupations than their previous full-time jobs... Women who are employed on a part-time basis are much more likely to work in low-skilled, low status and low paid occupations than in higher status and higher paid managerial and professional jobs.[34]

Two years later, Commission chair Kamlesh Bahl told the Secretary of State for Employment Michael Portillo that 'research showed that action is needed to encourage employers to adopt a high productivity, high quality strategy towards human resources and to improve the quality of part-time jobs'.[35] It was a problem that was never wholly solved. The Commission continued to ask that employers should make work more woman-friendly, especially in terms of hours, while at the same time understanding that women's greater representation amongst part-timers was a sign of their subordinate position in the labour market.

One answer to the question was put by Catherine Hakim, whose research first identified the segregation of women as a key factor in low pay. Hakim put the point the other way around, saying that when women choose to put their commitments to family first, it is wrong to see that as oppressive. If women choose domestic life over career, she was saying, it is wrong to dismiss that as 'false consciousness' on their part.[36] The point was reiterated by writer Rosalind Coward in her book *Our Treacherous Hearts*. Coming at the subject as a feminist, with a successful career, she interviewed women about how they felt about leaving work to bring up younger children. Coward was intrigued to find that many women, well aware of the feminist argument, had chosen to withdraw, and that 'women themselves desperately want to hang on to that central role in their children's lives'.[37] Perhaps the argument that Hakim and Coward were making was just a sign that women who were in the social position they were in preferred to see it their own choice, rather than one that was put upon them, and if they chose to make the most of it, then that is what people do. All the same, they raised a different way of looking at childcare as a responsibility in a society where, arguably, the task was not a marker of subjugation.

Maternity pay

In 1983 a breakdown of the General Household Survey, published by Equal Opportunities Commission, showed the unequal impact that children had on women's and men's working lives. Among couples where the woman was under 29, with no children, 72% worked full-time (a small number part-time). But if these couples had a child under four years of age, fully 63% were not working. Once the child was five, more mothers than not went back to work, though most of these worked part-time. The more children they had, the less likely women were to work full-time, and few women with children worked full-time at any age. It was a stark sign of the way that the priority of family limited women's prospects for work. A second indicator is the gender pay gap. While there has been much more advance among younger women, those over 30 show a disadvantage in relation to men's pay, which is greater the older they are. The evidence would seem to say that women can be on a level playing field with men, but that once children are born their careers will be derailed. It is for that reason that the women campaigners and the Equal Opportunities Commission paid special attention to the question of maternity pay and maternity rights at work.

William Beveridge's welfare plan included a payment, 'Maternity Benefit', given to all mothers for 13 weeks. The plan pictured mothers as home-bound and the payment supported them there. The picture was changed with the Employment Protection Act of 1975 which brought in a statutory right to 18 weeks' paid maternity leave (six weeks at 90% of full pay, the rest at a lower, flat rate) according to the Equal Opportunities Commission. There was also a right for women who had taken maternity leave to go back to their old job for up to 29 weeks after the day the baby was born — 'a significant landmark in the relationship between work and the family'. In 1984 the government pushed back on maternity rights and 'the Commission drew attention' to an extension in the 'qualifying period for protection against unfair dismissal from one to two years'. This would be a big problem because 'many women cannot meet the two-year service requirement necessary to qualify for a number of maternity rights'. [38]

Around 1988 the Labour opposition put the government under sustained pressure over the low rate of maternity pay, in comparison to other European countries, highlighted in a European Commission report.

Though the government was embarrassed, the Equal Opportunities Commission did offer some good news about a 'dramatic increase in the number of employed mothers'. They published a joint report with the Department of Employment and the Policy Studies Institute in 1991, titled *Maternity Rights: The experience of women and employers*.

'More and more young women are combining motherhood and paid employment', the Commission announced. The changes in the law helped, so that 'by the end of the 1980s, 60% of women in work during pregnancy met the statutory hours and length-of-service requirements for the right to reinstatement'. The report's findings 'demonstrate unambiguously that there has been a revolution in the position of working mothers since the beginning of the 1980s'. What is more, 'employers seem to be largely accepting of the change' with only a tenth reporting any problems.[39] It was a very positive, and possibly overstated, view. They did acknowledge that too few employers made definite plans to take women back after their maternity leave. Still, the results were important, marking the changing status of women in the labour market. After many years with little change, the Commission was in a position to report too that the pay gap was closing again:

> Over the 10-year period to 1990 the New Earnings Survey showed that the average hourly earnings of women remained around ¾ of those of men, although there was some narrowing of the gap towards the end of the decade.[40]

Change came with the 1993 Trade Union Reform and Employment Rights Bill. That changed the way that statutory maternity pay was administered, so that now it was paid out by the employer, who could claim it back from the government. The new law met some of the problems that had been raised by the European Commission, though the EOC objected that 'the burden of costs has been shifted to employers' (the cost of administration, that is), raising fears that employers would evade their responsibilities. The Commission wanted 'reform of the system of maternity rights with employers relieved of the burden of maternity pay'.[41]

Under the Labour government that took office in 1997 the Equal Opportunities Commission was consulted on 'the Government's review of maternity pay and parental leave arrangements', which were 'the main focus of the EOC's work in this field' in the year 2000-01. The major change for maternity rights was that they were to become 'gender neutral', parental rights, so that '450,000 new fathers will be eligible for paid paternity leave when it comes into effect in April 2003'.[42] As it turned out, very few men took up their right to paternity pay, which is too low to make it worthwhile to leave work.[43]

Swede Lars Jalmert taking paternity leave in the EOC News

The 'double-burden' in the twenty-first century

The evidence from the time-use studies is that the share of domestic work is unequal, but less than it has been, and that the amount of time people spend on housework has been greatly cut back. (Perhaps surprisingly, parents are spending more of their leisure time with their children than before.) The fall in the amount of time spent on domestic chores is both cause and consequence of women's much greater participation in the labour market. Also, the evidence shows that more women with young children are working and many of them are working full-time.

The changes have been spurred on and justified by the 'business case' for getting more women to work. But government also spent a lot to help women into work. For all the different ways of helping early-years childcare — tax relief on childcare vouchers, benefits for childcare, free nursery places — government was spending around £4.2 billion in 2012. A further £2.4 billion went towards statutory maternity pay — large-looking sums, though less than half a percentage point of Gross Domestic Product. [44] As much as government spends, parents spend more on childcare and other costs. And families spend money to save time on domestic chores in other ways, spending nearly £30 billion a year on takeaway food and eating out.

With couples spending more time at work there were fears that this might lead to more family break-ups. Divorce rates did rise in the 1980s and 1990s, to around 150,000, or 14 per thousand married people a year. More recently, though, they have fallen back to around 10 for every thousand.

Women still do almost twice as much housework as men do, and while there are nearly as many women as men in work, two fifths of those are in part-time work (compared to 12% of men). The hourly pay gap between men and women has effectively closed for workers under 30 but beyond the age of 30 it opens up. One interpretation of that is that women will continue to lose out when children are born. On the other hand, the penalty for childbirth is less than it was. As women who might be earning more than their male peers have children, they are less likely to withdraw permanently from their chosen career progression. On paper at least, employers and the law are committed to protecting the station they have earned. 'Average job tenure was falling for men', the Chartered Institute of Personnel and Development found, 'whereas it increased quite significantly for women':

> Improved maternity rights led to more women remaining with their employer after giving birth to a child and fewer women either leaving the labour market altogether or changing employers to find a job that suited their new circumstances.[45]

Moreover, the penalty that women face by leaving work to have a child is less marked when the model of a career for life is the accepted norm. As Beatrix Campbell argued:

> The assumption that people want to change careers, that they want time out of work, that they want to learn new things, go to college, have kids, move in and out of the labour market, rather than stay fixed in one place for forty years, with a gold watch at the end of it, all of those transformations are associated with women.[46]

Those changes are associated with women, but they are more and more models for men's employment, too. Overall, the evidence is that responsibility for domestic work is far less of a handicap to women's prospects in work than it was. Time outside of work is perhaps more pressured than it was, where two partners are both at work. People are spending less time on household chores, but also more time with their children.

The law has changed to reflect the changing position of women in society. In 1990 the Law Lords were asked to clarify the position of rape in marriage. The eighteenth-century Law Chief Justice Hale had set down the dictum that it was not possible for a man to rape his wife, on the grounds that she had already given her consent in the marriage vows. In 1990 the Law Lords thought that was unsustainable, and that the common law is 'capable of evolving in the light of changing social, economic and cultural developments'.[47] There were other changes in family law, such as the 1976 law against domestic violence, the 1989 Children Act giving public authorities power to act against parental authority in favour of the interests of children, further family law in 1996 that included a rule for police to detain any accused of domestic violence and the 2015 law against coercive and controlling behaviour in a marriage. All of these signalled the end of legal support for the patriarchal family as a privileged sphere.

The gender division of household and workplace that rose to pre-eminence in the period 1850-1950 survives today only as a shadow of its former self.

2. Race and Britishness

Trying to explain race discrimination, people often talk about the way a society needs 'scapegoats' to blame; or the point is developed by saying that communities shore up their collective identity by fixing a group as 'the other'. Put at that level of sociological abstraction, the argument is not so controversial. To look at the question of race in Britain historically, however, would mean seeing that the collective identity that was affirmed by emphasising the exclusion of black people was the identity of Britishness, which it might be more provocative to call into question. National identity, the assertion of a common British identity, for much of the twentieth century was understood as a white identity, with black people's foreignness highlighted to make that point.

National identity was not just an ideological question, but an all-too practical one for black people in the labour market. Large-scale black migration to Britain began in the 1950s with Afro-Caribbean and Asian labour recruitment. In the years that followed special laws to control immigration laid the basis for a two-tier labour market and a two-tier society. Officialdom treated black people differently from white, in the control of their movements, withholding citizenship status, demanding to see their papers, creating a special immigration police to track them, creating special detention centres for 'illegal immigrants', and in the assumption of the police that black people were to be treated differently, more harshly, because they were not a part of the law-abiding indigenous majority. All of these real manifestations of the second-class status of black immigrants in Britain were the basis for discrimination at work that was outside of work.

Race discrimination was ideological as well as being practical. It was bound closely to the idea of national identity. Discrimination was targeted at black people, but it was addressed to white people. The British elite were making an appeal to the wider white population, a promise that they were insiders, citizens. The real foundations of that national identity were the rights of citizens — their right to contracts to work or trade, to go freely where they wished, to organise to defend their interests, and to elect a government — all rights that were withheld to greater or lesser degree from black people. The long argument over national identity and British citizenship between 1945 and 1992 was an assertion of a community of interest between the working and the ruling classes. The foundations of that white national identity, though, were being undermined in the 1980s. The post-war consensus had recognised the participation of the working class as represented by the labour and trade union leaders in the 'tripartite system'. That system was under attack in the 1980s, and effectively dismantled by 1992.

The reason that the assertion of national identity was so shrill and forced in the 1980s was that the basis on which one might have claimed a community of interest between white citizens and elites was being dismantled. The Conservative government of the 1980s appealed stridently to national identity, and implicitly to a white identity, just as — and because — it was down-grading the rights of ordinary Britons. Targeting black and Asian immigrants was a way of reasserting the virtues of British citizenship as they were being emptied of substance. In time these shifts would lead to a big change in the general ideas of nation and community, in which colour played an altogether different role.

All through the 1980s, while the Conservative government was taking apart those institutions and agreements that bound British citizens to the national project, that same government projected a strident nationalism. The government claimed to defend 'British interests' in its dealings the European Economic Community, and in the Commonwealth of formerly British colonies. Prime Minister Thatcher fiercely defended British prestige abroad, sending troops to fight Argentina for possession of the Falkland Islands, as she berated the leaders in Brussels for taking 'our money'. This heightened call to nationalism added to the ill feelings towards foreigners and to immigrants settled in Britain.

It stands to reason that the Commission for Racial Equality could never accept the argument that black people were not British. The Commission saw its role as 'to help and encourage the minorities to confidently take their full place in the mainstream of British national life'. The Commission was grateful for 'the full commitment of this Government to the good race relations which are fundamental to the success of our British society', from Conservative Home Secretary William Whitelaw. The Home Secretary went on to say:

> [I]n the interests of the whole nation, and in particular to remove unjustified fears stirred up amongst ethnic minority groups, I wish to reaffirm the complete commitment of our Conservative Government to a society in which all individuals, whatever their race, colour or creed, have equal rights, responsibilities and opportunities.[48]

These words would ring hollow for the many who were asked to show their passports to get treatment in hospital, or singled out by their colour for special attention from the police, as well as those subjects of the British Empire who were refused the right to remain in Britain. The 'interests of the whole nation', 'the success of British society', seemed to be very much at odds with those of the black minority. They were denied a place 'in the mainstream of British life'.

Over time, though, attitudes changed. One effect of the much tighter controls on immigration in the 1980s and 1990s was, as Julian Clarke and Stuart Speeden noted, that 'the ethnic minority population is no longer immigrant' — more and more of the black population of Britain were born in Britain, and the pretext for denying their Britishness was becoming more and more tenuous.[49] As discriminatory as the Nationality Act was in its impact, the promise that those migrants who met its criteria would have their citizenship recognised did fix the idea that some Britons were black.

As we have seen, the growing number of asylum seekers shifted attitudes to black people in Britain.

Number of asylum applications received by year of application (including dependents)

2000	97,860
1999	91,200
1998	58,000
1997	41,500
1996	37,000
1995	55,000
1993	28,000
1992	73,400
1991	32,300
1990	38,195
1989	16,775
1988	5,739

Junior Minister Ann Widdecombe made the case for the restrictions on asylum-seekers' rights in Britain, when she warned that the 'opportunity to seek employment is a major incentive for economic migrants and undeserving asylum applicants'.[50] Official measures to curb and control 'asylum seekers' from overseas, like the opening of the Campsfield detention centre, searches at ports of entry, and police raids, all heightened hostility to more recent arrivals to Britain.

MP Martin Salter, a member of Reading Council for Racial Equality and long-standing supporter of the anti-racist magazine *Searchlight*, contrasted his 'ethnically mixed and proudly multicultural' constituency with the 'legally aided, corrupt abuse of the system' by 'deliberate overstayers' and 'stowaways', who 'can justifiably be regarded as economic migrants rather than refugees'. In Salter's telling, his black and Asian constituents, 'people, who are as British as I am, resent the fact that the debate on race and community relationships in this country has become skewed'; 'Someone whose skin is brown or who wears a turban might now, somehow, not be regarded as British any more, but as just another of those asylum seekers'.[51]

The Commission for Racial Equality had relatively little to say about the new asylum laws, keeping its criticism at the level of generalities. 'The questions being asked were "where is the fairness, where is the compassion, where is the justice?"' summarised Herman Ouseley, who had just taken over as Commission chair.[52]

In his 1981 book, *The New Racism*, Martin Barker anticipated the way that racial discrimination could be dissociated from biological 'race' as such, and attached instead to cultural differences. With the 'asylum seeker' panic of the 1990s, prejudice against the foreigner moved further away from the expected associations of black and brown migrants to Britain and hardened against the new dispossessed from Algeria, Somalia, and later Eastern Europe. The black but 'British as I am' were rendered more like insiders, in this way of looking at the question. But the shifts in racial thinking were not exhausted by this contrast of the good black Briton and 'bogus' asylum seeker.

The white underclass

Teenager Stephen Lawrence was murdered by a gang of white youths
in Eltham, South East London, on 22 April 1993. The case became
a turning point in British race relations. The police inquiry was a
farce, and it seemed likely that the killers would escape justice. A
determined campaign by the boy's parents, Doreen and Neville
Lawrence, won the support of everyone from the Anti-Racist Alliance
to the *Daily Mail*. This eventually led to an inquiry under Sir William
Macpherson. Below we consider the conclusions of the Macpherson
Inquiry, but let's look first at the way the killing was seen.

Racially motivated killings, tragically, were not unheard of in
Britain before 1993 and it seemed likely that Stephen Lawrence could
become just another grim statistic. The family's campaign to highlight
their son's death, though, struck a nerve. In the press the stereotypical
image of violent black youths and innocent white victims was more
or less reversed. Under the headline 'INTO HELL', *Daily Mirror*
reporter Brian Reade went to a largely white housing estate in Eltham
and 'found racism seeping from every pore' of this 'E-reg Escort land'
where racial hate is 'a way of life passed down from father to son'.[53]

The Lawrence killing became part of a new discourse on crime
initiated by the future Labour Party leader, then Shadow Home
Secretary, Tony Blair. Knowing that 'law and order' had been an issue
that the Conservative Party had dominated Blair was set to make it his
own, saying he would be 'tough on crime'. Blair pinned the cause of
crime on the free market and the way that it had destroyed community
cohesion. Talking about the Stephen Lawrence killing, and about the
murder by two children of the toddler Jamie Bulger, Blair painted
a picture of large swathes of society in a state of lawlessness. Even
Thatcher, no stranger to crime panics, was moved to protest that
'crime and violence are not the result of the great majority of people
being free — they are the result of a small minority of wicked men
and women abusing their freedom'.[54] Thatcher's crime panics targeted

outsiders and tended to reinforce Britishness as a positive, Blair saw crime as endemic in a sick society. The Labour politician hit a rich seam of middle-class fear, now expressed towards a burgeoning white underclass.

Music journalist (now novelist) Tony Parsons penned a vicious diatribe in the *Daily Mail* titled 'Why I hate the modern British working class' — 'treat them like humans... they still behave like animals' — and for Channel 4 authored a film on the same theme of denouncing the 'lumpens... dressed for the track, but built for the bar', called *The Tattooed Jungle*.[55] Jack Straw, then Shadow Home Secretary, gave a speech in 1995 about the 'Aggressive begging along with graffiti and in some cities "squeegee merchants" all heighten people's fear of crime on the streets', while radical journalist Beatrix Campbell writing about rioting in the North East and Liverpool in 1991 thought she saw a 'culture of crime' with 'coercive coteries... founded on bullying, intimidation and exclusive solidarity'.[56] These former socialists were venting their frustration on a working class that they felt had let them down. No longer the vehicle of socialism, the British working class was a big disappointment. These ways of thinking about the underclass were familiar to people who had paid attention to the racial insults thrown at black immigrants, except that now it was the white estate-dwellers who were being demonised, too. As Kenan Malik wrote at the time, paraphrasing the critics' argument: 'White yobbos, like black Yardies, are not part of civilised society.' As respectable society would see it, said Malik: 'Morally, socially and intellectually, the underclass, black and white, is inferior to the rest of us.'[57]

The coordinates of prejudice were shifting. Respectable society was not contiguous with white society any more. There were respectable black people, and less so, and there were degenerate white estates as there were good citizens. All of these prejudices floated on a very real social shift. The integration of organised labour into respectable society in the 1950s had come to an end as the century did. The furiously triangulating 'New Labour' party was putting a distance between itself and the working class in the 1990s as stridently as the Conservative Party had attacked them in the 1980s. The bond that tied the (largely white) labour movement to the nation state had been cut. All of that social change meant that the marked division between respectable white society and peripheral black migrants was breaking down.

The Macpherson Report and institutional racism

'In years to come 1998 will be seen as a watershed for race relations in Britain', Herman Ouseley wrote as chairman of the Commission for Racial Equality: 'No one will ever forget that it was the year of the Macpherson Inquiry into the racist murder of the black teenager, Stephen Lawrence.' The Commission played its part in the lead-up to Macpherson's report, and 'felt impelled to put the issue on the public agenda and decided to launch a hard-hitting advertising campaign': 'Our aim was to raise awareness of the extent to which racial prejudice still exists in Britain today and to suggest that everyone can and should do something to stop it.'[58]

Sir William Macpherson's conclusions were a considerable boost to the Commission's view. The conclusions that stood out were that the Metropolitan Police investigation into the teenager's death was compromised by the force's 'institutional racism'. It seemed to be a very hard-hitting phrase, one that was in common use among equal opportunity campaigners. The point of the term was to say that the problem of discrimination was deep-rooted, not just the matter of a few 'rotten apples' in the barrel. As he clarified the point, Macpherson made clear that he was not necessarily saying that individual officers were personally racist, but that they might *unwittingly* adopt practices that add up to institutional discrimination.

Macpherson's report had the unexpected result of excusing individual officers of responsibility for failings. At the same time it

Doreen Lawrence and Bernard Hogan-Howe

opened up the police service overall to a level of scrutiny and criticism from which the establishment had previously pledged to shield them. If the institution was racist, then it needed thorough-going reform. What was more, the 'report accepted the CRE's submission that institutional racism was not an issue solely for the police service, but for every institution public and private'.[59] Macpherson concluded that 'If racism is to be eliminated from our society there must be a co-ordinated effort to prevent its growth', and 'this need goes well beyond the Police Services'.

The Commission was pitched into the centre of public life, and the report's 'findings and recommendations have provided the CRE with a new framework for its work with organisations to eradicate racism and discrimination'. As they reported:

numerous copies of the CRE's leaflet on the implications of the inquiry for racial equality were distributed within three months, and we were inundated with requests for advice from public sector organisations all over the country.[60]

The impact of the Macpherson Report was consolidated in a far-reaching new amendment to the Race Relations Act that came into force in 2001. 'The amended Race Relations Act now includes all public functions', reported the Commission under its new chair Gurbux Singh. 'It gives some 40,000 public bodies in Britain a new, enforceable, statutory duty to promote racial equality and good race relations.'[61]

For the government Angela Eagle, Home Office minister for race relations, said:

> The changes are aimed at the hearts and minds of organisations. The government wants public organisations to make race equality core to their work. These new measures build a robust framework to help public bodies provide services to the public in a way that is fair and accessible to all, irrespective of colour or ethnicity.

The focus was on public institutions, but the goal was to make race equality a core British value throughout society: 'By placing the public sector at the forefront of the driver for race equality in British society, we hope to create a powerful lever to raise standards in all sectors of society.'[62]

The shift in attitudes at work that was initiated in the 1980s under equal opportunities policies had come to be a foundation stone of public policy in the '00s. Some might object that these were rhetorical commitments, though in fact the changes were far-reaching, with public institutions committed to ongoing reform. A conference called to check on progress two years after the report concluded that 'public authorities have a long way to go before they can say that their policies and practice are promoting racial equality' — the Macpherson reforms were framed as a process, rather than a result.[63]

More to the point, the general declaration behind the 2000 Race Relations Amendment was that racial equality was an established goal of British society.

Community cohesion

As if to underscore the importance of the question of race relations, just as the authorities and the experts were talking about the ongoing reform of public institutions, 'violent confrontations broke out between white and Asian people and the police in Oldham, Burnley and Bradford' between April and July of 2001.[64]

Home Office Minister John Denham commissioned a report into the disturbances from government advisor Ted Cantle, of the Institute for Community Cohesion. Running alongside Cantle's investigation, Herman Ouseley, having handed over the chairmanship of the Commission for Racial Equality, undertook an investigation at the request of the community and local government project 'Bradford Vision'. Coming out of Ouseley's and Cantle's reports there was a debate about the merits of 'multiculturalism' that we look at in the next chapter. But here it is worth taking note of the proposals that Ouseley made coming out of the riots. He called first for:

A coherent response for Bradford's public services (including the Police and all agencies) to meet their obligations under the new Race Relations (Amendment) Act 2000 and to promote social interaction and mixing.

Secondly, Ouseley hoped for:

Ways in which leadership at institutional, organisational and community levels must promote and carry forward the mission, vision and values for greater community, cultural and social interaction across the different cultural communities.[65]

These proposals read like timeless platitudes, and would hardly be remarkable read alongside the many local authority policies that Ouseley and others have authored over the years. What is noteworthy is that in the context that it was made this vision of 'community cohesion' was what stood in the place once occupied by national identity. Kyriakides and Torres call this policy 'Third Way Anti-Racism', showing that it comes out of the 'Third Way' political programme worked up by Labour party reformer Tony Blair. The 'Third Way became a means by which the state attempted to relegitimise itself in a world without alternatives to the capitalist system', they argue.[66]

In the technocratic language that was commonly adopted during the years that Tony Blair's 'Third Way' government ruled, Ouseley's abstract appeal to 'community cohesion' is doing the work that a more atavistic 'national identity' promoted under previous governments once did. It expresses a wish for social solidarity that would overcome division. In this version of 'community cohesion', though, people are not excluded on the grounds of their colour.

Where the Conservative governments of the 1980s and '90s jealously protected British national interests, the Blair and Brown governments were much more sympathetic to transnational institutions like the European Union and the United Nations. At least in the way they explained themselves, they were not following selfish national interests, but rather working with other nations towards humanitarian ends. Tony Blair seemed to be a lot more comfortable among other world leaders than he did with the British public, and much of the elite derived more authority from inter-governmental agreements than they did from any popular mandate. Cosmopolitan internationalism rather than national sovereignty was the clarion call of the elite.[67]

The end point of the Macpherson report and the Race Relations Act that followed it was, paradoxically, that Britain became institutionally anti-racist. Formally, at least, its institutions were committed to the goal of racial equality. Whereas in the past the moment of 'community cohesion' would be exemplified in the national anthem, the flag and the Queen, post Macpherson, the value most leant upon to emphasise social solidarity was diversity and tolerance in a multicultural society. Just how successful that could be would be tested in the years that followed. Still, it is worth underlining that the substantial reassertion of national identity that so pointedly excluded black and Asian people in the post-war years, was by the new century officially inclusive and diverse.

Limits to equal opportunities

Frustration with the lack of progress on equal opportunities led researchers to try to understand the more deeply-rooted, social bases of discrimination beyond the workplace. Those were valuable explorations that highlighted the way that women's unequal responsibility for housework on the one hand, and the institutional racism in British institutions on the other, worked against equality at work. To investigators it often seems as if the identification of these barriers shows that progress can only go so far, and that discrimination is as endemic as ever. To the contrary, though, the identification of these barriers to equality is itself a sign that they are being shifted.

It would be wrong to argue that discrimination has been brought to an end. No serious examination of the outcomes of the gender and ethnic pay gap, or employment prospects, would support such a conclusion. What is clear, though, is that many barriers that looked insurmountable are being moved.

There is a formula that activists used to explain — 'oppression is prejudice plus power'. The saying was coined to show that prejudice is not just a psychological attitude, but one that can be powerfully reinforced by the social and institutional distribution of power. Today there are as many, if not more, prejudices at large in British society. On top of the mainstream prejudices of white and male superiority, there are a whole welter of misanthropic ideas about the underclass, alongside prejudices about asylum seekers and Muslims, as well as many ideas about the pathological collapse of masculinity. All of these prejudices are expressive of a less robust democratic culture in Britain, and the decline of the status of organised labour as a social partner.

What is less true of today, though, is that prejudice against women, and against black people, is reinforced by institutional power. Indeed, the one remarkable thing about Britain at the turn of the new century has been its institutional commitment to build an equal opportunities society.

— NINE —

International and Historical Precedents

The people who drew up the laws and policies on equal opportunities had many examples to draw on, in history and also around the world.

Empire

The most important historical precedents for equal opportunities policies were about coping with other races in the British Empire. As we have seen, the first ideas about race relations laws in Britain, those that led to the 1965 Act, drew on the times when Britain governed many races in the Empire.

Ideas about racial hierarchy came about because of the British experience of Empire. Writers like Thomas Carlyle and Anthony Trollope, explorers like Sir Richard Burton and Henry Morton Stanley, and colonial officers like Sir Charles Gordon and Edward Eyre all gave voice to a strong sense of white superiority over native peoples. Later these ideas were made more systematic in the administration of the colonies, where pseudo-scientific doctrines of social Darwinism were commonly used to give grounds for the higher standing of white settlers over natives.

Not all ideas about natives were derogatory. Many colonial officers had a genuine sympathy with natives, though this was usually patrician and often a romanticised idea of the 'noble savage'.

Sir Arthur Gordon, who governed the Fiji Islands, was one of many who romanticised the traditional society of native peoples — the Fijians — though largely as a better, 'chiefly' counterweight to the growing number of Indian labourers brought into the colony. Gordon's ideas about native self-government, where the colony was run through traditional leaders, organised in a High Council of chiefs, was later taken up by Theophilus Shepstone, in Zululand, and Lord Lugard in Northern Nigeria. Lugard called this the 'dual mandate', where Britain ruled through local chiefs, deriving authority for British rule from the dual mandate of the Crown and the best interests of the native peoples.[1] One of the unintended outcomes of 'native self-government' was that the exercise of power through tribes and their presumed chiefs led native peoples to organise themselves as tribes, and offer up chiefs to meet the expectations of the colonial authorities.[2] These systems of rule through native leaders were copied all across the Empire. They were also in the back of the minds of the government officials who first organised the Community Relations Councils where church leaders and other elders from ethnic minority communities acted as intermediaries with the British authorities.

Native self-government was mostly about driving labour, and the ideas about tribes and peoples neatly fitted the needs of organising a division of labour. So it was that the Empire found different peoples with natural talents for waging war (Sikhs, Fijians, Pashtun), field labour (African slaves and Indian indentured labourers in the West Indies and Fiji), trade (Indians in Zanzibar and Chinese in Malaya), and the Tonga of the Zambezi Valley were held to have 'a natural affinity to night soil work'.[3] Handing out different kinds of jobs to different groups, marked out by their race, was a handy way of playing them off against each other, and so staying on top.

The colonial ways were also brought into the mother country at those times that colonial labour was recruited to fill jobs that English labourers could not or would not do. As we have seen, Ireland's rural surplus played the part of the unskilled itinerant labourers in Britain's industrial revolution. Indian ('lascar') and Chinese seamen were called on when the merchant marine lost English sailors to the navy in times of war. Not only were the lascars paid less, they were given smaller bunks in ship rules. Native labourers were treated with harsh indifference at times, and after the Second World War, many

Liverpool wives of Chinese seamen were shocked to find they and their children had been abandoned — only later learning that their partners had been rounded up and sent back to China on Churchill's orders, to make way for the British merchant seamen released from the Royal Navy. The West Indians who came to Tilbury and London from 1950 onwards were at first billeted in church halls, and put to work labouring, on the buses and in hospitals. Workplace segregation had its roots in colonial labour organisation, and the colour bar was for a while followed in Britain.

Many of Britain's old colonies, like Malaya, Fiji, and Hong Kong, carried on the system of a racial division of labour, and the corresponding distribution of political power, too. Indo-Fijians, whose grandparents had come as indentured labourers, still farm the sugar cane owned by Fijian tribal groups (called Mataqali), though these same Fijians are employed by the lease-holding Indian farmers to cut the cane at harvest time. In both Singapore and Malaysia, a delicate balance between Chinese business and native Malayan farmers is kept, with special laws obliging companies to employ a quota of Malays. Article 153 of the Malaysia Constitution protects the 'special position' of indigenous Malays, while Fiji's Deed of Cession makes the interests of native Fijians 'paramount' (though that has been much argued over, since). Hong Kong's Equal Opportunities Commission is tasked first and foremost with stopping sex discrimination, but also 'protects people against discrimination, harassment and vilification on the ground of their race'. In all these places the older colonial models of a racial division of labour are changing into modern systems of 'equal opportunity' legislation and the protection of minorities. These systems are supposed to manage race relations, but they have often themselves been the terrain over which ethnic conflicts have arisen (particularly in Fiji, but also in Malaysia and elsewhere), and may even have entrenched the divisions that generate these conflicts.

Northern Ireland

Though it is officially a part of the United Kingdom, Northern Ireland has different laws on equal opportunities than Britain. In 1976 a Fair Employment Act created the Fair Employment Agency, a body to oversee the law forbidding discrimination in employment (in 1999, the law was repealed and a new Act created the Equality Agency). The reason for the special legislation was that Northern Ireland was built around sectarian discrimination against its large Catholic minority. The Northern Ireland state was an artificial creation, made up of six of the nine counties of the historic province of Ulster, cut off from the rest of Ireland, which asserted its independence in 1920. The six counties were set apart on the basis that this was the territory that

Refugees from the 1920 Belfast pogrom arrive in Dublin

the predominantly Protestant and loyal community of the area could hold against the Irish rebels. In the six counties in 1920, 840,000 Protestants dominated 430,000 Catholics. To consolidate their hold on what their leader James Craig called 'a protestant parliament and a protestant state', all Catholics were driven out of the shipyards and most industries in a long campaign of terror. Jobs in Northern Ireland were allocated according to religion, on the assumption that the Catholic minority were disloyal. Many Catholics, and some Protestants, did protest at the discrimination, and in 1969, inspired by Martin Luther King, a civil rights campaign was launched — only to be beaten back by armed force. The suppression of political protest led to an armed conflict, with the Irish Republican Army waging a guerrilla war to free Ireland from British rule. The repression that followed further entrenched the sectarian division, as Protestant loyalists were recruited to man the burgeoning security services.

The 1976 Fair Employment Act was a sop to the civil rights agitation, but substantially a failure as the UK government leant heavily on the loyal Protestant population to defeat the challenge. By 1978 the proportion of Catholics to Protestants was closer to 40:60, but employment in industry was 72.5% Protestant, in vehicle building it was 80%, and in the shipyards 90% were Protestant.[4] After 16 years of the Fair Employment Agency, the position was hardly better. The aircraft manufacturer Shorts' workforce was only 11% Catholic, while major shipbuilders Harland and Woolf's had a workforce that was just 4.5% Catholic. Local authority employer Craigavon Council, pulled up by the Fair Employment Agency for drawing only 4% of its senior officers from the Catholic community (while 12% of its manual workers are Catholics), simply tossed the report in the bin. So damning was the Fair Employment Agency's report into Larne District Council, where no senior officer was Catholic, and most Catholics were employed on the very lowest grade, that the FEA itself suppressed the report. Even where discrimination was clearly shown, as in Northern Ireland Electricity, with its 3.5% Catholic workforce in

1992, the Secretary of State stepped in to stop the FEA's investigation and gave the electricity company permission to carry on.[5]

Oliver Kearney was chairman of a grassroots campaign in Northern Ireland called Equality, set up to highlight the problem of discrimination. 'We've had eighteen years of this legislation and there's been no improvement', he said in 1992. Though 'the legislation has been trumpeted by the British Government throughout the international community as being the complete answer to discrimination', Kearney explained, 'in fact the legislation actually provides for discrimination on a political basis'. There are two sections in the Fair Employment Act which protect the employer from discrimination if the employee is suspected of 'holding views which may be in support of or in sympathy with political violence'. The clause was important because all the Catholic population at the time was considered disloyal, and any employer could avoid a judgment from the FEA. Another section of the 1976 Act permits the Secretary of State to issue a certificate denying the Fair Employment Commission the right to conduct an investigation on the grounds that 'the security of the state is considered to be endangered' — and again, this was interpreted pretty broadly, since the security of the State rested on discrimination. As Kearney saw it, the FEA was not there to stop discrimination, but to uphold it. 'The Northern Irish state was specifically constructed with the objective of securing' the Protestant community 'as their reward for securing Britain's control of Ireland following partition'.[6]

In 1998 after a long stalemate between the insurrectionary Irish Republican Army, along with its political wing, Sinn Fein, and the British security forces, they came to the 'Good Friday Agreement'. The 1998 Agreement put a statutory obligation on public authorities to 'carry out all their functions with due regard to the need to promote equality of opportunity in relation to religion and political opinion', and also 'gender; race; disability; age; marital status; dependents; and sexual orientation'. These goals were also set down in Section

75 of the 1998 Northern Ireland Act along with the injunction to have 'regard to the desirability of promoting good relations between persons of different religious belief, political opinion or racial group'. The Fair Employment Commission was replaced by a new Equality Commission in Northern Ireland. Bronagh Hinds and Ciaran Kelly say that 'government departments and public bodies took a restricted approach to questions of equality'. All the same, 154 equality schemes were set up for public bodies under Section 75 by March 2003. There was also a clause creating 'contract compliance' as a motive for companies to adopt equal opportunities policies.

While the 20 years up to 1990 had been stagnant, employment began to grow, and faster in the Catholic community, so that their share of jobs grew from 38% to 41% in 1999, and the unemployment gap between the two communities fell. In 1990 about three quarters of all the firms that were covered by Fair Employment Commission agreements were more than three quarters Protestant, or in some cases, three quarters Catholic. By 2000 that was true of just under two thirds of all firms covered, which did suggest that the policies were beginning to work. The share of Catholic workers who were in monitored workplaces grew from 33% to 37.8%. Though more jobs did a lot to moderate the longstanding problem of Catholic unemployment, income statistics still showed that poverty was concentrated in that section of the community.[7]

Even with the winding down of the shooting war between the IRA insurgents and the security forces, Northern Ireland remains a deeply divided community with Belfast alone divided by 26 miles of 'peace walls'. The political settlement did not end the divisions, but rather entrenched them as the Northern Ireland Assembly works under a 'power-sharing' agreement that has institutionalised the 'nationalist' and 'unionist' political identities: all members of the legislative assembly must adopt 'a designation of identity, being "Nationalist", "Unionist" or "Other"'. Institutionalised sectarian divisions lead the politicians to compete for resources, widening the gaps even further.[8]

Affirmative action in the United States[9]

From the Second World War up to 1964 the United States' Congress and Executive made a number of acts and decrees to advance civil rights, under pressure from a burgeoning civil rights movement. A. Philip Randolph of the Brotherhood of Sleeping Car Porters and Bayard Rustin organised the first 'March on Washington Movement' with rallies for civil rights across the country in the 1940s. Later Martin Luther King, the Southern Christian Leadership Conference, and the Student Non-Violent Coordinating Committee all helped build a mass civil rights movement. Laws, beginning with Roosevelt's Executive Order 8802 desegregating the army, right up to the Civil Rights Act (1964) and the Voting Rights Act (1965), all aimed at dismantling the system of race discrimination in America. It was well understood that race discrimination was closely tied to jobs (the largest single demonstration, on 28 August 1963, was titled the 'March on Washington for Jobs and Freedom'). There were a number of local attempts to persuade employers to take on black workers specifically, through pickets and protests.[10] For the most part, civil rights supporters from Hubert Humphrey through to the Black Panther Party all saw progress as coming through full employment, and up until 1968 the idea of preferential treatment for minorities was a taboo. The civil rights movement argued that people should be judged by 'the content of their character not the colour of their skin' (King).

By the end of the 1960s, though, America's leaders were disturbed by the lack of progress towards equality. President Johnson gave a speech at Howard University saying that freedom and equal opportunities were not enough; there would have to be a new turn in civil rights, 'not just equality as a right and a theory but equality as a fact and equality as a result'.[11] Rioting in Watts in 1965 (following an arrest) and across urban America after Martin Luther King was assassinated in 1968 made the issue electric. A report on black schoolchildren's underachievement (Coleman Commission) was followed by a shocking conclusion from the Kerner Commission on Civil Disorders that 'our nation is moving toward two societies, one black, one white — separate and unequal'.

Surprisingly, the President who took the first step towards positive discrimination — or, as it would become known, affirmative action — was Richard Nixon. He tasked Secretary of State George Shultz with the revival of the 'Philadelphia Plan' — a plan to get Philadelphia construction firms to hire black workers by favouring those that did with government contracts. This was the original 'affirmative action' and the basis of all that came after. In 1972 Assistant Secretary of Labour Richard J. Grunewald went round the country promoting 'hometown plans' on the Philadelphia model, so that around 50 were running in different cities. At the time, the battle lines over affirmative action were not as sharply defined as they were later. The conservative William Buckley wrote that 'we must in fact encourage a pro-Negro discrimination'. Meanwhile the black congressman and civil rights activist Augustus Hawkins was sceptical about the Philadelphia Plan:

In the first year of the operation do you know how many blacks got jobs? Less than one hundred. Do you know how many women have gotten jobs in the history of the Philadelphia Plan? Not one.

Other civil rights supporters, like Democrat congresswoman Edith Green, opposed the Philadelphia Plan, because it introduced quotas for black recruits.[12] There is evidence that Nixon and his team were pleased to have set labour organisers and civil rights activists at odds, and caused some consternation amongst Democrats, who had the support of both of those constituencies, and certainly the prospect of holding down construction workers' wages would have been a consideration.[13] On the whole, though, it was fear of a widespread disaffection of black people from society that drove the initial introduction of affirmative action for the Nixon administration.

Pulling in the opposite direction, race discrimination got a new impetus in the 1970s. While Federal government had, at last, taken an active role in dismantling Southern segregation in the 1960s, the Federal Bureau of Investigations targeted black militants under its COINTELPRO campaign, most notoriously killing Black Panther leader Fred Hampton. Later, Nixon's government launched a 'war on drugs', which tended to criminalise black youth, leading to policing targeted at black communities and much more at black men in prison. Economic recession hurt all working people, but black communities in inner cities much more.

The success of affirmative action was always open to question. A 1973 Office of Federal Contract Compliance survey found that 3,243 minority placements in construction work had been made, though some of those lasted only 30 days.[14] J. Edward Kellough looked at many surveys of affirmative action outcomes in 2006, and the results were very mixed. There was evidence that firms with affirmative action policies hired more minorities, but overall the impact was very small. A number of different surveys found that women generally

US media portrayed black people as a violent threat

did better out of affirmative action policies, whereas black men did not, especially in times of recession. Employment in construction for black men had been positively influenced by affirmative action policies, and employment in the civil service for women also.[15] As far as black incomes went the impact of positive discrimination was overwhelmed by negative discrimination. In 1988 the median income for whites was $25,384; for blacks it was $15,630. Thus, on the whole black income was roughly 60% of white income, a percentage that had not changed substantially since 1980.[16]

Protesters for affirmative action against the Bakke decision

Affirmative action was a bitterly-fought-over political issue in the 1980s and '90s. Having taken up the idea of affirmative action for black Americans, Nixon went on to develop a politics of white American complaint against favouritism, under the label of the 'the silent majority' — an appeal to the country's white middle classes. Later, the Republican President Ronald Reagan (in office 1980-88) similarly appealed to white America's supposed sense of outrage at the special treatment afforded black Americans. Reagan played on prejudices against so-called 'welfare queens' living on state handouts in the ghettos. In 1984 the Supreme Court ruled that the Memphis Fire Department was within its rights to take length of service (seniority earned in days when whites were favoured over blacks) over ethnicity in its choice of who to lay off. The following summer the Reagan Justice Department set about overturning affirmative action plans in 56 cities, counties, and states. In the 1980s and 1990s affirmative action programs were more like an Aunt Sally for white complaints than a positive gain for blacks. The Supreme Court continued to curb them, and Democrat President Bill Clinton gave ground on much of the argument, with his affirmative action policy of 'mend it don't end it'. In February 1995 *Newsweek* ran a covers story proclaiming the 'End of Affirmative Action'.[17] The political debate over affirmative action in America had a tendency to treat employment as a zero-sum game, where black gains could only come at the expense of white workers, and vice versa. The historical record is that job competition really was a zero-sum game when the economy was poor. In 1982 black unemployment peaked at 18%, while white was at 9%. More people in jobs, as happened in the period 1995-2005, tends to help both black and white, so that in 2000, black unemployment was at 8%, and white at 4%.[18]

For all that, private industry, larger companies in particular, took a much more sanguine view of the question. A 'National Alliance of Businessmen' set up by Henry Ford undertook to give black candidates preference in hiring with the aim of creating '500,000 jobs in 50 cities'. They were following a lead given by Eastman Kodak in Rochester, which, after being picketed by activist Saul Alinsky's FIGHT organisation, offered to recruit 1,500 workers from black and poor communities. The CEO of Pitney-Bowes of Stamford, Connecticut announced a policy of preferential hiring shortly after President Kennedy's assassination. A survey of Fortune's 750 largest companies found that senior executives were mostly in favour of 'lowering the company's employment qualifications to hire more from disadvantaged groups', while junior managers were mostly against.[19] 'Affirmative Action is Deeply Ingrained in Corporate Culture', reported *Business Week* in 1991. They quoted AT&T chairman Robert Allen: 'Affirmative action is not just the right thing to do it is a business necessity.'[20] The difference between *Business Week*'s firm-oriented conclusion in 1991 and *Newsweek*'s politicised argument in 1995 is telling. Affirmative action was indeed part of corporate culture, but it remained politically sensitive.

In 1996 the State of California courts struck down college affirmative action programmes, forbidding the prestigious UCLA and UC Berkeley from taking race into account in awarding places. The ban on affirmative action had a marked impact on black enrolment which fell from around 10% to less than 5%. Other state judiciaries followed suit, with Michigan the latest to knock back affirmative action at its colleges in 2013. There was always a question as to whether affirmative action was supposed to be a limited or a permanent project. But the end point of the programme for US colleges is that black enrolment has fallen pointedly.

The Commission for Racial Equality in Britain drew on the American experience. At the 1986 TUC Annual Conference, the Commission organised a meeting on 'Britain's Cities and the Trade Union Movement'. The guest speaker was Ted Watkins, 'a US trades unionist and founder member of Watts Labour and Community Action Committee'.[21] It was often argued that the British legislation was different, because it was only positive action, that is preference in promotion and training, expressed in target, not affirmative action, meaning actual quotas for recruiting black candidates. British universities did better than US ones in recruiting black students, who are more likely to study beyond eighteen than the general population — a target achieved without US-style quotas.[22] But then again, as Barbara Bergmann, a defender of US-style affirmative action, argues, the difference between the British and American approaches is not as great as it seems.[23] Certainly programmes like the Creative Diversity Network's one-year trainee commissioner posts look like jobs, rather than targets. Perhaps the substantial difference between the US and UK experiences was that positive action did not become a political football.

The European Union and women

In 1957 France, Germany, Italy, Belgium, the Netherlands, and Luxemburg signed the Treaty of Rome, setting up the European Economic Community. In 1973 Britain, Ireland, and Denmark joined, and in the decades that followed so did the former dictatorships in Portugal, Spain, and Greece, and then the formerly neutral and Comecon states in East Europe. Over those decades the European Economic Community became more than a customs union, with common rules on social policy, a guiding Commission, a Parliament, and a European Court of Justice. To signal those changes the EEC changed its name to the European Community (1967), and then the European Union (1993).

The original Treaty of Rome had a clause, Article 119, that calls for each member state to 'ensure and subsequently maintain the application of the principle that men and women should receive equal pay for equal work'. The inclusion of the clause calls for some explanation, since, as Helsinki professor Johanna Kantola points out, 'the interests of women were not raised in the debate' over the Treaty of Rome: 'Article 119 was a piece of legislation by men, drafted in all-male working groups to which women had no access and no channels of influence.'[24] Equal pay for equal work had been an International Labour Organisation demand since shortly after the end of the First World War, and at the end of the Second, it was part of France's legislature. In the negotiations Holland and Germany were reluctant to agree to French demands that there should be parity in legislation so that France would not be at a disadvantage, but Germany's legal advice was that their own laws would meet the rule, so they agreed. For the most part the clause was not taken up by the national governments, as was clear in a survey by the Directorate General on Employment and Social Affairs, and a deadline for the implementation of equal pay provisions of 31 December 1964 passed without any changes.[25]

The social disturbances in Western Europe in the late Sixties led to a decade of disorder that led many governments to worry about disaffection and a perceived crisis of legitimacy. At the European level this led to a 'Social Action Plan' proposed by German Chancellor Willy Brandt and French President Pompidou, stressing that 'a common social policy was essential so that the population could identify with the [EEC]'. The Plan had equal pay and non-discrimination clauses.[26] Another influence was the case (two cases, in fact) brought to the European Court of Justice by lawyer Eliane Vogel-Polsky on behalf of a stewardess on Belgium's Sabena airline, Gabrielle Defrenne. Defrenne had been sacked on reaching the age of 40, while her male peers were allowed to work to 55, and had also been barred, as a stewardess, from the company pension. The Justices at the European Court were sympathetic, but said they did not have the powers to rule in her favour. The European Commission acted with three directives addressing women's inequality, on Equal Pay (1975), Equal Treatment (1976), and Social Security (1978).

The European Economic Community's — and its successors' — directives were a great source of confidence for the Equal Opportunities Commission in its push for equal opportunities, and they welcomed the news that 'The directives of the European Economic Community on equal treatment for men and women and on equal pay have come into effect'. The Commission took pride in the fact that 'the Equal Pay and Sex Discrimination Acts have generated a marked interest in Europe' and that 'the implementation and monitoring of the two EEC Directives provide a unique opportunity for this country to set the trend in the next phase of securing equality for women'.[27] European comparisons underlined the Commission's demands, as for example in 1979, when they were pointing out that 'Britain's mothers-to-be are getting a poor deal on maternity rights, in comparison with their European neighbours'.[28] Not only did the directives on equal pay and equal treatment help to secure the British laws on Equal Pay and Sex Discrimination, they also gave courage to the Commission in the years when it was at odds with the Conservative government in Westminster. From early on in the first Thatcher term, the Equal Opportunities Commission used the positive example of Europe to try to embarrass the government.

In 1982 they reported that 'by far the most important legal development during the year — and arguably in the lifetime of the Commission — was the judgment of the European Court of Justice in the infringement proceedings brought by the European Commission against the UK Government'. The European Commission charged that the United Kingdom was 'in breach of its obligations under the Treaty of Rome' for 'failing to provide in its national legislation for individuals to pursue claims of equal pay where they were engaged in work of equal value compared with other workers':

> The European Commission has maintained that these deficiencies in the Equal Pay Act constitute and infringement of the United Kingdom's Treaty obligations to give full effect to the provisions of Article 119 of the Treaty of Rome and, in particular, to the provisions of the Equal Pay Directive.[29]

The ruling led to the Equal Pay (Amendment) Regulations (1983, came into force in 1984), tightening up the law.[30] Looking back in 1985, the Commission underlined that it was 'conscious from the very outset of the European dimension of its work'. They knew that joint work between the European Commission and the EOC built confidence and influence:

The existence today of an Advisory Committee on Equal Opportunities at the Commission of the European Community in Brussels is due in no small measure to the European Conference, 'Equality for Women', which we organised on behalf of the European Commission in Manchester in 1980.[31]

In 1985 the Commission 'strongly supported the European Commission's proposal for a Directive to ensure that all Member States make a minimum provision for' parental leave from work, 'to take time off work following the end of maternity leave to care for a young child under two'. Though it was 'increasingly available within EEC countries'.[32]

It is worth bearing in mind that at the time the European Commission was clashing sharply with the British government. Prime Minister Thatcher had pilloried the European Community over the British contribution (which she pointedly called 'our money'). Shortly afterwards Commission President Jacques Delors went to the British Trade Union Congress, to tell trade unionists that if they were not loved by their government, they could rely on the protection of the European Community. For the Commission the European Community was a corridor around the truculent British government, to a higher power that could impose laws on Westminster.

In the 1990s that conflict reoccurred, after Thatcher had left office, and a rather weaker Prime Minister, John Major, struggled with a 'Eurosceptic' minority in his Cabinet (which he was once overheard calling 'the Bastards'). The European Community was also changing. In 1993 the Maastricht Treaty created the European Union. Major had to manufacture a row with Europe, over the 'Social Chapter' of the Treaty, guaranteeing some employment rights, which Britain opted out of to keep up the appearance of British defiance. Among the provisions of the Social Chapter in Article 2 were a commitment to 'equality between men and women with regard to labour market opportunities and treatment at work'. It was in that context that the

Equal Opportunities Commission chair, Kamlesh Bahl

Equal Opportunities Commission in the early Nineties, under its new chair Kamlesh Bahl, increased the appeal to European Union legislation to put pressure on the UK government. In 1993 Bahl celebrated 'the successful decision by the European Court of Justice, in the Marshall case', that 'confirmed the EOC's long-held view that the UK's upper limit to compensation for victims of sex discrimination was inadequate'. The Commission attached 'great importance to its membership of the European Commission's Advisory Committee on Equal Opportunities for Women and Men on which all Member States are represented'. They saw the EOC's work as part and parcel of the European Community's project:

> The EC's Third Action Programme on Equal Opportunities for Women and Men has three main objectives: developing and clarifying the legal base; the integration of women into the labour market and improving the status of women in society.[33]

The European Commission in Brussels was also interested in flattering the Equal Opportunities Commission in London, as part of its attempts to gain support in the clash with the British government.

So it was that 'the EOC's comments on the European Social Policy so impressed the European Commission it included many of them in its White Paper' in 1994. In truth the Equal Opportunity Commission's contribution to the European Commission's Social Policy were so much boiler-plate rhetoric:

- The need for a continuing, strong legal framework at European level.
- The need to move to the next phase focusing on equal treatment as well as equal opportunities.
- The urgent need to evaluate the economics of equal opportunity, especially the costs and disadvantages of inequality.
- All policies and proposals should be evaluated for their impact on women and men.
- The importance of women in all decision making spheres.
- The need for greater partnership and networking.

Still it helped both the European Commission and the Equal Opportunities Commission to have a British contribution to the Social Chapter, even if the British government was boycotting it.

Kamlesh Bahl wrote to Secretary of State for Employment, Michael Portillo:

I was delighted when you amended the employment protection laws to remove the discriminatory treatment of part-time workers. This followed the House of Lords decision in the Judicial Review the EOC brought on the matter and will help to stop part-timers being treated as second class citizens.

That was her way of telling him that the Equal Opportunities Commission had powerful allies in Europe.[34] The Commission wrote up the change in the Annual Report as an historic victory for the rights of part-time workers in Britain, 86% of whom were women:

Ruling on an EOC judicial review the House of Lords said that the existing qualifying thresholds applying to part-timers, for access to unfair dismissal and redundancy pay were incompatible with European Community Law.[35]

In 1997 Britain had a new government that signed up to the Social Chapter. That year the treaty of Amsterdam gave powers to the European Council to:

adopt measures to ensure the application of the principle of equal opportunities and equal treatment of men and women in matters of employment and occupation, including the principle of equal pay for equal work or work of equal value.

Under the following Labour and Conservative governments, European Directives on social policy and on equal opportunities in particular were followed.

To understand the trajectory of the European dimension of equal opportunities policies it is useful to look at what the European Commission's motives for challenging the British government were. The Commission, and all the institutions of the European Union (or EEC as was) were in a complicated position. Over time they were building up capacity for a Pan-European law, and social policy. But that project naturally clashed with the defence of national sovereignty in the member states. The European Union could not directly challenge member states' sovereignty since it was in the end a creation of those states. Still it had to innovate in ways that would lay the basis for a European administration. The Commission was unable to intervene directly in labour or welfare policies between 1973 and 1993 because these were very much at the core of national political debate. As an alternative the European Union agencies were drawn to new political movements and issues that were not well represented in national parliaments. So it was that the European Community was, for example, an early innovator in environmental regulation — an issue that was less controversial to member states.[36]

The question of equal pay and sex discrimination at work was one where the Commission was ahead of its member states. The directives on equal pay were influenced by the British laws of the 1970s, but later the governments of the 1980s were in defiance of these rulings. Ann Wickham explained in a far-sighted article, published in 1980, that the European Community 'has a need for subjects through which it can constitute its legitimacy, and therefore establish itself more firmly as an independent supranational body'. Class politics, Wickham explained, are 'unlikely to be successful because these… have already been constituted at a national level, particularly where there are social democratic parties appealing to the interest of the "working class"'. Women as political subjects, though, are attractive to European Community institutions: 'Women are available as political subjects precisely because they have not been widely constituted as political subjects at national level.'[37]

Equal opportunities for women at work were as important to the European Union, in seeking to enlarge its competence against national governments, as Europe was important to the Equal Opportunities Commission in finding another avenue of support that side-stepped Downing Street's intransigence.

A recent appraisal of the fortunes of women at work in the European Union was prepared by Professor Maria Corsi, of Universita 'La Sapienza' in Rome, for the 'FEMM Committee' of the European Parliament. Corsi is downbeat, saying that 'a sort of marginalisation toward the working woman still reigns', and that 'concentration of women in low value-added and thus low remuneration' industries is the norm. Her assessment of the relative positions of men and women, though, is more nuanced. She says that 'the current crisis presents aspects that no crisis has shown before'. By that she means that 'gender gaps are closing not because women have improved their situation, but because men saw theirs getting comparatively worse.'[38]

— TEN —

Mainstreaming Equal Opportunities

Equal opportunities policies have come of age. No longer a
nagging reform, they are at the heart of workplace relations
in the twenty-first century. The project though holds itself
to be unfinished. Dracula never dies, no matter how many times
you kill him. So it is with discrimination. The policy needs a
problem to address. Before we look at the problems that the equal
opportunities policies throw up, we ought first to understand just
how mainstream they are.

'Mainstreaming'

Mainstream is not just an adjective in the language of equal
opportunities policies, it is a verb. Under the heading 'mainstreaming',
the Equal Opportunities Commission pledged that it 'is working to
build equality considerations into all levels of government and all
services'. As they said, 'our objective is for the equality implications
of all policy to be considered from the start of the policy-making
process'.[1]

One example of how 'mainstreaming' works is the Athena SWAN
charter. The charter works as a commitment on the part of universities
and colleges 'to advancing women's careers in science, technology,
engineering, mathematics and medicine (STEMM) employment
in higher education'. Athena SWAN works as a kitemark or badge

awarded at different levels to universities and colleges by the Equality Challenge Unit: Bronze, Silver, and Gold. Sponsored by the Royal Society, the Department for Education, and the universities, the Equality Challenge Unit encourages universities to change 'cultures and attitudes across the organisation', on the grounds that 'to address gender inequalities requires commitment and action from everyone, at all levels of the organisation'.

These are laudable aims, but just as arresting are the means. The Equality Challenge Unit is a voluntary system of self-regulation on the part of the universities. It relies on the benchmark set by the charter, and on the competitive drive of institutions to match the standards achieved by rival universities. In practice it means that the charter is always the first point on the agenda of every meeting and decision — a formula that college administrations have adopted to earn their status as holders of the Athena SWAN Award, and to improve their rating, from Bronze to Silver, and on to Gold.

Universities have created the Athena SWAN charter, because it is a system of self-regulation that works — works both in the sense that it leads to consistent incremental advance towards a better representation of women in STEMM posts; but also in the sense that it works to give the organisations an overarching sense of purpose and reform. Lecturer Sara Ahmed, who worked on Goldsmiths College's equality charter, worried that 'the orientation towards writing good documents can block action, insofar as the document then gets taken up as evidence that we have "done it"'. Ahmed told the story of how her committee's work on the charter was lauded by a new Vice Chancellor, who showed off the Equality Challenge Unit's award to the College, 'informing the university that it had been given the "top rank" for its race equality policy', and thus '"We are good at race equality"'. 'But those of us who wrote the document did not feel so good', Ahmed explained: 'A document that documents the inequality of the university became usable as a measure of good performance.'[2]

Television broadcasters have often been criticised for the way they side-line or caricature black people. Tony Freeth, Stuart Hall, and the Black Workers' Association produced the show *It Ain't Half Racist, Mum* for BBC2 in 1979 which highlighted the problem. In the 1982 book of the same name Tony Freeth wrote that 'if there is to be significant change in the TV image of our black communities, there must be change in the production process', adding that 'there must be more black film-makers'.[3] Channel 4 and BBC both enhanced their minority-ethnic programme making, and a Commission for Racial Equality study of minority representation on TV found that while Asians were under-represented in proportion to their share of the UK population, 'black participants were more likely to be seen on TV than in the real world'.[4] In 2001 the BBC Director General said that the organisation was 'hideously white' and its management 98% white. The industry's Creative Diversity Network was founded by the major terrestrial and digital broadcasters to redress the imbalance. Amongst its many programmes are year-long placements for minorities amongst all the major commissioners. Channel 4 has committed itself to a 20% black and minority-ethnic workforce, and has also brought in Diversity Commissioning Guidelines — contract compliance for its independent television companies to employ minority production staff and talent. In June 2016 the BBC was criticised by MPs for advertising scriptwriting posts (for its drama *Holby City*) for black and minority-ethnic applicants only. The Corporation defended itself saying that the posts were training posts, and so covered by race equality law.[5]

'Mainstreaming' equal opportunities has been taken up by the institutions of the European Union, too. In 1998 the Council of Europe agreed that 'Gender mainstreaming is the (re) organisation, improvement, development and evaluation of policy processes so that a gender equality perspective is incorporated in all policies at all levels'. The Council set up the European Institute for Gender Equality, which as Director Virginia Landbakk explains 'has started working with selected tools which were considered good practice in the field of gender mainstreaming and at promoting gender equality'. What this adds up to is a commitment to 'gender training' — 'building gender capacity, competence and accountability', because:

> Gender mainstreaming requires decision-makers and public servants to support the goal of increasing gender equality, be aware of the mechanisms reproducing inequalities in general, and possess the skills and power to modify the public intervention for which they are responsible.[6]

Behind all of the prolixity, the point of this programme is mostly a training programme, whose unspoken purpose is to socialise European policy-makers into a certain way of thinking. The EIGE listed a number of different bodies who had already undergone the training, including the Andalusia Regional Government, the Swedish Association of Local Authorities and Regions, the European Commission DG for Research and Innovation, the Provincial Government of Styria in Austria, and Women in Councils in Northern Ireland.

Widening the equal opportunities model

One sign of the way that equal opportunities have become 'mainstream' is the way that other claims have been folded into the model of equal opportunities that were developed in the first instance to address discrimination against black and Asian people, and against women at work. Davina Cooper, a Haringey councillor in the 1980s, explains that equal opportunities 'provided a means of entry into the political agenda for lesbian and gay issues in the mid-1980s', and that it 'created an equivalence between identities — Black, female, disabled and homosexual' — which, she argues 'was frequently inappropriate'.[7]

Lesbian and gay rights

The question of the rights of gay men was raised in the 1950s and '60s as a question of civil liberties, by the Homosexual Law Reform Society and the Campaign for Homosexual Equality, leading to Lord Woolfenden's 1957 report favouring reform, and the 1967 Act that partially decriminalised homosexuality ('between consenting adults in private' and with a higher age of consent, 21 years). The Gay Liberation Front formed in 1970 was very much an outcome of the 'Sixties' generation of radicals that had also founded the Women's Liberation Front. The GLF's goal was to change society, and liberate not just gay men but all people from narrowly heterosexist norms, and to fight the still markedly repressive policing of gay men.

The Gay Liberation Front took up the cause of homosexuals persecuted at work as but one dimension of the general campaign for freedom. Gay rights (which were by this time coming to be coupled in the formula 'lesbian and gay rights') were only taken up as a specifically 'equal opportunities' campaign once the idea of equal opportunities for women and for black people had been set out. Principally, it was among the municipal left that inclusion of lesbian and gay rights at work came to be included in the equal opportunities policy. In the Spring of 1983 the Greater London Council announced its new Grievance Procedure in respect of discrimination: 'You can now take action against discrimination on grounds of sex, race, colour, nationality, ethnic or national origins, sexual orientation, age, trade union activity, political or religious belief.'[8] The inclusion of sexual orientation reflected the discussions that were taking place in the Women's Committee at County Hall, and the growing lobby for lesbian and gay rights among the municipal activists. In 1985 Phil Greasley published the book *Gay Men at Work*, 'A Report on discrimination against gay men in employment in London', with a foreword by the 'out' Labour MP for Islington South, Chris Smith.

Discrimination at work was without doubt a problem for lesbians and for gay men — as was discrimination in other settings too. However, there was no obvious sense in which lesbians or gay men as a cohort occupied a distinctive role in the workforce, as was the case with women and black people. Were gay people penalised in the labour market? What evidence there is seems to suggest that lesbians and gay men had average incomes higher than the average for the country.[9] Folding the rights of lesbians and gay men into the equal opportunities policy was one way that the logic of equal opportunities at work was coming to define liberation movements. The activists of gay liberation were reinterpreting their struggle as one of workplace discrimination to fit the preoccupations of the time. One councillor and gay rights activist despaired of the combative way that the issue had been raised, saying 'the gay issue has been dragged in by well-intentioned councillors who think it is the same as sexism and racism, when it's not, without realising the forces ranged against it'.[10]

Demonstration against Clause 28

That said, there was shortly afterwards a pointed struggle over gay rights that was indeed focused on the workplace, and that was the clash over Section 28 of the Local Government Act of 1988. The row took place in Haringey, after the education office circulated a booklet for schools called *Jenny Lives with Eric and Martin*, designed to familiarise children with the possibility that a child's carers — parents — might be two gay men. The council offices were picketed by an unhappy 'Parents' Rights Group', who did not want their children taught about homosexuality, which in their minds was associated with paedophilia. At the prompting of Dame Jill Knight, the Conservative government included the clause in its local government bill that forbade the 'promotion of homosexuality', and teaching the 'acceptability of homosexuality as a pretended family relationship' in schools. Large protests against the bill galvanised the lesbian and gay rights movement. Beatrix Campbell pointed out that Haringey Council was imperious in its attempts to bring about lesbian and gay equality from on high: 'in the absence of any public work within civil society, statism has replaced consciousness-raising', was the way she put it. She was right. As chair of the group Council Workers Against Clause 28, I helped to organise a day of action to oppose the government attack on gay rights. An officer in the Council's Lesbian and Gay Unit, who went round the council offices asking clerks for their support with me, berated those who were not sure, demanding to know why they worked for the Council if they did not support its equal opportunities policies. As she saw it, the task was to enforce compliance from employees, not to win over fellow workers to take solidarity action. In the way these things work out, when the bill became law, it was the Lesbian and Gay Unit itself that was tasked by the Council to ensure that its discriminatory clause was enforced. The contrast with the school secretaries in the local government union NALGO was marked. They were mostly working mothers and many were anxious about measures they saw undermining the family, and opening their children to undue sexual knowledge. On the other

hand, they could see that those teachers who were gay would be open to persecution under the law, and voted to oppose it.

The Section 28 episode showed that lesbian and gay rights did not really fit into the argument about equal opportunities at work, but was part of a larger, more ideological debate about the sanctity of the family, and the presumed pressures upon it. Section 28 stayed on the statute books from 1988 until 2003 when it was repealed (three years earlier in Scotland). Around that time governments of left and right moved quite quickly in the direction of lesbian and gay rights to equalise the law of consent (Sexual Offences Amendment Act, 2000), to outlaw discrimination (Equality Act (Sexual Orientation) Regulations, 2007), and eventually to legalise gay marriage (Civil Partnership in 2004, followed by the Marriage (Same Sex Couples) Act in 2013). The swift and surprising liberalisation of the laws on lesbian and gay rights comes about because, unlike the transformation of the position of women, gay rights do not require a reorganisation of the social order, but rather reflect the changing ideological position following on as 'family values' came to carry less weight.

Muslims in Britain

Over the last 20 years Britain's Islamic minority has been in the spotlight. Muslims in Britain had been addressed in social policy not as Muslims, but as a subset of an ethnic group, Asians (allowing that there are a small but growing number of ethnically European converts). The main Muslim populations in Britain have come from Pakistan (43% of the total), India (9%), Bangladesh (17%),[11] and more latterly from North and East Africa; as well as a smaller group from Arab nations. There are around three million Muslims living in Britain. Official policy to Muslims was not friendly or hostile, but the hostile attention to Asians by the immigration and police services, as well as by employers, often focused on Muslim beliefs and cultures.

In 1978 Dr Muhammed Iqbal and a member of the Home Secretary's Advisory Council on Race Relations argued the case for separate schools for Muslim boys and girls in the Commission for Racial Equality's newsletter, *New Equals*. Dr Iqbal understood the fear 'that separate schools for Muslim girls and boys may perpetuate under-achievement, hence alienate school-leavers from single-sex institutions from jobs commensurate with their attainments parallel to the English'. As he saw it, 'Westernisation may well bring about the desired results in terms of job opportunities'. But he asked 'what about the resultant and internecine secularisation, irreligiousness, materialism, pseudo-individualism and erosion of moral values?'[12]

Since the Khomeini revolution in Iran in 1979, the British state has often been in conflict with states and movements motivated by militant religious-political ideology in the Middle East, and these have had an impact on relations between Muslims, the authorities, and the wider population in Britain.

In 1988 British Muslims in Bradford protested at the satirical picture of the prophet set out in British-Indian author Salman Rushdie's novel *The Satanic Verses*. The cause was taken up by an imam in India, and then by the Ayatollah Khomeini, spiritual leader of the Islamic state in Iran, who issued a 'fatwa' or judgment against the apostate author, to the effect that it was acceptable to kill him. How rhetorical or serious the fatwa was, was open to question, but his Turkish publisher was killed, and Rushdie was allocated an armed guard by the British government. It was a moment when many Muslims in Britain came to organise around their religious identity more than their Asian heritage (the popular *Muslim News*, for example, was launched shortly afterwards).[13]

Increasing conflict in the Middle East, with British and American military intervention in Lebanon (1984), Libya (1986), the Persian Gulf (1988), two wars in Iraq (1991, 2003), and a prolonged participation in the occupation of Afghanistan (beginning in 2001), as well as British support for the Israeli occupation of Palestine, all added to the heightened tension between radical Islam and the British authorities. Terrorist attacks by small groups of radical Muslims against Western targets — most notably the World Trade Center in New York on 11 September 2001, but followed by bombing attacks in London on 7 July 2005 — heightened tensions between the authorities and British Muslims.

As well as the growing evidence of atrocities and torture carried out by British security services abroad, security measures to cope with 'home-grown' terrorism provoked anger. Anti-terrorism laws allowed for much longer time for those arrested to be interrogated before being released, for special orders imposing home curfews for 'terror suspects' and scores of early morning raids, and deportations of individuals — often to countries where they were at risk of torture.

The alienation of some Muslims, who were drawn to agitating for, and in some cases participating in, terror attacks against British targets, disturbed the British authorities. Alongside the surveillance and repressive measures undertaken against Muslims suspected of terrorist conspiracies, the British government has tried to build bridges with the broader Muslim population to reinforce more moderate beliefs. British support for mosque committees goes back to before the 1976 Act and the Community Relations Councils founded under the 1965 Act.

Mala Sen went to a day 'Conference of Bangladeshi Youth' organised by the Federation of Bangladeshi Associations and the Asian Centre in Islington in 1977, where 'a young Bengali, from the local Bangladesh Youth Association, stood up and criticised' their elders: 'we were not consulted', he said in Bengali, 'This thing has nothing to do with us. You've only come down here because you want to control us — you want us to follow you.' As Sen saw it back then, 'Unabashed, the elders, all of them professional community relations wallahs, proceeded'.[14]

Back then the generation gap saw younger Bangladeshis organised on the basis of their ethnic identity, in a political lobby, the Asian Youth Movement. In 1981, 12 members of the Asian Youth Movement were arrested and tried on conspiracy charges, after they organised to defend themselves and their community against racist attacks. Through the Commission for Racial Equality's grants to CRCs and through local government, the authorities shored up the influence of the mosques as a counter to the influence of the more political radicals. 'In March 1994', explains Kenan Malik, in the wake of the protests over *The Satanic Verses*, 'the Conservative Home Secretary Michael Howard appealed to Muslims to form a "representative body" that he could "support and recognize"'. Before then the Foreign Office had been supportive of Saudi-backed Muslim groups. In 1997 the Muslim Council of Britain under Iqbal Sacranie was founded.[15]

With Islamist movements inspiring more people around the world than radical nationalist movements did, the generational divide among British Muslims looked a bit different. The secular challenge of the Asian Youth Movement had fallen away. Instead young Muslims challenged their more moderate elders on the terrain of belief. The traditional religious identification that the authorities had encouraged became a battleground between radicals and moderates. When the congregants at the Finsbury Park Mosque, swelled by refugees from the civil war in Algeria, embraced the teachings of

Burning The Satanic Verses, *Bradford, 1989*

radical Abu Hamza it became a focal point for Islamists, until Hamza was forced out. In 2003 the security services raided the mosque.

Attempts to win over 'moderate' Muslims have led to more financial aid for mosque-based organisations that the government hope can act as interlocutors, like the Muslim Council of Britain. In 1997 the government changed the law so that Muslim schools could be state-aided along the same lines as Jewish, Catholic, and Church of England Schools. Some, though, have argued that the government's policy of funding religious organisations has tended to promote ethnic division. Kenan Malik explains that the government's preferred interlocutor, the Muslim Council of Britain, is in fact quite marginal to most Muslims and, being associated with the Pakistan-based organisation Jamaat-i-Islami, what most commentators would call 'radical'. As Malik says, 'if the prime minister believes that he can only engage them by appealing to their faith, rather than through their wider political or national affiliations, who are Muslims to disagree?' After the '7/7' bombings in July 2005 the government distanced itself from the MCB, thinking that it had not done enough to contain radicalism.[16]

Other than direct representation through Mosques and Muslim groups, British Muslims have tended to be Labour voters, and after some kicking back Muslims have won some standing in the Labour Party. In the 1990s Birmingham's nine sitting Labour MPs were all white though many of the party's voters and activists were Muslims of Pakistani origin. A membership fraud committee under Clare Short went through the party lists checking all the 'Muhammeds' they found there. Some popular Labour Party organisers of Bangladeshi background, like Jalal Uddin and Lutfur Rahman, were overlooked when parliamentary seats became available. In time some of these activists peeled away from the Labour Party to find a better welcome in the far-left RESPECT Coalition, the Liberal Democrats, or in Lutfur Rahman's case, setting up his own Tower Hamlets First Party. To the embarrassment of Labour, George Galloway won the Bethnal Green seat for RESPECT in 2005, with a large base of Bangladeshi support (a performance he repeated in the Bradford West by-election in 2012). Lutfur Rahman's Tower Hamlets First Party won control of the Council in 2014, but less than a year later was controversially thrown out of office by the electoral court on grounds of 'corruption'. When the electoral court handed its investigation over to the Metropolitan Police they judged that there was not enough evidence to carry on. In May 2016, Labour's candidate for the London Mayor Sadiq Khan beat the Conservative Party's Zac Goldsmith. Goldsmith was widely seen to have run a scurrilous campaign that tried to smear Khan as a friend of terrorism. Khan's own slogan, though — 'the British Muslim who can beat the extremists' — turned out to be very popular. The bond between Muslims and the Labour Party has been made strong again.

British Muslims are on average less well-paid, less economically active, and in less skilled posts than the rest of the population. They are overrepresented in the hotel and catering trades, and as cab drivers.[17] The think-tank Demos highlighted the statistical evidence that on average Muslims in Britain are less likely to hold a managerial or professional position, and that 'Muslims in England and Wales are also disproportionately likely to be unemployed and economically inactive'. Demos' report 'Rising to the Top' proposes a number of measures, including a plea for employers to:

> Do more to prevent discrimination and reduce the perception of discrimination — with the Government and organisations such as the CBI encouraging them to undertake contextual recruitment as part of their graduate recruitment process.[18]

The Demos report follows from the Runnymede Trust's 1997 proposal for monitoring of religious affiliation in employment and national statistics with a view to taking action to stop discrimination against Muslims.[19] The evidence that prejudice against Muslims has led to greater inequality is suggestive — though it is not easy to distinguish the effects of discrimination on racial grounds from those on religious grounds. The Employment Equality (Religion or Belief) Regulations of 2003 'extended legislative protection to individuals on the grounds of religion or belief' in the 'areas of employment and training'. The Commission for Racial Equality 'argued that new legislation should be introduced to give protection to individuals on the grounds of religion or belief not only in the area of employment, but also in provision of goods and services.' The Commission

> also considered that the introduction of new legislation to prohibit the incitement of religious hatred was necessary to protect individuals who were becoming increasingly vulnerable to verbal and racial attack, but who were not also protected by legislation that prohibited incitement to racial hatred, again due to the definition of racial groups.[20]

In 2006 Parliament passed the Racial and Religious Hatred Act, which largely expanded the definition of race hatred to encompass hatred against Muslims and Christians (Jews and Sikhs had both already been categorised as 'races' for the purpose of previous legislation). Some objected that the law would make proper criticism of religions illegal, that these were bodies of thought, not racial identities, which ought to be open to criticism.

Whether Britain's problematic treatment of its Muslim minority can be dealt with as a matter of extending anti-discrimination policy and enlarging the meaning of equal opportunities at work is not clear. What is clear is that the authorities have a problem persuading younger Muslims to identify with British society.

Disability rights

Long before disability was ever addressed as a question of rights, British society, like most others, had undertaken the care of the disabled as a charitable imperative. Edward Rushton's 'school for the indigent blind' was founded in Merseyside in 1791 after many lost their sight to smallpox.[21] Handicapped people in Britain were cared for in special schools like Chailey School in East Sussex. From 1944, under the Disabled Persons Employment Act, the government supported factories and workshops run by a dedicated corporation, Remploy, which opened its first factory in Bridgend in Wales in 1946, eventually managing some 83 factories around the country. From 1963 the Spastics Society ran workshops and day centres for people with cerebral palsy. Care and help for the disabled was for many years a voluntary activity undertaken by churches, Rotary Clubs, and the Variety Club.

In 1976 the Union of the Physically Impaired argued for a new way of looking at disability, which they defined as:

[T]he disadvantage or restriction of activity caused by a contemporary social organisation which takes no or little account of people who have physical impairments and thus excludes them from participation in the mainstream of social activities. Physical disability is therefore a particular form of social oppression.

The British Council of Organisations of Disabled People, launched in 1981, did a great deal to promote what they called the social model of disability, and to campaign against segregation and stigmatisation. The more activist approach to disability gave a lot of people with disabilities a greater dignity, and sense of ownership of their issue. In 1986 the British Association of Social Workers adopted the social model of disability and it has been influential in the bringing of disabled students into mainstream education, who would otherwise have been segregated.

The social model, though, is not wholly true. Physical disability is physical disability. Social action, whether attitudinal, or in the provision of ramps and other material infrastructure and equipment to mitigate disability, cannot overcome serious disability. Mainstreaming has many good outcomes, but in cases of serious disability, such as autism and blindness, mainstream schools and workplaces can only do so much to accommodate. The influence of the social model of disability, though, has led governments to move away from special schools and employment for the disabled. Both the Blair and Cameron administrations oversaw the winding down of Remploy with the loss of thousands of jobs for disabled people, the last three factories in Blackburn, Sheffield, and Neath, South Wales closing in 2013.

One of the more controversial interpretations of mainstreaming and the social model of disability has been the Conservative government's determination to get thousands of people off of incapacity benefit and into work. Lord Freud lauded the approach of government action 'to support people with health conditions and disabilities into work' and said that 'we want to ensure that we spend money responsibly in a way that improves individuals' life chances and helps them to achieve their ambitions, rather than paying for a lifetime wasted on benefits'.[22] The system of interviewing and reviewing claims under the workfare scheme has widely been seen as an attack on disabled welfare claimants.

Men's rights and 'Rights for Whites'

As a rhetorical response to equal opportunities policies aimed at helping women and ethnic minorities, some of those who had been thought of as privileged have tried to frame their ambitions in the language of equal opportunities. In a well-publicised exchange in a House of Commons Committee in October 2015, Tory MP Philip Davies asked for time to be set aside for a debate on a proposal for an International Men's Day, just as there was an International Women's Day. Labour MP Jess Phillips was withering, saying 'as the only woman on this committee, it seems like every day to me is International Men's Day'. Nonetheless men's rights campaigners have lobbied for greater access to children in divorce settlements as well as organising seminar series for picking up and dominating women. For the most part men's rights activists have been dismissed as creeps or weirdos.

There had been a different sort of 'men's movement' proposed in the late Seventies. The second national conference organised by Men Against Sexism took place at the Abraham Moss Centre in Crumpsall, Manchester in 1979:

> the 50 workshops spread over the weekend included the experience of fatherhood and child care; rape; the need for national men's campaign; therapy groups; sexuality; how feminism affects your daily life; and theoretical analyses of the role of men.[23]

The conference decided that a national men's campaign was not what they wanted, and no further conferences were planned. Later some researchers and activists argued that the damage done to men by changing gender relations, and by the ideology of masculinity, needs to be addressed. Books by Roger Horrocks (*Masculinity in Crisis*, 1996), Anthony Clare (*On Men: Masculinity in Crisis*, 2000), Susan Faludi (*Stiffed: The Betrayal of the American Man*, 1999), and R W Connell (*Masculinities*, 1995) all talked about the difficulties that men were having reconciling the ambition to domination in the ideal of masculinity, with the decline in the status of men.[24] Campaigners Diane Abbott, the Hackney MP, and feminist Laurie Penny both took up the call for action. 'We still don't have any positive models for post-patriarchal masculinity, and in this age of desperation and uncertainty, we need them more than ever', wrote Penny, while Abbott deplored what she imagined to be a culture of pornography, 'Viagra and Jack Daniels' on offer to men.[25] Not surprisingly few men took up this offer of an investigation of post-patriarchal masculinity. It seems unlikely that any call for a men's movement will be anything but a movement that blames women for the problems that individual men confront. But perhaps that is to be expected when the model for the negotiation of modern life is as a series of competing claims in a zero-sum game.

'Rights for Whites' was a slogan adopted by the far-right British National Party in the early 1990s, around the time that it won a seat on the Tower Hamlets Council for the Millwall ward. The BNP played on some feeling that white residents had lost out in the allocation of council services to Bangladeshis. The seat reverted to Labour at the next election. Investigating rioting in Bradford in 2001 Herman Ouseley found that 'many white people feel that their needs are neglected because they regard the minority ethnic communities as being prioritised for more favourable public assistance'. While Ouseley was a bit sceptical about the claims, some in the Committee for Racial Equality took note. Chair Trevor Phillips, in a television programme for Channel 4 and the associated press publicity, argued that many of the assumptions of redressing inequalities were wrong, and said for example that 'non-white school-leavers are more likely than their white peers to head for university', and that 'poor whites are the new blacks'.[26] In the programme Phillips pointed to the way that some schools were taking the kind of remedial measures to make sure that white working-class children prospered that once had been reserved for minorities.

The feeling that Britain's white working-class communities were losing out lay behind the remarkable vote in a referendum on Britain's membership of the European Union in June 2016. While most of the country's business and political leaders called for a vote to stay in the Union, widespread disaffection in the country among the less well-off led to a majority vote to leave. For the 'Remainers' it seemed as if there had been a revolt of the 'left-behind' against the multicultural society.

Whether men, or whites, considered as a group, could ever be the target of positive action on an equal opportunities model is hard to work out. The arguments for equal opportunities were always imagined as correctives to the advantages that whites and men had over black people and women respectively. 'Rights for whites', or 'rights for men' — by their controversial nature — seem to be claims that call into question the universalizability of the equal opportunities model.

Overall the equal opportunities model, in coming to fruition, has invited different groups to make claims within its logic. More recently, for example, transgendered individuals have been included in workplace policies over discrimination, and in 2016 the Women and Equalities Minister Maria Miller has been looking at legislation to help. Miller could not help but notice the outcry of protest from people that she said were 'purporting to be feminists' over the inclusion of transgender people's rights. But the transgender lobby is in many ways itself a creation of the logic of equality of opportunity. Inclusion in the list of those whose discrimination must be addressed is important for those individuals because it is the way that their broader social status is recognised.

Mainstreaming: the end of the CRE and the EOC

The generalisation of the case for equal opportunities, its adoption by business as equal opportunities policies, and the greater legislative framework supporting their adoption, was beginning to have some strange consequences for the special Commissions dedicated to them.

In Lewis Carroll's book, *Sylvie and Bruno Concluded*, the author has fun imagining a country where:

> '[W]e actually made a map of the country, on the scale of a mile to the mile!'
>
> 'Have you used it much?' I enquired.
>
> 'It has never been spread out, yet,' said Mein Herr: 'the farmers objected...'

With Britain largely committed, at least on paper, to the ideal of equal opportunities for people of different races and genders, the question of why you needed a special commission to advance the case was bound to come up. Or as Carroll's Mein Herr explains 'we now use the country itself, as its own map, and I assure you it does nearly as well'.

At a conference called by the Local Government Information Unit, 'Equalities', held in 1991, Gurbux Singh, who was then Haringey Council's Chief Executive, argued that the dedicated equal opportunities units that had been pioneered by Lambeth and adopted by local authorities all over the country 'were no longer appropriate'. What was needed was 'mainstreaming', getting all the local authority departments to 'take responsibility for equalities work'.[27] Singh's approach caught on, and the race, women's, and lesbian and gay units were closed. Haringey councillor Davina Cooper saw the changes as evidence of a downgrading of the importance of equality work. In some senses it was, as the revolutionary tide of 'equal opps' was giving way to more practical generalisation of the model. At Channel 4,

Commissioner of Multicultural Programming Yasmin Anwar made a similar point, saying that the real success would be when there was no need for multicultural programming.

The question of what the role of the Commission for Racial Equality would be in a country that had 'mainstreamed' equal opportunities was one that Gurbux Singh himself had to address, when he took over as its chair. Under Singh the Commission had some campaigns to carry on with, like one over the problem of rural racism. Talking about the 2000 Race Relations Act, Singh said that it was 'to make equality (as much as "value for money" and efficiency) an essential part of the way public services are conceived and delivered'. There was a private-sector focus, too, with the formation of a new business advisory group that was 'inaugurated in July 2001 to discuss policy and strategy with leading British businesses':

> Our aim was to create a forum where 'critical friends' could air their concerns. The group is made up of representatives from IBM, Shell, BP, Landrover, British Airways, HBOS, Barclays Bank, Lloyds TSB, J P Morgan and HSBC.

These initiatives were not a marked departure from the way that the CRE had worked since David Lane and Peter Newsam's day, except that all of the businesses that were signed up had by this point had equal opportunities policies in place for 15 years or more. The participating companies were those which were seeking to show their support for the government's initiatives. Most of them would in different ways, particularly at the time of the banking bailout in 2008, be grateful for the government's support in the years afterwards.

One initiative that the Commission sponsored was called 'The Leadership Challenge':

> In signing up to the Leadership Challenge, individual leaders make a personal commitment to promote racial equality, both in their

own organisation and more widely, through their sector, and to drive the creation and successful implementation of a corporate racial equality action plan.

The initiative was launched by Chancellor Gordon Brown in a speech in 1999. Brown told the assembled business leaders: 'this process — clearly nothing more than good practice — needs to become the ordinary way of doing business. This won't happen by itself — you as leaders need to make it happen.'[28] The business challenge was notionally about race equality, but substantially it was about business leadership, and a platform for motivational waffle of the kind that was so influential then. 'There is a duty upon all of us in positions of leadership', said Prime Minister Tony Blair, 'to try and offer a lead to everyone else. That includes government itself, and I am happy to take up the Leadership Challenge and to acknowledge that we've got more to do to make progress.'[29] Only very tangentially was the Leadership Challenge about race at all. It was really about geeing up business leaders, creating a sense of a cadre, with a mission and common goals.

The Commission for Racial Equality's work, like that of the Equal Opportunities Commission, was drifting. They no longer occupied the position of custodians of an ideal, or advocates for change. The changes that they had embodied were, by the new millennium, taken on by most people in Britain as if not an unalloyed good, at least the right direction to be going in. In May 2004, the government published a White Paper, 'Fairness for All', 'outlining its proposals for a Commission for Equality and Human Rights (CEHR) to replace the existing race, disability and sex equality commissions, with additional responsibility for religion or belief, sexual orientation, age and human rights'. The Commission for Racial Equality put up some resistance, but broadly the position was won without much argument. By comparison to the outcry over the vague threat to the CRE in 1981, when the Labour government wound up the Commission, it went almost unremarked.[30]

On 1 October 2007 the Equality and Human Rights Commission was set up, with Trevor Phillips as its first chairman. At the time of writing the chair is David Isaac, a lawyer and former Chair of the LGBT campaign Stonewall. The Commission takes up a broad range of issues, from those of travellers' rights to the impact of legislation on victims of domestic abuse. Its campaigning role, though, has proved more diffuse and less controversial than that of either of the two Commissions that it replaced.

— ELEVEN —

Contradictions in the System

Throughout the advance of the language of equality of opportunity there have been a number of sharp conflicts. To the proponents of change, it seemed clear that these were just the complaints of the old order, the backlash against progress. But that is not always the case. As with any emerging regulatory regime there are moments when the imposition of order provokes a reaction. Some of these early conflicts took place in the local authorities that first experimented with equal opportunities.

'Race spies'

In 1986 Brent Council suspended the popular head teacher of the Sudbury Infants School, Maureen McGoldrick, who had been accused of refusing to take on a teacher because she was black, which McGoldrick denied. McGoldrick was exonerated by a panel of the governing body, but the local authority overruled them and suspended her. The Brent Teachers Association supported McGoldrick, as did local parents; even the teaching candidate Miss Khan, who had later been taken on, joined the strike against McGoldrick's suspension. Only the Socialist Teachers' Alliance joined Brent LEA opposing the strike — a position they later regretted as they were denounced as 'parasites' on black parents' struggles. 'Brent appeared to be defending only its own prerogatives and procedures, rather than the community's rights', reported *Marxism Today*: 'the council appeared to be defending their own right to hire and fire, when they were defending their perfectly sound anti-racist policy'. But the Council were indeed defending their procedures when the community had already decided for McGoldrick.[1]

Ron Anderson, chair of the education committee in Brent, argued that the Brent Teachers Association was really pushing 'their own campaign against compulsory Race Awareness Training courses' and other anti-racist policies. RAT courses were often a source of conflict. In 1986 an inquiry into race relations in Manchester schools was launched under Ian Macdonald and Gus John after the murder of Ahmed Iqbal Ullah at the Burnage High School. The report looked at the culture of ethnically divided gangs in Manchester schools. They also drew attention to the way that Race Awareness Training had been put in place. 'In practice it has been an unmitigated disaster', they said, 'leading to polarisation between black and white and to a potentially greater racial conflict'. 'Since the assumption is that black students are the victims of immoral behaviour of the white students', Macdonald and John summed up, 'white students almost inevitably become the "baddies"'.[2]

In Lambeth a conflict broke out between social workers and the Council when 600 walked out in protest at disciplinary hearings called after the murder of a young girl, Tyra Henry, by her father in 1984. The issue was fraught with tensions over race. The girl and her father were black, the social workers mostly white. Under pressure to act, Lambeth Council set up an internal tribunal of four, two of them race advisers, to look at the case. Social workers felt that the first report, issued after two weeks, was unfair: 'Akin to a show trial in Eastern Europe', said the British Association of Social Workers Southwark chairman, John Wheeler: 'people were dragged forward and hectored and shouted at'. The chair of Lambeth Social Services argued that the black councillors understood the black community better: 'A lot of us are more in touch with communities than the social worker.' When the Council announced disciplinary action against three social workers a mass meeting of the department staff voted no confidence in Janet Boateng and her vice-chairman Stephen Bubb. An independent inquiry into Tyra Henry's death, under Stephen Sedley, QC, concluded that the issue of race had contributed to the child's death, but not in the way that was thought. The social workers' lack of confidence to confront the black parents meant that they did not take action in time. Sedley also found 'tension' between Boateng's social services committee and the social workers.[3] Arguably the climate of distrust at Lambeth compounded the social workers' caution.

The call-out culture

With the rise of equal opportunities, a number of sharp clashes over apparently rival claims and policies broke out. As the champions of these newer ways of understanding workplace relations were finding their feet, there were some ugly clashes. One gay activist described the mood at the Greater London Council, working on questions of equality around sexuality and class: 'It was', she wrote, 'a system that was ripe for guilt-tripping and denunciations', adding, 'GLC equalities at times resembled a wartime bunker or a city under siege, riven by internal strife.'[4]

Believing that the political issues being advanced were crucial and could brook no compromise without betrayal, many of the activists working around equality issues painted themselves into corners. These conflicts were particularly bitter once equality issues were put into grievance procedures and codes of conduct. It was quite common in the local authority offices in the 1980s to find two or more co-workers locked in mutually antagonistic grievances taken out against one another, alleging discrimination. Where the claims made were evenly balanced in justice, as between a white woman and a black man, each alleging discrimination against the other, these disputes could go on for months with the work in the office paralysed as each party called on all other employees to take sides, the two glowering at each other over mountains of paperwork, all relating to their case, rather than their employment, which consumed their every moment.

After the Greater London Council was abolished the London local authorities tried to keep its policy development alive in the London Strategic Policy Unit — but without practical questions of managing government to deal with, many in the Unit descended into mutual recriminations and grievance procedures. It was, say Stuart Lansley, Sue Goss, and Christian Wolmar, 'wracked by internal conflict', 'bedevilled by industrial disputes, mainly around minor complaints of racism', and 'much grinding of political axes'.[5] The generalisation of the tribunal model of moderating workplace conflict has been an inspiration for writers like Mark Lawson (who novelised his own investigation on charges of 'bullying' at the BBC as *The Allegations*), David Mamet (whose play *Oleanna* deals with sex-discrimination charges), and Philip Roth (on race charges in his novel *The Human Stain*).

In November 2014, Dr Matt Taylor led the Rosetta mission team, who landed a rocket, Philae on a Comet B67. It was a first that ought to have been widely celebrated. It was televised. For the recording Taylor wore a shirt, designed by his friend Elly Prizeman, that she had given him for his birthday. The shirt was in a rockabilly style, cut from a printed fabric with pattern of Fifties pin-up girls — the overall effect was camp, such as would not have looked out of place in a lesbian bar. Taylor was roundly denounced by a number of women scientists for his 'sexist shirt', which earned the hashtag 'shirtstorm'. Taylor went back on television the following day to make a tearful apology for the hurt he had caused, without intending to.

The following June, biologist Tim Hunt, part of a team that won the Nobel Prize for identifying the protein molecules that govern the sub-division of cells, was invited to give a talk in South Korea at the World Conference of Science Journalists about women in science. Hunt gave a self-mocking speech about being an old dinosaur with outmoded ideas, and hoping that people like him were not holding women scientists back. Irony-deficient science media lecturer Connie St Louis called Hunt on his 'sexism', and he was hauled over the coals. Back in London a senior official at University College London, where Hunt held an emeritus position, demanded he resign or be sacked, and he went, with his partner the immunologist Mary Collins.

These clashes were read very differently by people on either side of the argument. For those who were campaigning for more women in science Taylor's shirt and Tim Hunt's asides were just the tip of the iceberg of a culture of discrimination. For many, though, the targets seemed to be trivial, and the reaction intolerant.

Even the House of Commons was caught up in the 'call-out culture'. During a hotly fought election for London Mayor in April 2016, Prime Minister David Cameron tried to brand the Labour candidate Sadiq Khan an 'extremist' for having shared a platform with the Islamist Suliman Gani. Labour MPs shouted 'racist' at the Prime Minister. The following week the Tory politician Boris Johnson alluded to US President Barack Obama's Kenyan ancestry, drawing a stinging attack from Labour's John McDonnell: 'another example of dog-whistle racism from senior Tories'. The Conservative press retaliated by trawling through Labour MPs' Twitter feeds to find examples of anti-Semitic comments, such as Naz Shah's call for Israeli Jews to be relocated to New York. Defending Shah, Ken Livingstone blurted out in a radio interview that Hitler was a Zionist — an interpretation of history that was lost on most, sounding like an even worse example of anti-Semitism than the one he was defending. So it was that the architect of the Greater London Council's pioneering equal opportunities policies was himself suspended from the Labour Party on grounds of race discrimination. Clearly the accusations and counter-accusations of racism and anti-Semitism in these exchanges were a long way from a debate over policy, descending instead into a 'call-out culture' better suited to the National Union of Students' annual conference than the Palace of Westminster.[6]

The heightened fear of causing — or being seen to cause — discrimination has been called at various times 'political correctness', the 'call-out culture' (as in 'I am going to call you out on that'), the pitfalls of 'identity politics', and even the 'oppression Olympics'. Some right-wing commentators, like the *Daily Mail*'s Richard Littlejohn, have made hay with the allegation of 'political correctness gone mad'. Defenders of equal opportunities policies have replied that 'political correctness gone mad' is a formula that allows reactionaries to make light of discrimination. But all of the terms listed above were not coined by right-wing critics, but rather by anti-discrimination activists, trying to understand where they had gone wrong. It was not Richard Littlejohn who first coined the parody 'politically correct', but student activists fed up with being lectured by dogmatic Maoists; so too with the 'call-out culture', the 'oppression Olympics', and the problems of 'identity politics'.

Only in the rarefied atmosphere of 'identity politics' could it be ever thought of as an advantage to be discriminated against, or that to be so would grant you greater authority. Ordinarily to be discriminated against is to lose out, to lose rights and resources, and indeed to lose face. So it is in most of Britain. Failure is not something to be pleased about. Only in the hothouse atmosphere of equal opportunities does any advantage attach to being the victim of discrimination, where this is the basis of a claim laid against an employer, or a colleague. This advantage, let it be said, is both fleeting and illusory. Even where compensation is made for a wrong, the claimant must present themselves as the wronged party in a way that entrenches that wrong. The act of compensation, so far from hurting employers or higher authorities, enhances their power over the workforce. Where claims are made against peers the damage to all far outweighs any justice achieved. Mutual distrust has long been the quiet backdrop to liberal competition, and in equal opportunities policies that mutual distrust is given the force of just claims against discrimination. In the oppression Olympics, everyone loses.

Intersectionality

The American legal theorist Kimberlé Crenshaw developed a way of addressing the many levels of discrimination, which she called 'intersectional'. She was concerned with the way that black women were made invisible both in anti-racist and feminist movements. 'The problem with identity politics is not that it fails to transcend difference, as some critics charge', she wrote, 'but rather the opposite — that it frequently conflates or ignores intragroup differences'. Moreover, she thought, 'ignoring differences within groups contribute to tension among groups'.[7] Crenshaw's metaphor of an intersection recommended itself to many anti-discrimination activists because it seemed to suggest a way to manage the competing claims of different discriminations. The intersectional approach, though, only leads to more divisions.

The many rifts among the feminist collective that ran the magazine *Spare Rib* anticipated some of the debates that later would test college campuses. First there were arguments over the priority of heterosexual and lesbian feminists, and then, later, between white and black feminists. In 1980 the collective announced that 'personal rifts and political disagreements opened up that had until then lain relatively dormant', so that 'it has been difficult to produce work and get along in a sisterly spirit'. The argument broke out over an article 'about the gap in the movement between heterosexual women and lesbians and the dominance' as one contributor saw it 'of the idea that women should have nothing to do with men'. In reaction, three others thought that 'she expressed her views in anti-lesbian and heterosexist ways and so this article should not be published'.[8] By 1990 it was common for divisions to open up on race lines, so Thethani Sangoma wrote 'as African women we suffer a triple oppression of national, class and gender exploitation'. She chided that for black women, white feminists were one manifestation of the problem. The collective was clearly moved by the appeal of Third World liberation. An editorial in the July 1992 issue looked back over 20 years of *Spare Rib*, but curiously said nothing about women — concentrating instead on 'imperialism's brutal campaign of genocide'. But by that time much of the magazine's readership had fallen away, alienated by the guilt-tripping judgments. Soon afterwards *Spare Rib* closed.

The divisions amongst the feminists grew. Some hoped that socialist feminism would overcome the differences, but it just turned out to be another split. Among the socialist feminists Sheila Rowbotham, Lynne Segal, and Hilary Wainwright wrote a manifesto called *Beyond the Fragments*, which anticipated much of the intersectionality argument. Wainwright thought that it was wrong to merge the movements. 'There are good reasons for each movement controlling its own autonomy — women, blacks, gays, youth and national minorities have interests which may sometimes be antagonistic to each other both now and probably in a socialist society.'9

In 2013 'intersectional' feminism was pointedly excluding what they called 'Trans-Exclusionary Radical Feminists'. The intersectionalists thought that transgender women were women, and welcome in the women's movement, while the Radical Feminists thought they were men, who were not welcome in women-only spaces. The conference organised by the Radical Feminist group was chased underground, as the other camp told the Camden Irish Centre where it was to take place that it would not be safe. When journalists Suzanne Moore and Julie Burchill wrote strident attacks on transsexual demands to be treated as women in the *Guardian* newspaper they were vilified. There was even a protest organised outside the newspaper's office; and astonishingly the Guardian Media Group agreed to rewrite history by removing the article from their website. The struggle for intersectionality continued with the demand that journalist and Justice for Women founder Julie Bindel be refused a platform at a Manchester University Debating Union event on pornography, because she too was a 'TERF' (Bindel withdrew after death threats).

One of the drivers of the college-based debates over identity was the institution since the early 1990s of Student Union women's officers, and later diversity officers.[10] Student Unions have often been the sites of extreme and position-mongering arguments, so polarised because they are of relatively little moment. Student occupations and demonstrations carry less weight than strikes or walkouts in profitable businesses or essential services. All the same, student life has long been an important part of the intellectual culture of the country. Student activism in the 1990s, on the other hand, was in a downward spiral of apathy and disengagement. Women's officers and diversity officers struggled to organise campaigns that justified their offices. Talking to a relatively small group of active students who went to General Meetings, they were rhetorically strident as they were socially unimportant. Still they were fertile ground for the arguments over the intersection of racism and feminism.

In 2015 the whole argument over Trans-Exclusionary Radical Feminism blew up again when the veteran women's rights' activist Germaine Greer (who had written in a similar vein to Julie Burchill) was invited to speak at the University of Cardiff. Trans-activist Payton Quinn, along with the Student Union's women's officer, Rachel Melhuish, organised a petition to ban Greer, which attracted more than a thousand signatures (a counter-petition did similarly well, but was not much noticed). In the event Cardiff University went ahead with the meeting. A picket outside against the 'transphobic' Greer gathered at most 15 protestors.

It was a peculiar thing that the targets of these angry protests seemed more often to be radicals, like the feminists Julie Bindel and Germaine Greer, or like George Galloway and Tony Benn (both pilloried as 'rape apologists' for supporting the internet activist Julian Assange accused of rape), or veteran gay rights campaigner Peter Tatchell (attacked, nonsensically as a 'transphobe', for defending Germaine Greer's right to speak). So too, the films *Stonewall* (about a gay riot against police harassment) and *Suffragette* were both attacked for not including minorities (transgendered in the case of *Stonewall* and black women in the case of *Suffragette*). The champions of intersectionality are never happier than when they are taking down someone who is trying to make a radical case, just not radical enough. As Sigmund Freud told Sandor Ferenczi, 'there is no revolutionary who is not knocked out of the field by a more radical one'.[11]

These storms were largely ignored by the greater part of the population, galvanising only a small minority of activists around discrimination issues. The radical posturing was in inverse proportion to the importance they carried. Intersectionality looked like just another word for sectarianism.

Whiteness and white privilege

New ways of looking at the race question worked out by sociologists in the 1990s turned from investigating the social conditions of ethnic minorities to addressing the way that 'whiteness' was 'constructed'. The argument was that it was a mistake to look at the non-white ethnic group as the exceptional case, and to ignore the dominant race — white people, too, must be put under the microscope.[12] Some of these analyses were generous, even elegiac, like Darcus Howe's Channel 4 series *White Tribe*, or Michael Collins' book, *The Likes of Us* — as if marking the passing of a once-great people.

On the whole, though, the analysis of whiteness is critical, and emphasises the privileged position of whiteness. Ian Macdonald and Gus John outlined the base assumption behind the Race Awareness Training they found in Manchester schools, that 'there is uniform access to power by all whites, and a uniform denial of access and power to all blacks'.[13]

The argument that white Britons were privileged recovered a lot of nineteenth-century ideas, like 'white supremacy', the colour bar, and colonialism. These terms were now highlighted by the critics of 'whiteness' as problems to be attacked, where once they were ideals that were defended by colonists. The out-of-date words are supposed to highlight the way that things have not changed, at least not under the surface. But just as much they show us how much has changed. Colour bars have been illegal in Briton since 1965, and informal discrimination since 1976. Apartheid, the last systematic colour bar in the former Empire, was dismantled in 1994.

The charge that white people in Britain today gain by the disadvantage of black people is true if you look at the question as one of distribution and social averages. Statistical advantage can be demonstrated in the ethnic wage differential, wealth distribution, and employment. However, this is to look at average differentials rather than a substantial relation of exploitation. Working-class white people produce more goods than they ever get back in wages — they are exploited themselves, rather than privileged. Research by the Institute of Fiscal Studies shows that white Britons are less likely to go to university than black and Asian Britons. That recent differential advantage would not prove that black students were 'privileged' as against whites, and certainly not that black students gained at the expense of whites — rather, say the researchers, it is evidence of the underperformance of white working-class school leavers.[14]

The idea of white privilege in a modern setting was outlined by Peggy McIntosh, an associate director of the Wellesley College Center for Research on Women, in her short essay 'White Privilege: Unpacking the Invisible Knapsack'. McIntosh says that 'I have come to see white privilege as an invisible package of unearned assets that I can count on cashing in each day, but about which I was "meant" to remain oblivious'. The privileges that she thinks we take for granted are material goods, like 'I can be pretty sure of renting or purchasing housing in an area that I can afford and in which I would want to live'; and they also include assumptions of respect and civility, such as 'I can be pretty sure that my neighbours in such a location will be neutral or pleasant to me'; and they include spiritual resources, such as 'When I am told about our national heritage or about civilization, I am shown that people of my colour made it what it is'. The list, which includes many more points, is well-made and well-worth looking at, even in the knowledge that it could not be exhaustive.[15]

There is, however, a problem with casting the advantages of 'whiteness', as McIntosh presents them, as privileges. These are for the most part rights of citizenship, not privileges. The meaning of 'privilege' is a private law, such as were enjoyed by feudal lords in the medieval world, an elite minority. To move freely and organise independently, to strike contracts, including contracts of labour, and to take part in the election of the government in Westminster, and locally, as well as participation in the school board — all of these are not privileges, but rights, and rights that were fought for over many generations. Not the privileges of a minority, but the rights of the majority. The struggle against race discrimination has been a struggle to extend those rights so that they are not denied to people on the grounds of colour (as the struggle against sex discrimination was to extend those rights to women). Re-casting those rights as unearned 'privileges' diminishes their validity, in argument (just as these self-same rights are being diminished in fact, by successive government incursions on our civil liberties and rights of representation). A greater attention to the privileges of whiteness comes, ironically, at a time when racial differences carry less weight, and society has committed itself to remedial action to address such inequalities.

Labour's confusions over immigration

One area that remains heavily contested and crucially important is that of immigration to Britain. Under the Blair-Brown governments of 1997-2010 the mood towards immigration oscillated sharply between favourable and unfavourable, as the focus shifted from welcoming migrants, to harsh action against 'illegal' migrants. The UK welcomed an estimated net 1.5 million immigrants in the decade to 2008. Rates of migration changed markedly rising from around 50,000 a year in 1995 to something like three times that number in the years that followed.

In 2000 Minister Barbara Roche gave a speech at the Institute of Public Policy Research. Roche framed the question by contrasting Britain, and its perceived skills gap, and countries including the United States and Australia, who were using migration to grow their economies: 'We are in competition for the brightest and best talents. The market for skilled labour is a global market and not necessarily a buyers' market', she said. The answer was to relax immigration controls and let more in. Roche was cautious and there were some caveats, but the message was clear enough to irritate the opposition Conservative Party. Later, she recalled: 'I wanted to be the first minister to say that migration is a good thing. It is.'[16]

Roche's speech came after a discussion in the Performance and Innovation Unit, Tony Blair's Cabinet Office think-tank. A paper, titled 'RDS Occasional Paper no. 67, Migration: an economic and social analysis', made the argument that more migration was good for Britain. The argument was widely taken up by many. Will Hutton, citing the development economist Nigel Harris, argued that

> as long as demand for labour is buoyant, the existence of a supply of immigrant labour at lower wage rates in some sectors will so boost their fortunes that, by increasing employment overall, incomes and output in aggregate will, in turn, be lifted through spending, begetting more spending in a classic Keynesian multiplier.[17]

Professor of Social Policy Peter Taylor-Gooby wrote that 'immigrants are not a burden on the taxpayer, they are a benefit, because there are not enough children being born in the UK to work and finance our pensions and healthcare'.[18]

Some of the ways that the rules were changed to make them more liberal were: first, the repeal of the 'primary purpose rule' which had made it more difficult for men from the Indian sub-continent to bring their wives to Britain; second, the bringing in of a right of appeal (in 2000) where family visas were not allowed; and also the Human Rights Act (1998) which made it harder to deport people, and gave them rights in British courts from the point that they were in the country.[19]

One of the stranger outcomes of the Race Relations (Amendment) Act of 2000 was that it was 'legal to discriminate on the basis of nationality or ethnic or national origin (but not race or colour)' only 'when ministers expressly authorise this' — and this in particular 'covers the area of immigration, asylum and nationality law'. In other words, the immigration service had to ask express permission if they were going to discriminate. Following the letter of the law, perhaps to absurdity, as reported by the Commission for Racial Equality, 'since April 2001 there have been three ministerial

Labour's schizophrenia on immigration saw them scrambling to appear hard on the question in 2015

authorisations permitting immigration officers to discriminate'. 'The first authorisation allows discrimination when it can be shown that people of a particular nationality have broken, or will try to break, immigration laws', the Commission explained. Further, 'the second authorisation' — to discriminate — 'allows immigration officers to examine passengers from specified groups with particular care'. The groups identified were those of 'Chinese origin presenting a Malaysian or Japanese passport', Kurds, Roma, Albanians, Tamils, Somalis, and Afghans. The Commission registered their objection 'that this could amount to racially discriminatory treatment'. The third authorisation to discriminate allowed immigration officers to 'pilot a project to analyse the language used by asylum seekers from Afghanistan, Somalia and Sri Lanka'.[20] You might have thought that it was impossible to restrict immigration without discrimination. But such was the government's care over the new Race Relations Act that they thought it would be possible to have non-racist immigration controls, and where that was not possible, that it would be best if discrimination was specifically authorised.

According to one of the policy wonks that drew up the original Cabinet policy document, Andrew Neather, the original went even further before it was toned down. He wrote that 'earlier drafts I saw also included a driving political purpose: that mass immigration was the way that the Government was going to make the UK truly multicultural'. More, Neather said, 'I remember coming away from some discussions with the clear sense that the policy was intended — even if this wasn't its main purpose — to rub the Right's nose in diversity and render their arguments out of date'.[21]

These arguments were being made at the height of the re-motivation of the Labour Party as 'New Labour', and indeed the country as 'New Britain', by its youthful Prime Minister, Tony Blair. A speech he gave the year before the change in immigration policy contrasted his vision for a New Britain with the 'forces of conservatism'. The forces of conservatism were all those holding us back. As Blair said, he was for a 'progressive politics distinguishing itself from conservatism of left or right'. Blair argued that these were 'the old prejudices, where foreign means bad', and 'Where multiculturalism is not something to celebrate, but a left-wing conspiracy to destroy their way of life.' The future was coming whether we liked it or not, and 'these forces of change driving the future don't stop at national boundaries.'

In that moment of self-confidence, Blair and his Cabinet believed that increased immigration was a part of the new changes that were making Britain into a multicultural country, one in which the right would not win power again, and where the dinosaurs of 'Old Labour' — in particular the trade union defenders of state socialism — were relegated to obscurity.

The liberal intent of Labour's immigration policy, however, was undermined by their caution about winning over ordinary people to support immigration. They did not — perhaps could not — do that because they had defined their new political project in direct opposition to the party's own working-class base. The old Labour supporters were the 'forces of conservatism', too. A new multicultural Britain was conceived as an escape from Labour's commitments to its heartlands in the formerly industrial north of the country. The Labour Party's psephologists were telling them that most Britons did not like immigration.

One thing was for sure: they did not like the economic argument for immigration, since its premise was that immigration was good for the economy because it would keep wages down. Another kind of movement might have been able to win over working-class support for immigration. But Labour's dilemma was that it thought of immigration and multicultural Britain as a de-throning of the old Labour heartlands. It was for that reason that the Labour Party was nervous about race and immigration.

While Barbara Roche was talking about relaxing inward migration, Home Secretary Jack Straw was cracking down on illegal 'people trafficking'. In April 2000 Straw had himself filmed working alongside the immigration police in Dover. As a truck was searched and a Kosovan stowaway captured, Straw gurned for the cameras and blamed truck drivers for taking money for getting people in. The news that the police would be searching for stowaways had consequences — people took more desperate measures to get through. Fifty-eight Chinese men and women were being smuggled in inside a sealed refrigerated truck. When the lorry was opened all were suffocated. Straw said that the deaths were a 'stark warning to others' who might be tempted to come. It was an ugly moment that showed the other side of the government's immigration policy.

Over the winter of 2008-09, workers at the Lindsey oil refinery in North Lincolnshire walked out on strike, protesting at the company's preference for contract labour from Portugal and other European countries. Prime Minister Gordon Brown was at pains to say that he supported the case of 'British jobs for British workers'. A Downing Street spokesman explained that the contracts had been issued for foreign labour when there was a labour shortage in Britain, which was 'obviously not now the case'.[22]

Some Labour supporters were already hostile to immigration, before Gordon Brown's *volte face*. David Goodhart, the *Prospect* editor and most recently director of Demos, makes the argument that social democratic government must control its own borders. So, too, does the veteran commentator Polly Toynbee argue that immigrants 'hold down the pay rate for all other low-paid workers, keeping wage inflation remarkably low and the Bank of England very happy'. Of Tony Blair and Gordon Brown, Toynbee says they 'embrace the inevitability of globalisation, but make a deliberately class-blind analysis' — meaning that immigration hurts the working class. Toynbee's argument makes sense if you see the working class as bounded by national borders, and all of those migrants marooned in Calais as outside of the working class (the 'British working class', perhaps). The force of her argument is that the case for immigration that was being made by the government was a case for boosting profits at the expense of workers: 'Of course the wealthy want an immigration free-for-all', she writes.[23] But the case that should be made is the one that sees working-class solidarity that goes beyond national borders — which is a case for defending workers' rights to free movement alongside a defence of workers' wages, as well as their political right to be consulted about a change in policy, rather than have a policy surreptitiously foisted upon them.

In the election the following year, Labour were clearly on the defensive about their immigration policy. They were seen to have foisted an unwanted immigration on a sceptical public. To liberally-minded people it was a concession to listen to those who were sceptical about immigration. But that was the problem. Ordinary people needed to be won over if it was to be more than an elite policy to hold down wages. In the middle of the election campaign Gordon Brown was persuaded to talk to a voter, Gillian Duffy, who was critical of the policy. The exchange was forced, and the Prime Minister, not known for his personal touch, was struggling to make the case. Worse, when he moved on, he forgot that his television microphone was still attached to his lapel. In the car Brown was recorded telling his handlers 'that was a disaster'. But it was his view of Duffy that stood out: 'Ugh everything! She's just a sort of bigoted woman that said she used to be Labour. I mean it's just ridiculous. I don't know why Sue brought her up towards me.' It was a turning point in the election. Everyone could see that it was Brown who was bigoted — bigoted in his contempt for Gillian Duffy. For Labour, the idea of winning working-class voters over to immigration was too hard. First they tried to bring in the policy round the voters' backs. And then when that failed the party simply reversed its policy, and clamped down on immigration.

Since the Conservative-Liberal Democrat coalition government took office in 2010, and since the majority Conservative administration was elected in 2015, there has been a surprising continuity in policy over immigration. Government policy still remains committed to race equality in Britain — most recently launching a new campaign to advance progress towards equality early in 2016 — while at the same time promising to stem inward migration. Politicians were talking tough on immigration, but still people came, adding to the sense that the politicians were lying, and allowing it to happen without admitting that it was happening. The great weakness of those who favoured a more liberal immigration policy was that they had not won a political consensus in favour of greater migration, but were believed to have connived at that result. The widespread feeling that immigration had not helped poorer communities in the country's depressed industrial towns doubtless added to the vote to leave the European Union in the 2016 referendum. Fears that the referendum campaign itself would provoke greater hostility to migrants were demonstrated by a spike in recorded race attacks. The difficulty for the 'Vote to Remain' camp was that they were seen to be the establishment, whereas as the 'Leavers' spoke to a large swathe of England that felt that it had lost out in the globalised economy.

Multicultural Britain?

As we have seen, social disorder in Bradford and Oldham in 2001 caused something of a re-think on race in Britain, and in particular about the merits of the multicultural society. Herman Ouseley's report on the Bradford riots — cautiously — echoed some of the points that Gus John and Ian Macdonald made in their inquiry into Manchester's schools, that some of the policies to promote the social integration of ethnic minorities had had the opposite effect, leading to division, and even social apartheid. The point was taken up by Trevor Phillips when he took over at the Commission for Racial Equality. Are we, he asked, 'sleepwalking into segregation'?[24] It was an extended argument which, he despaired, had been edited down into three words 'Multiculturalism is dead'.

Phillips explained himself at length in an article, where he said:

The institutional response to the demand for inclusion has been cynical and bureaucratic — a series of bribes designed to appease community leaders coupled with gestures to assuage liberal guilt, while leaving systemic racism and inequality untouched. Multiculturalism is in danger of becoming a sleight of hand in which ethnic minorities are distracted by tokens of recognition, while being excluded from the real business. The smile of recognition has turned into a rictus grin on the face of institutional racism.[25]

Phillips' argument was not so different from the criticism of 'tokenism' that black activists made against the Commission for Racial Equality back in the late Seventies. This time, though, it was being made by the chair of the Commission for Racial Equality. Phillips was saying that the policy that was supposed to fix division was actually disguising it, even contributing to it.

Another approach was argued by Munira Mirza, London's Deputy Mayor for Education and Culture. Mirza talked about the improvements in the lot of black people in Britain, but asked whether the legislation was helping. She highlighted the Equality Act (2000) and the duty it put on 43,000 public authorities 'to promote good relations between persons of different racial groups'. As Mirza explained, this obligation has 'spawned an industry of behaviour management and control in workplaces, schools, fire stations, hospitals, councils and government departments'. As she saw it, 'Hard-pressed public institutions are required to employ ethnic monitors, diversity trainers and equality impact assessors in order to guard against costly legal action'. The question remained, 'does this heightened awareness of racism help to stamp it out?' Mirza's answer was surprising: 'Quite the opposite. It creates a climate of suspicion and anxiety. Suddenly your colleague is a potential victim of your

Trevor Phillips

unwitting racism. A minor slight can be seen as an offence.'[26] Mirza was pointing to one unexpected consequence of the way that society had changed to accommodate equal opportunities.

One way to understand the point is to look at the contradictory evidence on race prejudice. By one measure, the evidence would seem to be that race prejudice today is getting worse. That measure is the result of an opinion poll survey question: 'Do you think race relations in Britain are getting worse?' The answer is that nearly half think that race prejudice has got worse, while less than a third think it has got better. Those are depressing results. But they are not the whole story. They are questions about what people think other people are like. Other kinds of questions ask about what respondents themselves feel about race. These get different results. There are two questions: one is 'Would you mind working for an employer who was black or Asian?'; the other is 'Would you mind being married to someone who is black or Asian?' This question has been asked by pollsters for many years now, so that we have a time series mapping of this particular expression of prejudice. Two things stand out. The first is that over time fewer people are offended by the idea of working for someone of another race, as fewer are offended by the idea of marrying someone of another race. The second thing is that attitudes become consistently more liberal the younger the respondent.[27] Put together the two different poll results point to a remarkable outcome. First people are pessimistic about race relations, thinking that they are getting worse. The second is that individually, white people are becoming more liberal, less prejudiced against black and brown people. Munira Mirza's vision of a society that is managing racial divisions quite well on an informal basis in its own civil interactions, but at an institutional level is distrustful of people's abilities to cope with racial difference, is right.

The criticism of multiculturalism that Phillips and Mirza had made, that the policies might prove more divisive than unifying, were taken up by Britain's new Prime Minister David Cameron in February 2011. Cameron's speech was in part a response to the continuing challenge of Al Qaeda to British foreign policy, and the perception that Islamic extremists in Britain were not being confronted. Cameron argued that 'state multiculturalism has failed'.

A genuinely liberal country 'believes in certain values and actively promotes them', he said, outlining what he meant: 'Freedom of speech. Freedom of worship. Democracy. The rule of law. Equal rights, regardless of race, sex or sexuality.' Cameron went on to argue that under the 'doctrine of state multiculturalism', different cultures have been encouraged to live separate lives.

Reaction to Cameron's speech was dogmatic. Hassan Mahmadallie argued that Cameron was wrong because 'the notion that multiculturalism was ever an official state policy is simply not true' — and this in a volume entitled *Defending Multiculturalism*. Salma Yaqoob argued that 'Cameron's latest attack on our multicultural society is only a continuation' of Trevor Phillips' arguments.[28] Substantially, however, it was hard to see what the differences were between Cameron and his critics. Both sides believed in social solidarity, and both sides believed in defending minority rights. The argument just seemed to be another example of the 'call-out culture', where the Prime Minister's critics were keen to portray him as a racist, to score political points.

Looking back at the contradictions of the equal opportunities revolution, what stands out is that the top-down anti-discrimination measures reveal themselves to be instruments of labour discipline, in the hands of the employers and the authorities, to dominate employees. Even where these acts of domination are in favour of minorities, they enhance the power of the elite over the mass. More, the policies derive their power from division. Diversity in the workforce, diversity in society, must be managed. As Kimberlé Crenshaw argues it, diversity is not to be overcome, but maintained and formalised. Policies and organisations that were supposed to help to address inequality have ended up institutionalising it.

Conclusion

Between 1975 and 1995 Britain underwent a revolution in relations at work that saw women and black people overturn the subordinate role they had played in the workforce. Workplace reform echoed a wider debate in society about equality, and a change that came with far greater numbers of women and black and Asian people in the workplace.

Sexism and racism were not abolished, but discrimination at work was first outlawed, and then companies adopted policies to promote equal opportunities. In particular, the decade 1980-90 is the decade in which equal opportunities policies became the norm — at the beginning of that decade only Camden and Lambeth Councils had an equal opportunities policy, but by the end most employees in Britain were covered by equal opportunities policies.

The timing of the equal opportunities policy is surprising. It coincides with a government that was known for its hostility to workers' rights, for its aggressive policies of policing black youth and immigrants, and for its traditional, family-oriented outlook.

The settlement between labour and capital that was made in the late nineteenth century, and institutionalised in the twentieth, was dismantled from 1980 onwards. That settlement was based upon a hierarchy of working men, the idea at least of the family wage, with women as a reserve army of labour; further it bedded down a patriotic feeling for a corporatist state, with a promise to organised labour in Britain that it was more highly regarded than migrant labour. Though those two strands of sex and colour chauvinism were stated yet more firmly by government in the 1980s, the social institutions they were built upon were being dismantled in the name of a free market in labour. Against their explicit intentions, the Conservative government opened up the labour market to women and to black Britons, when it tore up the post-war social consensus. Equal opportunities policies seemed to be coming from a very different place than the anti-union laws. But they did make sense to employers who were looking for a new agreement with their workforces. The equal opportunities revolution supplanted the old social democratic consensus, which, while it was generous to labour, was hierarchical as regards sex and colour.

The first take-up of equal opportunities policies, by London's left-wing Labour councils, was in a spirit of opposition to the Conservative government, and their promotion by the two Commissions — for Racial Equality and Equal Opportunities — were cold-shouldered by Whitehall. Over time, though, many more employers in the private as well as the public sector took up equal opportunities policies. They did so for many reasons, often because they felt they had to comply with the law, and with European directives, but increasingly because they felt they were both morally right and also good business sense.

It is a view that has been backed up again and again. In 2015, McKinsey looked at what diversity did for business in '366 public companies across a range of industries in Canada, Latin America, the United Kingdom, and the United States'. They worked out that 'Companies in the top quartile for racial and ethnic diversity are 35 percent more likely to have financial returns above their respective national industry medians'. They found that gender diversity put you 15% ahead.[1]

Behind the business case for equal opportunities lay a fear on the part of employers that they needed a moral motivation for their authority. Gaining by the reorganisation of industry, and having shed their prior commitments to partnership with trade unions, employers' equal opportunities policies recreated a sense that both sides of industry were in it together. After a decade of harsh conflict at work, rebuilding their reputation as 'equal opportunity employers' was an important moral appeal to their own workers, and to wider society.

The old order that the new Human Resource Management replaced was one that had raised up the industrial worker as a partner at work. That old order was struck with organisations that had their roots in a workforce in which women and immigrant workers were second-class. The defeat of organised labour in the many struggles of the 1980s did have the surprising result of opening up the labour market to those formerly excluded women and migrant workers. Jamie Allinson says 'neo-liberal capitalism positing the rights of an abstract market individual against inherited practices, has permitted much more progress on "social" questions'.[2] It is worth noting that the progress on the social questions has not dislodged, but rather reinforced the authority of employers over the workforces.

The quasi-governmental commissions, the EOC and the CRE, were often mocked for their tokenistic and piecemeal approach. Much of that criticism was justified. But the shift in social attitudes that they register is an important measure of the real struggles that ordinary women and men engaged in to win their rights. The outcome of those struggles was mixed.

The equal opportunities revolution came about with the defeat of organised labour. Bringing more women and more migrants into a greatly expanded workforce has not hurt business, but on the contrary, helped it to grow. The relative social position of women and of migrants has improved — too slowly, but it has improved all the same. But the overall position of the working classes relative to their employers has greatly suffered. Inequality of incomes, and more so, inequality of wealth, has opened up while equal opportunities between sexes and races has improved.

The intensity of work has also got worse. And double-income households are time-poor as they are work-rich. Hugh Cunningham points to:

The entry of married women into the workforce, the increase in hours of work in key sectors of the economy, the evidence of greater intensity of that work, the removal since the 1970s of what were regarded as impediments to a flexible labour force, but were actually means of preventing the crisis in time use that is wrapped up and concealed by talking about work-life balance.[3]

To be employed is to be used. What we call equality in employment is the right to be used. We measure the increase in equal opportunities in the subordination of ever greater numbers of people to the wage labour-capital relation.

At work, and in society generally, the questions of sex and race are in one sense greatly improved. Discrimination at work as in wider society is largely illegal and morally repugnant to most. But our perceptions are that these relations are more difficult than ever. The formal systems for managing sex and race relations at work have problematized them, and increased our sensitivity to conflict. Ironically, the real positions of the sexes, and of people of different races, are much closer than they have been. The divisions of the past, where men worked and women stayed at home, are long gone. There are many more racially mixed relationships and racially mixed people than before. But at the same time there is a greater pessimism about race relations, and also about relations between the sexes.

The aspiration to equality is a powerful driving force in a modern society. It has pushed forward the equal opportunities revolution. The yearning for equality is strong first because it is already present in the mutual respect that people feel they owe one another, as the basis of all possible interaction; but at the same time, we feel defensive of equality because it is so often thwarted by the great inequalities of wealth and social power. Most people feel a strong affinity with the stories of oppression and liberation that we tell ourselves again and again. We identify with the struggle of the civil rights leaders in America and the anti-Apartheid movement in South Africa, as we do with the Suffragettes' fight for the vote, the Dagenham women's struggle for equal pay, and the Stonewall rioters' fight for respect. That identification comes from the real sense that many feel that their own status is undermined, and that the dominant fist hides behind the façade of equality. The structures of inequality are changing all the time. To meet the challenges of the twenty-first century we must address what is emerging, as well as the decaying order that has held us back.

Notes

Introduction

1 Barbara Kersley et al, *Inside the Workplace: Findings from the 2004 WERS,* London, Routledge, 2006, p 237; *New Equals,* Commission for Racial Equality, 11 April 1980

2 1.76 million Asians; 757,010 black Africans and Afro-Caribbeans; and 700,000 mixed-race and other non-white people. Office for National Statistics, 'Ethnicity and the Labour Market', 2011 Census, England and Wales, 13 November 2014

3 Jen Beaumont Population, *Social Trends* 41, London, Office for National Statistics, 2011, p 6

4 'Life in the United Kingdom', Home Office, HMSO, 2002, p 42, 45

5 *Derby Daily Telegraph*, 25 November 1885

6 *Coventry Standard*, 14 June 1918

7 *Yorkshire Post*, 13 March 1943

8 *Free to Choose*, Harcourt Brace Jovanovich, New York, 1980, p 128

9 Ibid, p 133

10 Ibid, p 128

11 *Western Mail*, 31 January 1914

12 *Walsall Observer*, 24 March 1917

13 *Western Daily Press*, 1 July 1927

14 *Hull Daily Mail*, 31 December 1929

15 *Western Morning News*, 18 June 1936

16 Labour Party Manifesto, 1950

17 Conservative Manifesto, 1950, http://www.politicsresources.net/area/uk/man/con50.htm

18 Labour Manifesto, 1955

19 Nancy Seear, Veronica Roberts, John Brock, *A Career for Women in Industry*, London, LSE, 1964, p 2

20 Beatrix Campbell, *Iron Ladies*, London, Virago, 1987 gives a good account of the Conservative Party's appeal to housewives

21 TUC Congress Report, 1965

22 Conservative Party Manifesto, 1970, http://www.politicsresources.net/area/uk/man/con70.htm

23 February 1974, http://www.politicsresources.net/area/uk/man/lab74feb.htm

24 Rebecca Solnit, *Hope in the Dark*, Nation Books, 2005, p 82

25 David Perfect, 'Briefing paper 2, Gender pay gaps', Equality and Human Rights Commission

26 Brynin and Güveli, 'Understanding the ethnic pay gap in Britain', *Work, employment and society* 26(4), p 574–87

Chapter One

1 Eric Hobsbawm, *Industry and Empire*, London, Weidenfeld and Nicholson, 1969, p 93, 94; Richard Croucher, *Engineers at War*, London, Merlin Press, 1982, p 2

2 'Ethnicity and National Identity in England and Wales 2011', Office for National Statistics, 11 December 2012; 'A Vision of Britain through time' University of Portsmouth, 2009-2014, http://www.visionofbritain.org.uk/census/SRC_P/5/EW1911GEN

3 Minqi Li, Feng Xiao, and Andong Zhu, *Long Waves, Institutional Changes, and Historical Trends: A Study of the Long-Term Movement of the Profit Rate in the Capitalist World-Economy*, p 40 — they define: 'Profit rate = profit / net stock of private non-residential fixed capital'; Eric Williams wrote in his account of slavery's contribution

to capitalist take-off, *Capitalism and Slavery*, that 'it must not be inferred that the triangular trade was solely and entirely responsible for the economic development. The growth of the internal market in England, the ploughing-in of the profits from industry to generate still further capital and achieve a still greater expansion, played a large part. But this industrial development, stimulated by mercantilism, later outgrew mercantilism and destroyed it.' New York, Capricorn Books, 1966, p 105–6

4 Karl Marx, *Capital* I, Chapter 16, Progress, Moscow, 1974, p 477

5 Maxine Berg, 'Women's Work, Mechanisation and the early phases of industrialisation in Britain', in *The Historical Meanings of Work*, Patrick Joyce (ed), Cambridge University Press, 1987, p 73

6 Marx to Siegfried Mayer, 9 April 1870, https://www.marxists.org/archive/marx/works/1870/letters/70_04_09.htm

7 30 August 1883, https://www.marxists.org/archive/marx/works/1883/letters/83_08_30.htm

8 Christopher Kyriakides and Rodolfo Torres, *Race Defaced: Paradigms of Pessimism, Politics of Possibility*, Stanford University Press, 2012, p 55

9 Marx to Siegfried Mayer, 9 April 1870, https://www.marxists.org/archive/marx/works/1870/letters/70_04_09.htm

10 'Gendered Discourses and the Making of Protective Labor Legislation in England, 1830–1914', *Journal of British Studies* 37(2), April 1998, p 166; Harriet Martineau, *Illustrations of Political Economy*

11 Quoted in Marx, *Capital* I, p 267

12 House of Commons, 12 March 1869, Hansard, vol. 194 § 1209

13 Hugh Cunningham, *The Invention of Childhood*, London, BBC, 2006, p 166, 172

14 Jane Lewis, *Labour and Love: Women's Experience of Home and Family, 1850-1940*, Basil Blackwell, 1986, p 104

15 G. D. H. Cole and Raymond Postgate, *The Common People*, London, Methuen, 1961, p 426; Gareth Stedman Jones, *Outcast London*, Harmondsworth, Penguin, 1976, p 318

16 HC Deb, 26 April 1876, vol 228, §1697; HC Deb, 16 March 1886, vol 303, §1016; HC Deb, 14 March 1884, vol 285, §1596

17 Hilary Land, 'The Family Wage', *Feminist Review* 6, 1980, p 72 (Beveridge quoted), 60 (Arthur Howley quoted); Sara Horrell and Jane Humphries, 'The origins and expansion of the male breadwinner family', *International Review of Social History* 42, 1997, supplement, p 31

18 Catherine Hakim, *Work-Lifestyle Choices in the Twentieth Century*, Oxford, University Press, 2000, p 59; Chiozza Money, *Riches and Poverty*, London, Methuen, 1905, p 169; Alison Wolf, 'Working Girls', *Prospect*, April 2006

19 Richard Price, *Labour in British Society*, London, Routledge, 1986, p 158, 145

20 J.T. Murphy, *Modern Trade Unionism*, London, Routledge, 1935, p 7

21 To the *Daily Mail*, in 1909, quoted in José Harris, *Unemployment and Politics*, Oxford, Clarendon, 1972, p 346

22 R. Michels, *Political Parties*, London, Simon and Schuster, 1966, p 282

23 Quoted in Bill Fishman, *East End Jewish Radicals*, London, Duckworth, 1995, p 77

24 Quoted in ibid, p 78

25 Joseph Buckman, *Immigrants and the Class Struggle: The Jewish Immigrant in Leeds, 1880-1914*, Manchester University Press, 1983, p 132

26 HL Deb, 3 August 1905, vol 151, §19

27 Christopher Addison, *Four and A Half Years*, vol I, London, Hutchinson, 1934, p 225, 163

28 Ibid, p 168; Charlotte Drake, 13 April 1915, in *Sylvia Pankhurst: The Home Front*, London, Cresset Library, 1987, p 160

29 J. T. Murphy, *Modern Trade Unionism*, London, Routledge, 1935, p 7

30 Quotes taken from Robert Clough, *Labour: A Party Fit for Imperialism*, London, Larkin, 1992, p 90, 92, 97

31 Ralph Darlington, Dave Lyddon, *Glorious Summer*, London, Bookmarks, 2001, p 6, 9

32 Huw Benyon, *Working for Ford*, Harmondsworth, Penguin, 1973, p 66

33 'The Institutional Face at Ministerial Level', in *The Changing Institutional Face of British Employment Relations*, Linda Dickens, Alan Neal (eds), Biggleswade, Kluwer, 2006, p 19

34 HC Deb, 8 November 1976, vol 919, §27

35 Keith Middlemas, *Politics in Industrial Society*, London, Andre Deutsch, 1979, p 422, 408; 'Mr. Butskell's Dilemma', *Economist*, 13 February 1954, p 439

36 Sir William Beveridge, *Social Insurance and Allied Services*, London, HMSO, reprinted 1966, p 7

37 Ibid, p 10–11

38 Ibid, p 49

39 Ibid, p 50

40 Ibid, p 51–2

41 Peter Yuen, *Compendium of Health Statistics- 2005-2006*, Office of Health Economics, Oxford, Radcliffe Publishing, 2005, p 142

42 Quoted in Irene Bruegel, 'Anne Gray, The Future of Work and the Division of Childcare between Parents', *Social Science Research Papers* 18, London South Bank University, March 2004

43 Keith Middlemas, *Politics in Industrial Society*, London, Andre Deutsch, 1979, p 391, 392

44 Kate Marshall, *Real Freedom*, London, Junius, 1982, p 79

45 Kathleen Paul, *Whitewashing Britain: Race and Citizenship in the Postwar Era*, Ithaca, Cornell University Press, 1997, p 115

46 Ibid, p 127; P. Hennessy, *Prime Minister: the office and its holders since 1945*, London, Penguin, 2001, p 205

47 House of Commons, 23 March 1964

48 Commission for Racial Equality Annual Report, 1986, p 18

49 Published in 1971 by New Beacon Books; see also Beverly Bryan et al, *The Heart of the Race*, London, Virago, 1985, p 70–71. My mother, who was a teacher in Effra Road Junior School at the time,

knew the book and Coard's argument well. For contemporary segregation in schools by choice, see Sean Coughlan, 'Study reveals school segregation', BBC, 6 July 2015, http://www.bbc.co.uk/news/education-33409111

50 Robert Clough, *Labour: A Party Fit for Imperialism*, London, Larkin, 1992, p 158

51 Race Today Collective, *"The Struggles of Asian Workers in Britain"*, London, Race Today, 1983, p 8

52 *Race Today*, May/June 1982, p 96

53 *Race Today*, March 1983, p 210

54 Beverly Bryan et al, *The Heart of the Race*, London, Virago, 1985, p 45

55 Ann Kramer, *Many Rivers to Cross*, London, The Stationery Office, 2006; BBC: On This Day, '1966: Euston staff 'colour bar ended', http://news.bbc.co.uk/onthisday/hi/dates/stories/july/15/newsid_3043000/3043439.stm; Keith Thompson, *Under Siege*, London, Penguin, 1988, p 72

56 Barbara Castle, *The Castle Diaries 1964-70*, London, Weidenfeld and Nicolson, 1984, p 562

57 HL Deb, 18 March 1969, vol 300, §743

58 'The Institutional Face at Ministerial Level', in *The Changing Institutional Face of British Employment Relations*, Linda Dickens, Alan Neal (eds), Biggleswade, Kluwer, 2006, p 19

59 Will Podmore, *Reg Birch*, London, Bellman Books, 2004, p 161–2

60 *Guardian*, 11 July 2012, http://www.theguardian.com/commentisfree/2012/jul/11/frances-ogrady-tuc-sexism-union

61 Race Today Collective, *The Struggles of Asian Workers in Britain*, London, Race Today, 1983, p 21–22

62 *Sunday Times*, 2 November 1975

63 Neil Millward, Alex Bryson, and John Forth, *All Change at Work?*, London, Routledge, p 224

64 Margaret Thatcher on 'tripartism', *The Downing Street Years*, London, Harper Collins, 1995, p 7, 141; Nigel Lawson, *The View from Number 11*, London, Corgi, 1993, p 432

65 Linda Dickens and Alan Neal, 'Changing Times, Changing Needs' in *The Changing Institutional Face of British Employment Relations*, Linda Dickens, Alan Neal (eds), Biggleswade, Kluwer, 2006, p 5

66 Neil Millward, Alex Bryson, and John Forth, *All Change at Work?*, London, Routledge, p 225

67 Richard Cracknell and Rob Clements, 'Acts and Statutory Instruments: the volume of UK legislation 1950 to 2014', House of Commons library, 19 March 2014, http://researchbriefings.files.parliament.uk/documents/SN02911/SN02911.pdf

68 Kathleen Paul, *Whitewashing Britain: Race and Citizenship in the Postwar Era*, Ithaca, Cornell University Press, 1997, p 182, 183

69 Keith Thompson, *Under Siege*, London Penguin, 1988, p 77–9

70 Ibid, p 80

71 Ibid, p 21

72 'Ethnic unemployment in Britain (1972-2012)', 15 January 2014, http://www.racecard.org.uk/finance/ethnic-unemployment-in-britain/

73 Margaret Thatcher, *The Downing Street Years*, London, Harper Collins, 1995, p 628, 627

74 *Guardian*, 9 September 1979

Chapter Two

1 H. Hodson, 'Race Relation in the Commonwealth', *International Affairs* 26(3), July 1950, p 305

2 HC Deb, 3 May 1965, vol 711, §926

3 *Guardian*, 28 November 1963; Robin G. D. Kelley and Stephen Tuck, *The Other Special Relationship*, Palgrave Macmillan, 2015, p 48

4 Speech to the Lord Mayor's Banquet, reported in the *Guardian*, 17 November 1964

5 Commonwealth Immigrants Bill, HL Deb, 29 February 1968, vol 289, cc917–1217

6 'Wilson Hits Out on Housing', *Observer*, 20 Sept 1964

7 'Mr Wilson Blamed on Colour', *Guardian*, 9 October 1964

8 Robin G. D. Kelley and Stephen Tuck, *The Other Special Relationship*, Palgrave Macmillan, 2015, p 51

9 See Gavin Schaffer, *The Vision of a Nation: Making Multiculturalism on British Television, 1960-80*, Palgrave, 2014, footnote 226, p 142

10 Race Relations Bill, HC Deb, 23 April 1968, vol 763, §53

11 Race Relations Bill, HC Deb, 4 March 1976, vol 906

12 See John Williams' biography, *Michael X*, London, 2008; and Robin Bunce and Paul Field, *Darcus Howe*, London, Bloomsbury, London, 2014

13 Robin Bunce and Paul Field, *Darcus Howe*, London, Bloomsbury, London, 2014, p 157

14 The Moonshot Club had been the target of many attempts to burn it down, and was set on fire in 1978. *New Equals* 2, February 1978

15 *Race Today*, February/March 1982, p 68

16 This preamble is taken from 'Draft Code of Practice', Commission for Racial Equality, November 1982, and is reproduced in many of their documents around that time

17 *New Equals* 1(1), November 1977, p 1

18 Ibid, p 4

19 'Draft Code of Practice', Commission for Racial Equality, November 1982, p 3

20 '1.1 The Responsibility of Employers, Draft Code of Practice', Commission for Racial Equality, November 1982, p 4

21 See Norman Tebbit, *Upwardly Mobile*, London, Futura, 1989, for a defence of management's right to manage

22 HC Deb, 15 July 1981, vol 8, cc407-8W 407W

23 In M. Anwar, P. Roach, R. Sondhi, *From Legislation to Integration? Race Relations in Britain*, Basingstoke, Macmillan in association with Centre for Research in Ethnic Relations, University of Warwick, 2000, p. 84

24 Margaret Thatcher saved James Anderton from moves to sack him in 1986, state documents revealed. *Manchester Evening News*, 17 January 2013, http://www.manchestereveningnews.co.uk/news/greater-manchester-news/revealed-secret-documents-show-how-678786

25 John Torode, 'Interview: Herman Ouseley', *Independent*, 24 April 1993, http://www.independent.co.uk/voices/interview-a-victim-takes-control-herman-ouseley-the-commission-for-racial-equality-is-riven-by-1457330.html

Chapter Three

1 Anne Perkins, *Red Queen*, London, Macmillan, 2003, p 327

2 26 January 1941, in Sheila Lahr, *Yealm*, London, Unkant, 2015, p 374

3 Mary Davis, 'An Historical Introduction to the Campaign for Equal Pay', http://unionhistory.info/equalpay/roaddisplay.php?irn=820

4 Anne Perkins, *Red Queen*, p 327

5 Industrial Charter for Women and Report of the 33rd Annual Conference of Representatives of Trade Unions Catering for Women Workers, TUC, 1963

6 Anne Perkins, *Red Queen*, p 328

7 J. Hunt and S. Adams, *Women, Work and Trade Union Organisation*, London, 1980, p 15

8 Nancy Seear, Veronica Roberts, John Brock, *A Career for Women in Industry*, LSE, 1964, p 2

9 Tony Cliff, *Class Struggle and Women's Liberation*, Chapter 11, https://www.marxists.org/archive/cliff/works/1984/women/11-wmvmtb.htm

10 Anne Perkins, *Red Queen*, p 328

11 Barbara Castle, *Diaries, 1964-70*, London, Weidenfeld and Nicolson, 1984, p 465–6, entry for 22 June 1968

12 Anne Perkins, *Red Queen*, p 328

13 *Diaries, 1964-70*, London, Weidenfeld and Nicolson, 1984, p 475, entry for 27 June 1968

14 Ibid, p 476

15 Ibid, p 532–5, entries for 18 October 1968

16 Ibid, p 711, 713, entries for 25 September and 29 September 1969; p 756, entry for 27 January 1970

17 Ibid, p 707, 9 December 1969

18 *EOC News*, December 1978, p 3

19 *EOC News*, October/November 1980, p 2

20 EOC Annual Report, 1977, p 53

21 EOC Annual Report, 1977, p 4

22 *EOC News*, June 1979, p 4–5; Alan Marsh, *Women and Shiftwork: The Protective Legislation*, survey by HMSO, 1979

23 EOC Annual Report, 1977, p 11

24 *EOC News*, March 1978, p 8; May 1978, p 7; July 1978, p 4

25 *EOC News*, July 1978, p 7

26 Quoted in *EOC News*, May 1978, p 8

27 EOC Annual Report, 1977, p 10; *EOC News*, December 1978, p 1

28 'Equality between the sexes in industry: how far have we come?', EOC, 1978, p 13, 14

29 Ibid, p 15

30 *EOC News*, December 1978, p 1

31 EOC Annual Report, 1977, p 10

32 EOC Annual Report, 1985, p 1, 2

33 EOC Annual Report, 1985, p 5

34 'Putting Gender on the Agenda — EOC — Annual Report and Accounts 2000/2001', p 15

35 Irene Bruegel and Diane Perrons, 'Deregulation and Woman's Employment: the diverse experience of women in Britain', LSE Gender Institute, Discussion Paper Series, October 1996, p 12

36 EOC Annual Report, 1985, p 1

37 *EOC News*, 2 May 1978, p 5

38 EOC Annual Report, 1982, p 2

39 J. Earle and J. Phillips, 'Equal Pay: Why the Acts Don't Work', *Spare Rib* 86, September 1979, p 22

40 EOC Annual Report, 1985, p 10–11

41 'Equality in the 21st Century, Annual Report and Accounts, 1999-2000', Equal Opportunities Commission, 7 December 2000, p 4

42 According to Ina Zweiniger-Bargielowska, *Women in Twentieth-Century Britain: Social, Cultural and Political Change*, London, Routledge 2014, p 286

43 Beatrix Campbell, *Iron Ladies*, London, Virago, 1987, p 213

44 See reports in the *Independent*, 31 January 1995, by Barrie Clement; and 21 January 1996, by Nick Cohen

45 Listen to the discussion with Dr Steve Davies, *Women's Hour*, 9 June 2011, http://www.bbc.co.uk/programmes/b011pldp; and see Sue Jackson, *Networking Women... Women's Studies International Forum* 23(1), 2000, p 1–11

Chapter Four

1 Commission for Racial Equality, 'Annual Report', 1986, p 26, 24

2 Martin Boddy and Colin Fudge, *Local Socialism*, London, Macmillan, 1985, p 5, 7; see also David Regan, *The Local Left*, Centre for Policy Studies, London, 1987

3 In Martin Boddy and Colin Fudge, *Local Socialism*, London, Macmillan, 1985, p 270

4 John Carvel, *Turn Again Livingstone*, London, Profile, 1999, p 4

5 'Policy Invitation', *New Equals* 18, Summer 1982, p 2

6 'Living and Working Together', Islington Council, produced by Islington Council's Press, Campaign and Publicity Unit and the Race Equality Unit [n.d.]

7 'Racial Disadvantage in Lambeth — A Council for Community Relations in Lambeth', Report to Lambeth Council, May 1978, p 1. Today black people make up one quarter of 310,000 residents, the

major difference is that there are as many black Africans as Afro-Caribbeans today, whereas most in 1977 were Afro-Caribbean, Lambeth State of the Borough, 2014.

8 Herman Ouseley with Daniel Silverstone and Usha Prashar, *The System*, London, Runnymede Trust, and South London Equal Rights Consultancy, 1983, p 101

9 'The Spitalfields Survey: Housing and Social Conditions in 1980', CHAS, reported in *New Equals* 17, Spring 1982, p 11

10 'Racial Disadvantage in Lambeth — A Council for Community Relations in Lambeth', Report to Lambeth Council, May 1978, p 3

11 *New Equals*, August 1978, p 6

12 *New Equals* 2, February 1978, p 8; 'EOC News', March 1978, p 2

13 'Racial Disadvantage in Lambeth – A Council for Community Relations in Lambeth', Report to Lambeth Council, May 1978, p 3

14 Herman Ouseley with Daniel Silverstone and Usha Prashar, *The System*, London, Runnymede Trust, and South London Equal Rights Consultancy, 1983, p 22

15 Ted Knight, *Marxism Today*, January 1981, p 12

16 *Equals* 1, July 1983, p 1

17 Livingstone Interview, Martin Boddy and Colin Fudge, *Local Socialism*, London, Macmillan, 1985, p 270

18 Sue Goss, 'Women's Initiatives in Local Government', in Boddy and Fudge, *Local Socialism*, London Macmillan, 1985, p 111

19 'Women and training', *Equals* 1, July 1983, p 2

20 *Equals* 2, October 1983, p 2

21 'Women and training', *Equals* 1, July 1983, p 2

22 Quoted in Sheila Rowbotham, *The Past is Before Us*, London, Pandora, 1989, p 140

23 Sue Goss, 'Women's Initiatives in Local Government', in Boddy and Fudge, *Local Socialism*, London, Macmillan, 1985, p 110

24 *Equals* 1, July 1983, p 3

25 'On the Road to Equality', First Annual Equal Opportunities Monitoring Report 1983-4, GLC, p 1

26 Labour Research, May 1986

27 'Equality Moves Forward', GLC Equal Opportunities Second Annual Monitoring Report, p 2

28 Keith Thompson, *Under Siege*, London, 1988, p 123

29 Richard Aldrich, *Public or Private Education*, London, Routledge, 2004, p 93

30 Commission for Race Equality, 'From Words to Action: progress on the Code of Practice', London, CRE, 1985, p 1, 2

31 CBI Conference on Equality at Work, 24 September 1985, held at Centre Point, Conference notes on 'Equal Pay for Work of Equal Value', p 1

32 EOC Annual Report, 1986, p 26; EOC Annual Report, 1987, p 26

33 EOC Annual Report, 1987, p 27

34 EOC Annual Report, 1987, p 7

35 CRE Annual Report, 1987, p 26; CRE Annual Report, 1986, p 28

36 Nick Jewson, David Mason, Chris Lambkin, and Frank Taylor, 'Ethnic Monitoring Policy and Practice: A Study of Employers' Experiences', Ethnic Minority Employment Research Centre, University of Leicester, p 12

37 Ibid, p 3, 10

38 CBI, 1996, p 3

39 Cynthia Cockburn, *In the Way of Women*, London, Macmillan, 1991, p 91

40 Lesley Mackay and Derek Torrington, *The Changing Nature of Personnel Management*, London, Institute of Personnel Management, 1986, p 79–80

41 Commission for Race Equality, 'From Words to Action: progress on the Code of Practice', 1985, p 1

42 Nick Jewson, David Mason, Chris Lambkin, and Frank Taylor, 'Ethnic Monitoring Policy and Practice: A Study of Employers' Experiences', Ethnic Minority Employment Research Centre, University of Leicester, p 11

43 Ibid, p 35

44 Ibid, p 34

45 Ibid, p 35

46 Ibid, p 150–151

Chapter Five

1 Interview on 27 Jan 1978

2 Walden Interview, *Weekend World*, ITV, 16 January 1983; *Daily Express*, 4 December 1980

3 Reported in the *Guardian*, 'Thatcher team plot their future for the family', Malcolm Dean, 17 February 1983

4 Margaret Thatcher, *The Downing Street Years*, London, Harper Collins, 1995, p 144–6

5 Ibid, p 144

6 'Inner Cities', HC Deb, 9 December 1981, vol 14

7 'Race and Sex Discrimination', HL Deb, 10 June 1981, vol 421

8 *New Equals* 17, Spring 1982, p 1

9 'Commission for Racial Equality', HC Deb, 23 December 1981, vol 15, cc423-4W

10 *New Equals* 17, Spring 1982, p 8

11 'So much to build on', EOC Annual Report, 1985, p 10

12 Ibid, p 2

13 Martin Kettle, 'The Drift to Law and Order', *Marxism Today*, October 1980, p 21

14 Margaret Thatcher, *The Downing Street Years*, p 339, 563

15 David Regan, *The Local Left and its National Pretensions*, Centre for Policy Studies, 1987, p 46–7, 48

16 *New Equals* 2, February 1978, p 8

17 'Director attacks equal pay board', *Guardian*, 4 July 1981

18 See James Curran, Julian Petley, and Ivor Gaber, *Culture Wars: The Media and the British Left*, Edinburgh University Press, 2005, especially Chapter Nine

19 Quoted in Keith Thompson, *Under Siege*, London, 1988, p 128

20 Anna Coote, 'Labour: The Feminist Touch', *Marxism Today*, November 1985, p 12

21 CRE Annual Report, 1986, p 18

22 CRE Annual Report, 1987, p 23

23 Ibid, p 9, 21

24 Ibid, p 28

25 HC Deb, 21 July 1987, vol 120, cc159–60, 159

26 HC Deb, 14 December 1987, vol 124, cc828–67

27 'Government's Decision Deplored', *New Equals* 16, April 1981, p 2

28 CRE Annual Report, 1986, p 25

29 King Edwards Hospital Fund for London Equal Opportunities Task Force, 'The Work of the Equal Opportunities Task Force 1986-1990 — a final report', p 2

30 CRE Annual Report, 1986, p 26

31 King Edwards Hospital Fund for London Equal Opportunities Task Force, 'The Work of the Equal Opportunities Task Force 1986-1990 — a final report', p 3

32 Later on the Institute for Race Relations became more radical, under the leadership of A. Sivanandan.

33 'Race Relations Industry', *Red Mole*, 1 May 1972, p 5; the article drew on a pamphlet by Robin Jenkins (*The Production of Knowledge at the Institute of Race Relations*, London, Independent Labour Party, 1971) who had been a researcher at the organisation, but turned against it

34 *Race Today*, April/May 1977, p 67

35 Reproduced in *Black Voice* 12 (newspaper of the Black Unity and Freedom Party), c. 1981, p 2

36 'Without Malice', February/March 1982, p 60

37 *New Equals* 18, Summer 1982, p 1

38 *Race Today*, May 1983, p 21. Dhondy's sarcasm about the GLC meeting was only slightly tempered by the fact that C. L. R. James, grand old man of the Race Today Collective, was flattered enough to accept the invitation to speak there.

39 Leonora Brito, 'Protest: Positive Discrimination: Who Needs It?', *Race Today*, January 1984, p 43

40 'Rashid Mufti', *Race and Class* 28, 1987, p 104–6 — Mufti makes his attack on municipal anti-racism in reply to a pamphlet attacking the militant-led Liverpool Council for its failure to implement an equal opportunities policy, among other things; Lee Bridges, 'Keeping the Lid On: British urban social policy, 1975-81', *Race and Class* 23, 1981, p 181

41 'Challenging Racism', *Race and Class*, Autumn 1983, p 2, 9

42 'Black Workers in the North West', Report of a conference held on 3 November 1984, Black Workers Planning Group in Conjunction with Tube (WEA NW District), p 8

43 Cynthia Cockburn, *In the Way of Women*, London, Macmillan, p 16

44 Linda Dickens, 'Beyond the business case', *Human Resource Management Journal* Vol 9, No. 1, January 1999

45 Linda Dickens, 'Walking the Talk?' in *Managing Human Resources*, Stephen Bach (ed), Blackwell (Fourth Edition), 2005, p 189

46 Irene Bruegel and Diane Perrons, 'Deregulation and Woman's Employment: the diverse experience of women in Britain', LSE Gender Institute, Discussion Paper Series, October 1996, p 12; citing Clement, 'How to Make Opportunity Knock', *Independent*, 29 April 1992, p 28

47 Dickens, 'Walking the Talk?' in *Managing Human Resources*, Stephen Bach (ed), Blackwell (Fourth Edition), p 189

48 EOC Annual Report, 1992, p 2

49 Cynthia Cockburn, *In the Way of Women*, London, Macmillan, p 91

50 EOC Annual Report, 1980, p 1

51 Interview: Herman Ouseley, *Open Democracy*, 6 January 2014, https://www.opendemocracy.net/5050/beatrix-campbell/neoliberal-neopatriarchy-case-for-gender-revolution

52 Interview: Herman Ouseley, *Sociology Review*, September 2003, p 26

Chapter Six

1 Tom Peters, *Thriving on Chaos*, Dorling Kindersley, 2000, p 52

2 Ronald Burke, Cary Cooper, *The Human Resources Revolution: Why Putting People First Matters*, London, Elsevier, p 13, 14

3 Master of Arts in Human Resource Management (M.A. HRM), Program Overview, http://metro.cua.edu/masters/mahrm.cfm

4 'The place and shape of HRD in a globalised and turbulent workplace', 13 July 2009.

5 Tom Keenoy, 'Human Resource Management' in *The Critical Management Studies Handbook*, p 454, 456

6 Brigid van Wanrooy et al, 'Employment Relations in the Shadow of the Recession — findings from the 2011 Workplace Employment Relations Survey', p 57

7 Neil Millward et al, *All Change at Work*, Chapter Three; Brigid van Wanrooy et al, 'Employment Relations in the Shadow of the Recession — findings from the 2011 Workplace Employment Relations Survey', p 51

8 Millward et al, *All Change at Work*, London, Routledge, 2000, p 12, citing D. Guest and K. Sisson as representative of each view respectively

9 At the time of writing Standard Chartered is going through a severe downsizing, so these figures are changing

10 'Looking for HRM/union substitution: evidence from British workplaces', LSE, 2004

11 Tom Keenoy, *Human Resource Management*, p 460, 461, 464; Mike Beer et al, *Managing Human Assets*, 1984; Mike Beer et al, *HRM: A General Manager's Perspective*, 1985

12 Bogdan Costea, Norman Crump, and Kostas Amiridis, 'Managerialism: the therapeutic habitus and the self', *Human Relations* 61, 2008

13 Graham Hollinshead and Mike Leat, *Human Resource Management*, London, Pitman Publishing, 1995, p 24

14 Brigid van Wanrooy et al, 'Employment Relations in the Shadow of the Recession — findings from the 2011 Workplace Employment Relations Survey', Basingstoke, Palgrave Macmillan, 2013, p 53

15 Michael Porter and Christian H. M. Ketels, 'UK competitiveness: moving to the next stage', *DTI Economics Paper* 3, May 2003, p 12, 36; 'UK Productivity and competitiveness indicators', *DTI Economics Paper 9*, 2003, p 72

16 Quoted in James Heartfield, *Creativity Gap*, London, Blueprint, 2005, p 20

17 Sue Fernie and Helen Gray, 'It's a Family Affair — the effect of union recognition and Human Resource Management on the provision of equal opportunities in Britain', LSE Centre for Economic Performance, April 2002, p 11

18 Baroness Seear, 'Training: the fulcrum of change', Seventh Willis Jackson Lecture, British Association for Commercial and Industrial Education, July 1976, p 2

19 Dennis J Kravetz, *The Human Resources Revolution*, London, Jossey-Bass, p 129–131, 127

20 Nick Jewson, David Mason, Chris Lambkin, and Frank Taylor, 'Ethnic Monitoring Policy and Practice: A Study of Employers' Experiences', Ethnic Minority Employment Research Centre, University of Leicester, p 5

21 Ali Dizaei, *Not One of Us*, London, Serpents Tail, p 232 (Dizaei was eventually jailed on questionable charges of impropriety)

22 http://www.independent.co.uk/news/uk/crime/hundreds-of-police-officers-investigated-for-racist-or-threatening-social-media-posts-9677195.html

23 Chip Chapman, 'An Independent Review of the Police Disciplinary System in England and Wales', October 2014, p 26; Report on Metropolitan Police Service handling of complaints alleging race discrimination, Statistical Information, July 2013

24 House of Commons, 18 January 1999

25 Herman Ouseley with Daniel Silverstone and Usha Prashar, *The System*, 1983, p 22

26 Brigid van Wanrooy et al, 'Employment Relations in the Shadow of the Recession — findings from the 2011 Workplace Employment Relations Survey', Basingstoke, Palgrave Macmillan, 2013, p 59, 51; Barbara Kersley et al, *Inside the Workplace: Findings from the 2004 WERS*, London, Routledge, 2006, p 44; Women in management, says Cynthia Cockburn, 'will become the personnel managers and public relations officers rather than production managers, staff the line', *In the Way of Women*, p 64

27 Luc Boltanski and Eve Chiapello, *The New Spirit of Capitalism*, London, Verso, 2007, p 73

28 Cynthia Cockburn, *In the Way of Women*, 1991, p 71, 98

29 Chuck Pettis, *Technobrands: How to Create and Use Brand Identity to Market, Advertise and Sell Technology Products*, American Management Association, 1995, p 121

30 Fiona Gilmore, *Brand Warriors*, London: Harper CollinsBusiness, 1999, p 31, 33

31 Simon Caulkin, 'The Bosses We Love to Hate', *Observer*, 6 July 2003

32 Herman Ouseley with Daniel Silverstone and Usha Prashar, *The System*, London, Runnymede Trust, and South London Equal Rights Consultancy, 1983, p 91–6

33 'Emotional Labor around the World: An Interview with Arlie Hochschild', *Global Dialogue*, Newsletter of the International Sociological Association, http://isa-global-dialogue.net/emotional-labor-around-the-world-an-interview-with-arlie-hochschild/

34 Kerry McDermott, 'Revealed: Pret a Manger's bizarre 'emotional labour' rules for workers',
Daily Mail, 2 February 2013, http://www.dailymail.co.uk/news/article-2272400/Revealed-Pret-Mangers-bizarre-emotional-labour-rules-workers-told-happy-touch-NEVER-act-moody.html

35 'So much to build on', EOC Annual Report, 1985, p 4; EOC Annual Report, 1987, p 27; CRE Annual Report, 1986, p 24–5;

36 *Equals* 1(1), Spring 1983, p 2

37 Lesley Mackay and Derek Torrington, *The Changing Nature of Personnel Management*, London, Institute of Personnel Management, 1986, p 80

38 Sheila Cohen, *Notoriously Militant*, London, Merlin, 2013, p 144–5

39 *Training: The Implementation of Equal Opportunities at Work Vol 1: Planning and Policy*, Commission for Racial Equality, December 1987, p 7–10

40 Barbara Castle, *The Castle Diaries 1964-70*, London, Weidenfeld and Nicolson, London, 1984, p 704

41 M. W. Snell, P. Glucklich, and M. Povall, 'Equal Pay and Opportunities — A Study of the Implementation and Effects of the Equal Pay and Sex Discrimination Acts in 26 Organisations', Research Paper 20, Department of Employment, April 1981, p 1

42 EOC Annual Report 1982, p 4; and see also EOC Annual Report, 1978, p 2

43 Huw Benyon, *Working for Ford*, Penguin, 1973, p 31–3

44 Nick Jewson, David Mason, Chris Lambkin, and Frank Taylor, 'Ethnic Monitoring Policy and Practice: A Study of Employers' Experiences', Ethnic Minority Employment Research Centre, University of Leicester, p 5

45 'Why Race Records are Important: Living and Working Together', Islington Council, produced by Islington Council's Press, Campaign and Publicity Unit and the Race Equality Unit [n.d.], p 4

46 Nick Jewson, David Mason, Chris Lambkin, Frank Taylor, 'Ethnic Monitoring Policy and Practice: A Study of Employers' Experiences', Ethnic Minority Employment Research Centre, University of Leicester, p 36

47 Irene Bruegel and Diane Perrons, 'Deregulation and Woman's Employment: the diverse experience of women in Britain', LSE Gender Institute, Discussion Paper Series, October 1996, p 14, ii, citing Bevan and Thompson, 'Merit Pay, Performance Appraisal and Attitudes to Women's Work', IMS Report 234, IMS, 1992; on

opposition to PRP see Lesley Mackay and Derek Torrington, *The Changing Nature of Personnel Management*, Institute of Personnel Management, 1986, p 131

48 Lesley Mackay and Derek Torrington, *The Changing Nature of Personnel Management*, Institute of Personnel Management, 1986, p 134

Chapter Seven

1 M. W. Snell, P. Glucklich, and M. Povall, 'Equal Pay and Opportunities — A Study of the Implementation and Effects of the Equal Pay and Sex Discrimination Acts in 26 Organisations', Research Paper 20, Department of Employment, April 1981, p 3

2 *Financial Times*, 16 August 1985

3 *EOC News*, October 1979, p 6

4 *EOC News*, October 1979, p 2

5 EOC Annual Report, 1978, p 2

6 *EOC News*, December 1978, p 1

7 *EOC News*, October 1979, p 4

8 *EOC News*, December 1978, p 6

9 Cynthia Cockburn, *Brothers*, London, Pluto Press, London, 1991 edition, p 248–9

10 'TUC plans "black equality charter"', *Guardian*, 30 September 1980, p 2

11 CRE Annual Report 1986, p 28; *New Equals*, Summer 1984, Special insert, p iii

12 CRE Annual Report, 1986, p 15–16

13 EOC Annual Report, 1985, p 7

14 *Marxism Today*, London, December 1984; and in a more recent profile of TUC President Frances O'Grady, in the *Guardian*, 11 July 2012, http://www.theguardian.com/commentisfree/2012/jul/11/frances-ogrady-tuc-sexism-union

15　EOC Annual Report, 1989, p 15

16　Trade Union Reform and Employment Rights Bill, HL Deb, 1 March 1993, vol 543, cc420–508

17　EOC Annual Report, 1992, p 21–2

18　Paul Cheston, 'Over half of tribunal cases involve sex discrimination, research finds', *Evening Standard*, 24 July 2014, http://www.standard.co.uk/news/uk/over-half-of-tribunal-cases-involve-sex-discrimination-research-finds-9626292.html

19　EOC Annual Report, 1986, p 26

20　Cynthia Cockburn, *Brothers*, London, Pluto Press, 1991 edition, p 75, 77; the EOC investigation is described on p 170

21　'Formal Investigation Report: The Society of Graphical and Allied Trades — The London Central Branch and the London Women's Branch', Equal Opportunities Commission, p 1, 4, 5

22　EOC Annual Report, 1986, p 16

23　Cynthia Cockburn, *Brothers*, London, Pluto Press, 1991 edition, p 93

24　Brenda Dean, *Hot Mettle*, London, Politico's, 2007, p 58, 68

25　Ibid, p 38, 47, 92

26　Beatrix Campbell, *Iron Ladies*, London, Virago, 1987, p 237

27　John Lang and Graham Dodkins, *Bad News: The Wapping Dispute*, Spokesman, Nottingham, 2011, p 169–171

28　*Spare Rib*, August 1986, p 11

29　Brenda Dean, *Hot Mettle*, London, Politico's, 2007, p 177

30　http://www.ford.co.uk/experience-ford/AboutFord/FordCareers

31　http://www.ford.co.uk/experience-ford/AboutFord/News/CompanyNews/2011/Anti-Racism

32　Sheila Cohen, *Notoriously Militant*, London, Merlin, 2013, p 140–1; and see Daniel Trilling, *Bloody Nasty People: The Rise of Britain's Far Right*, London, Verso, p 201

33　Ibid, p 141

34　Ibid, p 150

35　Ibid, p 153, 154, 169

36　Ibid, p 174

37 Ibid, p 180–2

38 Ibid, p 182–3

39 CRE Annual Report, 1999–2000, p 24; 'Ford: Driving Diversity Forward', Michael Rubenstein Publishing, 2003, http://www.rubensteinpublishing.com/default.aspx?id=1057727

40 Sheila Cohen, *Notoriously Militant*, London, Merlin, 2013, p 183–4

41 Ibid, p 197

42 'Female Jobless Figure May Be Higher', *EOC News*, October/November 1980, p 1; Craig Lindsay and Paul Doyle, 'Experimental consistent time series of historical Labour Force Survey data', Labour Market Division, Office for National Statistics, in *Labour Market Trends*, 2003, p 467

43 EOC Annual Report, 1989, p 15

44 On the persistence of the theory of the economic cycle, see David Cannadine, 'The Present and the Past in the English Industrial Revolution 1880-1980', *Past & Present* 103, May 1984, p 131–172

45 Marian Ramelson, *Petticoat Rebellion*, London, Lawrence and Wishart, 1976, p 178; and see also Irene Bruegel, 'Women as a Reserve Army of Labour', in *The Changing Experience of Women*, Elizabeth Whitelegg et al (eds), Open University/Basil Blackwell, 1985, p 105

46 Directorate-General for Economic and Financial Affairs, 'Report on the Implementation of the 1999 Broad Economic Policy Guidelines', *European Economy: Reports and Studies* 1, 2000, p 11, http://ec.europa.eu/economy_finance/publications/european_economy/2000/eers0100en.pdf. See also 'Rules-based Fiscal Policy and Job-rich Growth in France, Germany, Italy and Spain', *IMF Country Report* 1(203), November 2001

47 *EOC News*, January 1981, p 2

48 *EOC News*, October/November 1980, p 2

49 Beatrix Campbell, quoted in Cynthia Cockburn, *In the Way of Women*, Macmillan, 1991, p 129

50 See Sylvia Ann Hewlett and Cornel West, *The War Against Parents: What We Can Do for America's Beleaguered Moms and Dads*, New York, Mariner Books, 1999

51 D. H. Blackaby, D. G. Leslie, P. D. Murphy, and N. C. O'Leary, 'The ethnic wage gap and employment differentials in the 1990s: evidence for Britain', *Economic Letters* Vol, 58, No 1, 1998, p 97

52 Ibid, p 99–100

53 Kathleen Paul, *Whitewashing Britain: Race and Citizenship in the Postwar Era*, Ithaca, Cornell University Press, 1997

54 'Racially Motivated Incidents Reported to the Police', Home Office Research and Planning Unit 54, London, Home Office, 1989

55 Charles Leadbeater, 'In the Land of the Dispossessed', *Marxism Today*, April 1987, p 21

56 Luc Boltanski and Eve Chiapello, *The New Spirit of Capitalism*, London, Verso, 2007, p 229   57   Gill Kirton and Anne-Marie Greene, *The Dynamics of Managing Diversity: A Critical Approach*, Second Edition, Elsevier, 2007, p 58–9

58 Asma Bajawa and Jean Woodall, 'Equal Opportunity and Diversity management meet downsizing', *Employee Relations* 28(1), 2006, p 52

59 Ibid, p 54–5

60 Department of Employment and Pensions, Employment by Sector and Ethnic Group, ONS, 2013, https://www.gov.uk/government/uploads/system/uploads/attachment_data/file/269607/employment-by-sector-and-ethnic-group.xls

61 http://www.dailymail.co.uk/news/article-2417031/Middle-class-Not-60-say-working-class--1983.html

Chapter Eight

1 Carole Pateman, *The Sexual Contract*, Cambridge, Polity, 1988, p 11

2 Catharine Mackinnon, *Towards a Feminist Theory of the State*, London, Harvard University Press, 1989 p 165

3 *The System*, Runnymede Trust, and South London Equal Rights Consultancy, 1983, p 11

4 'So much to build on', EOC Annual Report, 1985, p 8

5 EOC Annual Report, 1996, p 21

6 Dr Jennifer Somerville, *Feminism and the Family: Politics and Society in the UK and USA*, Palgrave Macmillan, 2000, p 138

7 'So much to build on', EOC Annual Report, 1985, p 10; Caroline Flint, later an MP, was chair of the Workplace Nurseries Campaign; Jill Insley, 'Workplace nurseries feel the squeeze', *Guardian*, 30 September 2011, http://www.theguardian.com/money/2011/sep/30/workplace-nurseries-squeeze

8 EOC Annual Report, 1989, p 13

9 Ibid, p 15

10 'The Equality Challenge', EOC Annual Report, 1991, p 3

11 EOC Annual Report, 1992, p 12

12 EOC Annual Report, 1996, p 23–4

13 Jennifer Somerville, *Feminism and the Family: Politics and Society in the UK and USA*, Palgrave Macmillan, 2000, p 138

14 Sally Holtermann, 'Investing in Young Children', London, National Children's Bureau, 1995, p 5, 55

15 Jennifer Somerville, *Feminism and the Family: Politics and Society in the UK and USA*, Palgrave Macmillan, 2000, p 138

16 EOC, 'Women and Men in Britain: The Work-Life Balance', 2000, p 5

17 Ibid, p 13

18 Ruth Smith et al, 'Childcare and Early Years Survey of Parents', Department for Education, Research Report DFE-RR054, 2009, p 9

19 Katy Morton, 'Ofsted statistics show drop in childcare providers and places', *Nursery World*, 25 October 2013; in fact the Department for Education committed itself to expand the free nursery hours for three to four year olds to 30 a week — see 'Review of childcare costs: an executive summary of the analytical report', DFE, DFE-00296-2015, 25 November 2015

20 Man Yee Kan, Oriel Sullivan, and Jonathan Gershuny, 'Gender Convergence in Domestic Work: Discerning the Effects of Interactional and Institutional Barriers in Large-Scale Data', Sociology Working Papers, 2010-03, University of Oxford, p 6, Table 1; 'The Time Use Survey', 2005, Office for National Statistics, July 2006, p 38; Louisa Peacock, 'Women spend half as much time on housework today compared to 1960s', Daily Telegraph, 5 December 2012, http://www.telegraph.co.uk/women/womens-life/9721147/ Women-spend-half-as-much-time-on-housework-today-compared-to-1960s.html

21 Catherine Hakim, '(How) can social policy and fiscal policy recognise unpaid family work?', Renewal 18(1/2), 2010, http://www.lse.ac.uk/ newsAndMedia/news/archives/2010/08/CatherineHakimRenewal. pdf; Nicholas Hellen, 'Women Catch Up With Men on Playtime', Sunday Times, 2 November 2014, p 8; also, amongst ethnic minorities, where women do more work, the men tend do to more housework — see 'Black men "best in Britain" at sharing household chores', Observer, 6 February 2016, http://www.theguardian.com/ society/2016/feb/06/black-men-best-britain-sharing-housework

22 Thanks to James Woudhuysen for explaining this point; and see Joanna Bourke, Working-Class Culture in Britain, 1890-1960, London, Routledge, 1994, p 69

23 Patricia Hewitt, About Time, London, Rivers Oram Press, 1993, Chapter Two

24 EOC Annual Report, 1992, p 2

25 EOC Annual Report, 1996, p 21

26 'Putting Gender on the Agenda', EOC Annual Report and Accounts, 2000/2001, p 4; Hugh Cunningham, Time, Work and Leisure, Manchester University Press, 2016, p 194

27 Patricia Hewitt, About Time, London, Rivers Oram Press, 1993, p 79

28 EOC News, December 1978, p 1

29 EOC News, February 1979, p 4

30 EOC News, Feb 1979, p 4

31 'The Equality Challenge', EOC Annual Report, 1991, p 6

32 EOC Annual Report, 1992, p 29

33 'The Equality Challenge', EOC Annual Report, 1991, p 6

34 EOC Annual Report, 1992, p 29

35 EOC Annual Report, 1994, p 1

36 Catherine Hakim, *Work-Lifestyle Choices in the Twenty-First Century: Preference Theory*, Oxford, 2000

37 Rosalind Coward, *Sacred Cows: Is Feminism Relevant to the New Millennium?*, London, Harper Collins, 2000, p 163

38 Patricia Hewitt, *About Time*, Rivers Oram Press, 1993, p 48; 'So much to build on', EOC Annual Report, 1985, p 8

39 'The Equality Challenge', EOC Annual Report, 1991, p 18

40 Ibid, p 6

41 EOC Annual Report, 1993, p 6, 17

42 'Putting Gender on the Agenda', EOC Annual Report and Accounts, 2000/2001, p 9, 17

43 Around 1% according to a TUC survey, http://www.bbc.co.uk/news/uk-22924708

44 Mike Brewer, Sarah Cattan, and Claire Crawford, 'State support for early childhood education and care in England', Institute of Fiscal Studies, 2014, p 176

45 Chartered Institute for Personnel and Development, *Megatrends*, London, CIPD, 2013, p 4, https://www.cipd.co.uk/binaries/megatrends_2013-trends-shaping-work.pdf

46 On Radio 4's Analysis, in 1994, quoted in Ros Coward, *Sacred Cows*, London, Harper Collins, 2000, p 47

47 The Law Commission, 'Criminal Law Rape Within Marriage', Law Com 205, 13 January 1992, p 2

48 *New Equals* 17, Spring 1982, p 8

49 CRE, 'Then and Now: Change for the Better?', London, CRE, 2001, p 17

50 HC Deb, 8 February 1996, vol 271

51 'Asylum Applications', HC Deb, 8 July 2004, vol 423

52 CRE Annual Report, 1993, p 3

53 Quoted in Mick Hume, 'Keeping our wits about us', LM issue 119, April 1999

54 Ridley Memorial Lecture, 22 November 1996, reproduced in the *Sun*, 7 February 1997

55 Published 6 October 1992

56 Jack Straw, *Independent*, 6 September 1995; Beatrix Campbell, 'Lessons from the Riots', in *Families, Children and Crime*, Anna Coote (ed), London, IPPR, 1994, p 45

57 *Independent*, 3 November 1993

58 CRE Annual Report, 1998, p 3

59 CRE Annual Report, 1999–2000, p 15

60 Sir William Macpherson of Cluny, 'The Stephen Lawrence Inquiry: Report of an Inquiry', February 1999, p 46, 34

61 CRE Annual Report, 2001, p 5

62 Ibid

63 Ibid, p 10

64 CRE Annual Report, 1999–2000, p 29

65 Sir Herman Ouseley, 'Community Pride Not Prejudice — Making Diversity Work in Bradford', presented to Bradford Vision, 2001, foreword

66 Christopher Kyriakides and Rodolfo Torres, *Race Defaced: Paradigms of Pessimism, Politics of Possibility*, Stanford University Press, 2012, p 131

67 See David Goodhart, *The British Dream*, Atlantic, London, p xxxv

Chapter Nine

1 See James Heartfield, *The Aborigines' Protection Society*, London, Hurst, 2011; Suke Wolton, *Lord Hailey, the Colonial Office and the Politics of Race and Empire in the Second World War: The Loss of White Prestige*, Macmillan, 2000

2   See Rusiate Nayacakalou, *Tradition and Change in the Fijian Village*, Suva, 1978; Peter France, *The Charter of the Land: Custom and colonization in Fiji*, Oxford University Press, 1969; Terence Ranger, 'The Tribalization of Africa and the Retribalization of Europe', unpublished paper, c. 1994

3   Terence Ranger, 'The Tribalization of Africa and the Retribalization of Europe', unpublished paper, c. 1994, p 5

4   Fair Employment Agency Report, 1978, quoted in *Irish Freedom Movement Handbook*, Second Edition, London, Junius, 1987, p 82

5   See Janet Sugden, 'The Sectarian State', *Irish Freedom*, Spring 1992, p 10

6   See 'Apartheid in all but name', Oliver Kearney Interview, *Irish Freedom*, Autumn 1992, p 8

7   Bronagh Hinds and Ciaran O'Kelly, 'Affirmative Action in Northern Ireland', in *Race and Inequality: World Perspectives on Affirmative Action*, Elaine Kennedy-Dubourdieu (ed), Aldershot, Ashgate, 2006, p 115–6, 120, 121, 122; Northern Ireland Office, *The Belfast Agreement*, 1998, p 16

8   See James Heartfield and Kevin Rooney, *Who's Afraid of the Easter Rising*, London, Zero, 2015

9   Kevin Yuill's *Richard Nixon and the Rise of Affirmative Action*, Rowman and Littlefield, 2006 is very good on this, and I have leant on it here

10 Thomas Sugrue, 'Affirmative Action from Below', *The Journal of American History* 91(1), June 2004, p 145

11 Lyndon Baines Johnson, Commencement Address, Howard University, 4 June 1965, http://www.heritage.org/initiatives/first-principles/primary-sources/from-opportunity-to-outcomes-lbj-expands-the-meaning-of-equality

12 Kevin Yuill, *Richard Nixon and the Rise of Affirmative Action*, Rowman and Littlefield, 2006, p 93, 147

13 Hugh Davis Graham, *The Civil Rights Era*, New York, Oxford UP, 1990, p 325

14 Kevin Yuill, *Richard Nixon and the Rise of Affirmative Action*, Rowman and Littlefield, 2006, p 149

15 J. Edward Kellough, *Understanding Affirmative Action*, Georgetown University Press, 2006, p 131–43; Harry Holzer and David Neumark, 'Assessing Affirmative Action', *Journal of Economic Literature* 38(3), September 2000; Harry Holzer and David Neumark, 'Affirmative Action: What do we know?', *Journal of Policy Analysis and Management*, November 2005

16 Stephen Steinberg, 'Occupational Apartheid in America', in *Without Justice for All*, Adolph Reed Jr (ed), Westview Press, 1999, p 229

17 Rev. Jesse L. Jackson, 'Reagan and Affirmative Action', *Chicago Tribune*, 19 May 1985; Philip Klinker, 'Bill Clinton and the New Liberalism', in *Without Justice for All*, Adolph Reed Jr (ed), Westview Press, 1999

18 Drew DeSilver, 'Black Unemployment Rate is Consistently Twice that of Whites', Pew Research, 21 August 2013, http://www.pewresearch.org/fact-tank/2013/08/21/through-good-times-and-bad-black-unemployment-is-consistently-double-that-of-whites/

19 Kevin Yuill, *Richard Nixon and the Rise of Affirmative Action*, Rowman and Littlefield, 2006, p 94–5

20 Jo Ann Ooiman Robinson, 'Race in the Workplace: Is Affirmative Action working?', in *Race and Inequality: World Perspectives on Affirmative Action*, Elaine Kennedy-Dubourdieu (ed), Aldershot, Ashgate, 2006, p 38; 'Affirmative Action in the United States', *Business Week*, 8 July 1991, p 53–6

21 CRE Annual Report, 1986, p 28

22 Claire Crawford and Ellen Greaves, 'Ethnic minorities substantially more likely to go to university than their White British peers', Institute for Fiscal Studies, 10 November 2015, https://www.ifs.org.uk/publications/8042

23 Barbara Bergmann, *In Defence of Affirmative Action*, New York, Basic Books, 1996, p 31

24 Johanna Kantola, *Gender and the European Union*, Palgrave Macmillan, 2010, p 28

25 Ibid, p 29

26 Ibid, p 31

27 EOC Annual Report, 1977, p 4

28 'Maternity Rights Call — Britain's Expectant Mothers Come Off Second Best in European Table', *EOC News*, June 1979, p 8

29 EOC Annual Report, 1982, p 4

30 See Baroness Writtle's speech in the House of Lords, 5 December 1983, vol 445, cc894-930, http://hansard.millbanksystems.com/lords/1983/dec/05/equal-pay-amendment-regulations-1983-1

31 'So much to build on', EOC Annual Report, 1985, p 2

32 Ibid, p 10

33 EOC Annual Report, 1993, p 4, 14–5

34 EOC Annual Report, 1994, introduction, p 1, 2

35 EOC Annual Report, 1994, p 6

36 See James Heartfield, *The European Union and the End of Politics*, London, Zero, 2013

37 Ann Wickham, 'Engendering Social Policy in the EEC', *m/f — the feminist journal* 4, 1980, p 9, 10

38 'Economic Independence and the Position of Women on the Labour Market of the European Union', Directorate General for Internal Policies, 2014, p 6

Chapter Ten

1 'Putting Gender on the Agenda', EOC Annual Report and Accounts, 2000/2001, p 15

2 Sara Ahmed 'Equality Credentials', 10 June 2016, https://feministkilljoys.com/2016/06/10/equality-credentials/ — Ahmed resigned from the college in frustration at the sidelining of her committee's work on harassment

3 In Phil Cohen and Carl Gardner (eds), *It Ain't Half Racist, Mum: Fighting Racism in the Media*, London, Comedia, 1982, p 32

4 'Ethnic minority group representation on popular television', CRE/ Communications Research Group, London, 2001, p 203

5 *360° Diversity Charter*, Channel 4, 2015; Harry Yorke, 'BBC Criticised…', *Telegraph*, 3 June 2016, http://www.telegraph.co.uk/ news/2016/06/03/bbc-criticised-by-mps-and-job-applicants-over- training-placement/

6 'Mainstreaming Gender into the Policies and the Programmes of the Institutions of European Union and EU Member States', European Institute for Gender Equality, 28 November 2011, p 5, 10, 15

7 Davina Cooper, *Sexing the City*, London, Rivers Oram, 1994, p 22

8 *Equals* 1(1), Spring 1983, p 3

9 Polly Curtis, 'Gay men earn £10k more than national average', *Guardian*, 23 January 2006, http://www.theguardian.com/uk/2006/ jan/23/money.gayrights

10 Quoted in Beatrix Campbell, 'The Charge of the Light Brigade', *Marxism Today*, February 1987, p 13

11 Sophie Gilliat-Ray, *Muslims in Britain*, Cambridge University Press, 2010, p 120

12 'Education For Life: Here And Hereafter', *New Equals*, April 1978, p 7

13 Sophie Gilliat-Ray, *Muslims in Britain*, Cambridge University Press, 2010, p 237

14 Writing as Mala Dhondy, 'Facing the Asian Youth', *Race Today*, April 1977, p 67

15 Kenan Malik, *From Fatwa to Jihad*, Atlantic Books, 2009, p 126; Sophie Gilliat-Ray, *Muslims in Britain*, Cambridge University Press, 2010, p 108

16 Kenan Malik, *From Fatwa to Jihad*, Atlantic Books, 2009, p 129, 130; Sophie Gilliat-Ray, *Muslims in Britain*, 2010, p 109

17 Sophie Gilliat-Ray, *Muslims in Britain*, 2010, p 125–6

18 'Time to Tackle the Under-Representation of British Muslims in Top Professions', press release, December 2015, http://www.demos.co.uk/press-release/rising-to-the-top/

19 *Islamophobia: A Challenge for Us All*, London, Runnymede Trust, 1997, p 33

20 CRE Annual Report, 2004, p 7

21 Bill Hunter, *Forgotten Hero: The Life and Times of Edward Rushton*, Liverpool, Living History Library, 2002, p 3 — latterly the Merseyside Trade Union and Unemployed Resource Centre has been housed in the school buildings

22 Welfare Reform and Work Bill, 27 January 2016, House of Lords, Hansard, vol 768

23 *EOC News*, June 1979, p 6

24 See James Heartfield, 'There is no Masculinity Crisis', *Genders* 35, 2002, for a commentary

25 Laurie Penny, 'We Need to Talk About Masculinity', *Guardian*, 16 May 2013

26 Daniel Martin, 'At Last!', *Daily Mail*, 15 March 2015

27 Davina Cooper, *Sexing the City*, London, Rivers Oram Press, 1994, p 169

28 CRE Annual Report, 1999–2000, p 16

29 CRE Annual Report, 1998, p 6

30 Some years later, when the outgoing CRE Chief Trevor Phillips raised questions about the policy of multiculturalism in Britain, he was branded as the man who had 'closed down the CRE', by Lee Jasper, for example, https://twitter.com/LeeJasper/status/575880562356940800

Chapter Eleven

1 'Charge of the Light Brigade', *Marxism Today*, February 1987, p 12; and see Michael Crabtree, 'Strategies Against Racism', Thesis submitted for Ph. D. Aston University, 1988, p 67

2 Ian Macdonald and Gus John, *Murder in the Playground: The Burnage Report*, Longsight Press, 1989, p 347–8

3 Sarah Boseley, 'Social Workers Denounce Councils', *Guardian*, 27 July 1985; 'Whose Child? The Report of the Panel of Inquiry into the death of Tyra Henry', London Borough of Lambeth, 1987 chaired by Mr Stephen Sedley QC, p 135–6

4 Ann Tobin, quoted in Davina Cooper, *Sexing the City*, London, Rivers Oram, 1994, p 37

5 Stuart Lansley, Sue Goss, and Christian Wolmar, *Councils in Conflict*, London, Macmillan, 1989, p 65

6 'PM Brand Racist for Attack on Labour's Khan', *Sky News*, 20 April 2016, http://news.sky.com/story/1682129/pm-branded-racist-for-attack-on-labours-khan; John McDonnell's tweet, 22 April 2016, https://twitter.com/johnmcdonnellMP/status/723481596096090112; see Jeremy Corbyn: 'I am completely against anti-Semitism', in the *Guardian*, 29 April 2016, http://www.theguardian.com/politics/2016/apr/29/jeremy-corbyn-i-am-totally-completely-and-absolutely-against-antisemitism

7 Kimberlé Crenshaw, 'Mapping the Margins', *Stanford Law Review* 43, July 1991, p 1242

8 Editorial, *Spare Rib*, London, September 1980

9 Sheila Rowbotham, Lynne Segal, and Hilary Wainwright, *Beyond the Fragments*, London, Merlin, 1979, p 5–6

10 On 29 November 1989, the *Guardian* newspaper carried an advertisement for a 'women's adviser' that the NUS was seeking to appoint, to 'maintain and develop the Union's work on women and promote the participation of women students in their students union'; on 24 April 1991, the *Guardian* reported that 'the Oxford University Students Union has a full-time women's officer for the first time this year' — Karen Mathieson — and on 8 March 1994, a *Guardian* article welcomed women's officers at Warwick (Marisa Bailey), Northumbria (Kate Skipworth), the Organisation of Labour Students' national women's officer (Clair Wilcox); there were

women's officers at LSE (Tesher Fitzpatrick) and Essex (Françoise Humphrey) shortly afterwards and by the mid-Nineties it was the norm.

11 *The Correspondence of Sigmund Freud and Sándor Ferenczi: 1920-1933*, Harvard University Press, 1993, p 422

12 David Roediger, *Towards the Abolition of Whiteness*, London, Verso, 1994; Theodore Allen, *The Invention of the White Race*, London, Verso, 1994; and see James Heartfield, review of *White Mythologies* by Robert Young, *Living Marxism*, May 1991

13 Ian Macdonald and Gus John, *Murder in the Playground: The Burnage Report*, Longsight Press, 1989, p 347–8

14 Javier Espinoza, 'Ethnic minorities "more likely to go to university" than white working-class British children', *Telegraph*, 10 November 2015

15 From the Winter 1990 issue of *Independent School*, and reproduced online at http://ted.coe.wayne.edu/ele3600/mcintosh.html

16 Talking to Hugh Muir, *Guardian*, 2 March 2011; and see BBC, 'Call for rethink on immigration', 12 September 2000, http://news.bbc.co.uk/1/hi/uk_politics/920182.stm

17 Will Hutton, 'The unholy alliance against immigrants', *Guardian*, 23 June 2002

18 Letters, *Guardian*, 24 June 2002

19 David Goodhart, *The British Dream*, London, Atlantic Books, 2014, p 41

20 'Immigration and the Amended Act', CRE Annual Report 2001, p 6

21 *Evening Standard*, 23 October 2009

22 *Guardian*, 30 January 2009

23 Polly Toynbee, 'Of course the wealthy want an immigration free-for-all', *Guardian*, 11 October 2005; and see Goodhart's book *The British Dream*, London, Atlantic Books, 2014

24 CRE Annual Report, 2004, p 4

25 *Guardian*, 28 May 2004

26 Munira Mirza, *Rethinking Race*, Prospect, 22 September 2010

27 Robert Ford, 'Is racial prejudice declining in Britain?', *The British Journal of Sociology* 59(4), 2008; Vikram Dodd, 'Poll pessimism on race relations', *Guardian*, 13 May 2002
28 Hassan Mahmadallie, *Defending Multiculturalism*, London, Bookmarks, 2011, p 21; and Salma Yaqoob, in the same collection, p 167

Conclusion

1 Vivien Hunt et al, 'Why Diversity Matters', McKinsey, January 2015, http://www.mckinsey.com/business-functions/organization/our-insights/why-diversity-matters
2 Jamie Allinson, 'Don't Mourn, Accelerate', *Salvage* 1, July 2015, p 15
3 Hugh Cunningham, *Time, Work and Leisure*, Manchester University Press, 2016, p 194

Index

Repeater Books

is dedicated to the creation of a new reality. The landscape of twenty-first-century arts and letters is faded and inert, riven by fashionable cynicism, egotistical self-reference and a nostalgia for the recent past. Repeater intends to add its voice to those movements that wish to enter history and assert control over its currents, gathering together scattered and isolated voices with those who have already called for an escape from Capitalist Realism. Our desire is to publish in every sphere and genre, combining vigorous dissent and a pragmatic willingness to succeed where messianic abstraction and quiescent co-option have stalled: abstention is not an option: we are alive and we don't agree.